Adam Smi
New in

First published in 177
much more than just
market economics; it is a founding text for the organisation
of Western society in its broadest sense.

In order to understand the impact of Smith's text across the
academic disciplines, this volume brings together leading
scholars from the fields of economics, politics, history,
sociology and literature. Each essay offers a different reading of *Wealth of Nations* and its legacy.

Contributors consider the historical context in which
Wealth of Nations was written, its reception and its
profound impact on contemporary concepts of market liberalism, on education, on gender relations and on environmental debates. The volume also offers deconstructive
analyses of the text and a feminist critique of Smith's
construction of the economy.

This volume will be the ideal companion to Smith's work
for all students of literature, politics and economic history.

*Stephen Copley is Lecturer in English at the University of York,
and Kathryn Sutherland is Professor of Modern English
Literature at the University of Nottingham.*

TEXTS · IN · CULTURE

Series editors

Stephen Copley and Jeff Wallace

Advisory editors

David Aers, University of East Anglia
Lynda Nead, Birkbeck College, London
Gillian Beer, Girton College, Cambridge
Roy Porter, Wellcome Institute for the
History of Medicine
Anne Janowitz, University of Warwick
Bernard Sharratt, University of Kent

This new series offers a set of specially commissioned, cross-disciplinary essays on a text of seminal importance to Western culture. Each text has had an impact on the way we think, write and live beyond the confines of its original discipline, and it is only through an understanding of its multiple meanings that we can fully appreciate its importance.

Adam Smith's *Wealth of Nations*
Stephen Copley, Kathryn Sutherland (eds)

Charles Darwin's *The Origin of Species*
David Amigoni, Jeff Wallace (eds)

Sigmund Freud's *Interpretation of Dreams*
Laura Marcus (ed.)

Simone de Beauvoir's *The Second Sex*
Ruth Evans (ed.)

Niccolo Machiavelli's *The Prince*
Martin Coyle (ed.)

(TEXTS·IN·CULTURE

Adam Smith's

WEALTH
OF NATIONS

New interdisciplinary essays

STEPHEN COPLEY
KATHRYN SUTHERLAND

editors

Manchester University Press
Manchester and New York

*distributed exclusively in the USA
and Canada by St Martin's Press*

Published by Manchester University Press
Oxford Road, Manchester M13 9NR, UK
and Room 400, 175 Fifth Avenue, New York, NY 10010, USA

Distributed exclusively in the USA and Canada
by St Martin's Press, Inc.,
175 Fifth Avenue, New York, NY 10010, USA

British Library Cataloguing-in-Publication Data
A catalogue record is available from the British Library

Library of Congress Cataloging-in-publication Data
Smith, Adam, 1723-1790
    Adam Smith's The wealth of nations : new interdisciplinary essays /
edited by Stephen Copley and Kathryn Sutherland.
        p.   c.m. — (Texts in culture)
    ISBN 0-7190-3942-8. — ISBN 0-7190-3943-6 (pbk.)
    1. Economics. 2. Smith, Adam, 1723-1790. Inquiry into the nature
and causes of the wealth of nations. I. Copley, Stephen, 1954–
II. Sutherland, Kathryn. III. Title. IV. Series.
HB161.S66914 1995
330.15'3—dc20   94-16671
                                                              CIP

ISBN 0-7190-3942-8 *hardback*
ISBN 0-7190-3943-6 *paperback*

Typeset in Apollo by Koinonia, Manchester
Printed in Great Britain by Biddles Limited, Guildford and King's Lynn

Contents

Series introduction

Texts are produced in particular cultures and in particular historical circumstances. In turn, they shape and are shaped by those cultures as they are read and re-read in changing circumstances by different groups with different commitments, engagements and interests. Such readings are themselves then re-absorbed into the ideological frameworks within which the cultures develop. The seminal works drawn on by cultures thus have multiple existences within them, exerting their influence in distinct and perhaps contradictory ways. As these texts have been 'claimed' by particular academic disciplines, however, their larger cultural significance has often been obscured.

Recent work in cultural history and textual theory has stimulated critical awareness of the complex relations between texts and cultures, highlighting the limits of current academic formations and opening the possibility of new approaches to interdisciplinarity. At the same time, however, the difficulties of interdisciplinary work have become increasingly apparent at all levels of research and teaching. On the one hand the abandonment of disciplinary specialisms may lead to amorphousness rather than challenging interdisciplinarity: on the other, interdisciplinary approaches may in the end simply create new specialisms or sub-specialisms, with their own well guarded boundaries. In these circumstances, yesterday's ground-breaking interdisciplinary study may become today's autonomous (and so potentially circumscribed) discipline, as has happened, it might be argued, in the case of some forms of History of Ideas.

The volumes in this series highlight the advantages of interdisciplinary work while at the same time encouraging a critical reflexiveness about its limits and possibilities; they seek to stimulate consideration both of the distinctiveness and integrity of individual disciplines, and of the transgressive potential of interdisciplinarity. Each volume offers a collection of new essays on a text of seminal intellectual and cultural importance, displaying the insights to be gained from the juxtaposition of disciplinary perspectives and from the negotiation of disciplinary boundaries. Our editorial stance is avowedly 'cultural', and in this sense the volumes represent a challenge to the conception of authorship which locates the significance of the text in the individual act of creation; but we assume that no issues (including those of disciplinarity and authorship) are foreclosed, and that individual volumes, drawing contributions from a broad range of disciplinary standpoints, will raise questions about the texts they examine more by the perceived disparities of approach that they encompass than by any interpretative consensus that they demonstrate.

All essays are specially commissioned for the series and are designed to be approachable to non-specialist as well as specialist readers: substantial editorial introductions provide a framework for the debates conducted in each volume, and highlight the issues involved.

Stephen Copley, University of York
Jeff Wallace, University of Glamorgan

Abbreviations

All references to works by Adam Smith are to *The Glasgow Edition of the Works and Correspondence of Adam Smith* and adopt the abbreviations and system of reference employed in that edition as follows:

Corr: *Correspondence of Adam Smith*, ed. E. C. Mossner and I. S. Ross

EPS: *Essays on Philosophical Subjects*, ed. W. P. D. Wightman, J. C. Bryce and I. S. Ross

LJ (A), LJ (B): *Lectures on Jurisprudence*, ed. R. L. Meek, D. D. Raphael and P. G. Stein

LRBL: *Lectures on Rhetoric and Belles Lettres*, ed. J. C. Bryce

TMS: *The Theory of Moral Sentiments*, ed. A. L. Macfie and D. D. Raphael

WN: *An Inquiry into the Nature and Causes of the Wealth of Nations*, ed. R. H. Campbell, A. S. Skinner and W. B. Todd

Chronology of contexts for, and developments of, the *Wealth of Nations*

1676 William Petty, *Political Arithmetic* (published 1690).

1691 John Locke, *Consequences of the Lowering of Interest.*

Dudley North, *Discourses upon Trade.*

1698 Charles Davenant, *Discourses on the Public Revenues and on Trade.*

1705 John Law, *Money and Trade Considered.*

1714–25 Bernard Mandeville, *The Fable of the Bees.*

1723 Adam Smith born at Kirkcaldy, Fife.

1734 Jean François Melon, *Essai politique sur le commerce.*

1737 Adam Smith enters Glasgow University as a student and as the pupil of the philosopher Francis Hutcheson.

1740–46 Adam Smith in Oxford.

1748–51 Adam Smith gives public lectures in Edinburgh on rhetoric and belles lettres, and on civil law.

1749 Josiah Tucker, *Essay on Trade.*

1751 Jean Le Rond d'Alembert *et al.*, *Encyclopédie.*

Ferdinand Galiani, *Della moneta.*

Malachy Postelthwayt, *Universal Dictionary of Trade and Commerce.*

1751 Adam Smith appointed to the chair of logic at Glasgow University.

1752 David Hume, *Essays Moral, Political, and Literary; Political Discourses.*

1752 Adam Smith appointed to the chair of moral philosophy at Glasgow University.

1755 Richard Cantillon, *Essai sur la nature du commerce en général* (written 1734).

Josiah Tucker, *The Elements of Commerce.*

1756 François Quesnay, *Fermiers.*

1757 Malachy Postelthwayt, *Great Britain's True System.*

1758 François Quesnay, *Tableau économique.*

1759 Adam Smith, *The Theory of Moral Sentiments.*

1764 Adam Smith travels on the Continent. Meets François Quesnay and other physiocrats. Begins work on *Wealth of Nations*.

1767 Adam Ferguson, *An Essay on the History of Civil Society*.

1767 James Steuart, *Principles of Political Economy*.

1766 Anne Robert Jean Turgot, *Réflexions sur la formation et la distribution des richesses* (published 1769–70).

1769 English translation of Cesare Beccaria, *A Discourse on Public Economy and Commerce*.

Benjamin Franklin, *Concerning National Wealth*.

1771 Pietro Verri, *Meditazioni sulla economia politica*.

1773–7 Adam Smith mainly in London. Admitted to the Royal Society and extends acquaintance with Edmund Burke, Samuel Johnson, Edward Gibbon and possibly Benjamin Franklin.

1776 Adam Smith, *An Inquiry into the Nature and Causes of the Wealth of Nations*, first edition.

1776 Etienne Bonnot, Abbé de Condillac, *Le commerce et le gouvernement*.

1776–c.1848 'Classical' political economy and economics.

1776–8 First German translation of *Wealth of Nations*.

1778 Second edition of *Wealth of Nations*.

1778–9 First French translation of *Wealth of Nations*.

1784 Third edition of *Wealth of Nations*, considerably expanded.

1786 Fourth edition of *Wealth of Nations*.

1789 Fifth edition of *Wealth of Nations*.

1790 Adam Smith dies in Edinburgh.

1794 Dugald Stewart, 'An Account of the Life and Writings of Adam Smith'.

1795 Posthumous publication of Adam Smith's *Essays on Philosophical Subjects*.

1798 (expanded edition 1803) Thomas Robert Malthus, *An Essay on the Principle of Population*.

1803 Jean-Baptiste Say, *Traité d'économie politique pratique*.

1816 [Jane Marcet], *Conversations on Political Economy*.

1817 David Ricardo, *The Principles of Political Economy and Taxation*.

c. **1820–50** 'Manchester School' economic liberalism.

1824 J. R. McCulloch, *A Discourse on the Rise, Progress, Peculiar Objects and Importance of Political Economy*.

1832 Harriet Martineau, *Illustrations of Political Economy*.

1848 John Stuart Mill, *Principles of Political Economy*.

1859 Karl Marx, *A Contribution to the Critique of Political Economy*.

*c.***1870–** 'Neoclassical' economic theory developed.

1871 W. Stanley Jevons, *The Theory of Political Economy.*

1890 Alfred Marshall, *The Principles of Economics.*

1912 Arthur Cecil Pigou, *Wealth and Welfare.*

1936 John Maynard Keynes, *The General Theory of Employment, Interest and Money.*

1930s–40s 'Keynesian revolution'.

1948 Friedrich A. von Hayek, *Individualism and Economic Order.*

1953 Milton Friedman, *Essays in Positive Economics.*

1977 Foundation of the Adam Smith Institute.

1979– Economic programmes of the 'New Right' adopted by governments in Britain and USA.

1

Introduction:
reading the *Wealth of Nations*

STEPHEN COPLEY

Few works of economic and political analysis have exerted a more profound influence on European, American and latterly world economic and social policy than Adam Smith's *Wealth of Nations*. Or rather, few works have been more extensively appealed to in support of economic policy decisions and in confirmation of the underlying political, social and ideological objectives that have informed those decisions. Inevitably in this context the book has borne widely differing interpretations in the practical field of policy making, in academic debate and in popular reputation. These differences have never been more marked than in the last twenty years. The 1976 bicentenary of the publication of the *Wealth of Nations* was celebrated with the appearance of the new standard Glasgow edition, and with a plethora of scholarly commentaries on and analysis of the economic and social programmes that Smith develops within it. This body of work offers a striking index of the changing ideological climate of its time. On the one hand, many commentators read Smith's arguments through the filter of Keynes and his successors. On the other hand, the bicentenary occurred just before the major political changes in Britain and the United States which produced the right-wing free-marketeering administrations of the 1980s in both countries. These administrations, owing their intellectual allegiances to economic and political theorists of the new right, gave practical expression to quite different readings of Smith, harking back in their emphasis to the nineteenth century. Indeed, much of the crusading zeal shown by the governments of the 1980s on both sides of the Atlantic in economic and in social policy was justified in the name of Adam Smith, whether through public claims by politicians such as Margaret Thatcher to have taken the *Wealth of Nations* as their inspiration, or through the emergence of bodies such as the Adam Smith Institute (founded in 1977) as influential centres for the promulgation of free-market doctrines.

The statements of loyalty to Smith's supposed principles made by British government ministers in this period are legion. In 1975, in a speech in Chicago, for instance, Margaret Thatcher linked the publication of *Wealth of Nations* with the Declaration of Independence and announced that 'Adam Smith, in fact, heralded the end of the strait-jacket of feudalism and released all the innate energy of private initiative and enterprise which enables wealth to be created on a scale never before contemplated'. Furthermore, Hugo Young records her comment, 'in what was believed to be a reference to Adam Smith, the economist, and possibly the philosopher David Hume', that '"The Scots invented Thatcherism, long before I was thought of"' – a reading of Scottish Enlightenment thought which explains the surprise that she expresses in her memoirs when she notes that 'there was no Tartan Thatcherite revolution' during her period of office, and writes: 'That might seem strange. For Scotland in the eighteenth century was the home of the very same Scottish Enlightenment which produced Adam Smith, the greatest exponent of free enterprise economics till Hayek and Friedman.' In the early 1980s Keith Joseph's reading list of twenty-nine titles to brief civil servants at the Department of Industry in 'free-market principles' ranged 'from Adam Smith to eight of his own pamphlets'; and in 1980 the union leader Len Murray complained that meetings with government ministers involved 'arid lectures on Adam Smith and the need to reduce pay settlements'. A striking visual embodiment of this claimed link with Smith occurs in the shape of a china figurine of this period, produced (I assume) for a local Conservative Association, which shows Margaret Thatcher, dressed in blue, carrying a copy of the *Wealth of Nations*.[1]

At the time of preparing this volume, the influence of the

new right seems to be on the wane. Intellectually, John Gray, one of its leading apologists in political science during the 1980s, has recently dissociated himself from its dogmatic faith in the efficacy of markets, and has instead moved towards advocating a mixture of 'traditional' conservatism and green politics.[2] At the same time, administrations in Britain and the United States seem uncertainly poised between abandonment of the strident public advocacy of *laissez faire* that marked the 1980s, on the one hand, and pursuit of policies which still show every sign of having been shaped under the influence of that doctrine, on the other. In Britain, for instance, the cult of entrepreneurship and the rhetorical attacks on social welfarism which characterised 'Thatcherite' advocacy of 'enterprise culture' have been toned down, but the present (1994) government's policy of privatisation continues to be extended into areas where it was not pursued even under Margaret Thatcher: in the USA the policies of the Reagan/Bush years have been superseded by new, but as yet undelivered, promises of attention to public social welfare provision. The prominence which has been accorded to claims and counter-claims for Smith's ideas in a wide range of political and cultural debates in this period means that now is a particularly appropriate moment to reconsider both the historical Adam Smith and the interpretations and appropriations of the *Wealth of Nations* that have been produced in various contexts and across various disciplines in the last 220 years.

At the same time, it is an appropriate moment to survey some of the problems that have characterised different disciplinary approaches to Smith's text in that period. At the most general level, readings of the book have treated it in one of two ways. On the one hand, it has been taken as a source of economic principles with continuing relevance outside its own historical period, and, on the other, it has been read historically. Of course these projects overlap; each can be traced under different guises in a variety of distinct forms of commentary and analysis; and each has spawned problems of its own. Historical readings have themselves taken two broad directions. Traditionally, historians of economic theory have read Smith as a pivotal figure in the development of classical economics – the systematiser of many strands of English, French and Scottish economic thought developed in the late seventeenth and eighteenth centuries, whose conclusions and preoccupations were complemented and further systematised by Malthus and Ricardo as the foundation of classical political economy, and refined by a sequence of later commentators in the nineteenth century. There is a considerable difference, however, between the projects and scale of inquiries of the Scottish political economy of which Smith was a leading proponent, and those of the nineteenth-century versions of the discipline, which adopted some of its procedures and conclusions, and canonised its major work of economic analysis, but excluded many of its concerns. In this volume, Keith Tribe details the changes of emphasis (as well as of language) that occurred when Smith's work was incorporated into the nineteenth-century German tradition of political economy, and so eventually into a developing international discipline of economics; and other contributors consider various aspects of the disparity between the Scottish study and later political economy and economics. As Noel Parker points out, Smith's version of Scottish political economy draws on Enlightenment debates about political questions and social values rather than resting on the later assumption that economics constitutes a separate and autonomous domain of knowledge; as Andrew Skinner demonstrates, it includes detailed consideration of a range of areas (such as the ends, and means of provision, of education) which are no part of the later discipline; and as Heinz Lubasz suggests, its concern with 'commercial society' cannot simply be equated with later economists' concern with 'the market'.

Commentators in the nineteenth and earlier twentieth centuries who narrowed their focus on Smith to include only the disciplinary concerns of classical economics excluded large parts of his argument, and in doing so effectively realigned and reshaped what remained. The famous 'Adam Smith problem' debated at length in the nineteenth century - the 'problem' being the supposed incompatibility between the arguments developed in various areas of his work - thus seemed to be a problem to commentators of the time only because of their adherence to later, and in the context of the Scottish Enlightenment anachronistic, disciplinary demarcations. In this context, more recent intellectual historians in various disciplines, particularly since the 1970s, have stressed the need to read Smith with a broader sense of historical period, and in the light of the varied concerns and projects of the Scottish Enlightenment, not only as they are reflected in his other published works, but also as they are integral to the *Wealth of Nations* itself.

The assumptions which underlie the approach of these historians are summarised in the introduction to a recent study in which Maurice Brown, writing as a sociologist, attempts to take discussion of Smith beyond the disciplinary bounds of classical economics, while avoiding any attempt to abstract trans-historical principles from his work.[3] He sets 'absolutist' readings of Smith's texts, which do attempt to trace such principles, against what he calls 'relativist' readings such as his own (and, whatever their methodological differences, those of a number of historians of the Scottish Enlightenment); and writes that these latter readings attempt 'to take a thinker's work as a whole, and analyse it within the context of the perspectives and objectives of his own particular time' (p. 2), which may be quite different from those which inform the later disciplinary traditions into which the work has been incorporated. He thus suggests that his own project involves 'attempting to reconstruct Smith's epistemology' (p. 25) in order to find the terms in which his 'approach to science is fundamentally homogeneous' (p. 39). In this context, many of the problems discovered or constructed in later readings are irrelevant: once he has suggested that 'I am not concerned with the Neo-classical economists' Adam Smith and have virtually nothing to say about him' (p. 4), for instance, he can claim that, for him, 'The "Adam Smith Problem" is not therefore a problem at all' (p. 5).

The danger in this approach, of course, is that, in rejecting trans-historical abstraction, it may instead place undue confidence in the retrievability of a single, historically authenticated, reading of the work under consideration. If histories are, as Michel Foucault suggests, inevitably histories of the present, this is never clearer than in readings of historical texts in which so much of the present is invested – and historical readings themselves, no matter how scrupulous in scholarly terms, can never be incontestably neutral and uncharged with explicit or implicit ideological commitments.

This point is well illustrated in an extended argument between historians, which has continued from the early 1970s to the present, over a passsage from the *Wealth of Nations*, in the course of which the participants have raised important questions about the various disciplinary frameworks within the broad field of history in which the work might be read. In 1971 E. P. Thompson proposed that the late eighteenth century saw the demise of a traditional rhetoric of social regulation which posited a 'moral economy' of paternalist interventionism on the one hand, and deferential obligation on the other, in the face of the new claims of political economy. This new science demoralised economic transactions in society, and spoke instead in terms of the primacy of the market in social and political affairs.[4] Thompson claimed that, as well as being deployed as a rhetoric in the legislative and political writings of the earlier eighteenth century, the 'moral economy' functioned in practical terms in the period, in however vitiated a form, when, for instance, it was appealed to by 'the crowd' as a means of exerting pressure on the regulators of society to intervene in the supply of grain in order to relieve suffering in times of dearth. According to him, this point of popular leverage was lost once the new arguments of political economy prevailed in treating famine as the consequence of the impersonal operations of the market, and once they had persuaded governments and social legislators of the overriding need to refrain from any sort of intervention in those operations.

The seminal instance of the arguments of political economy, for Thompson, is the twenty-page 'Digression Concerning the Corn Trade and Corn Laws' from the *Wealth of Nations* (IV.v.b), in which Smith argues against regulatory intervention in the grain market, and in favour of 'The unlimited, unrestrained freedom of the corn trade' as 'the only effectual preventative of the miseries of a famine' and as 'the best palliative of the inconveniencies of a dearth' (IV.v.b.7). In Thompson's eyes, although this recommendation may offer long-term solutions to scarcity, it is, crucially, hostile to the short-term measures to relieve suffering which had earlier been countenanced as aspects of governmental regulatory policy. He does not suggest that the 'Digression' is entirely typical of Smith's work in this respect, but he does argue that it was enormously and directly influential on the formulation of British government policy in the late eighteenth and nineteenth centuries, domestically and in the colonies. Indeed he suggests that 'These pages ... were among the most influential writings in history' (p. 283), and that, in this respect at least, there was a direct continuity between the arguments of Smith and the practical policies of his successors, which had enormous consequences in the real world in which people lived – or, in this case, in the world in which they starved as the result of the non-interventionism advocated by Smith and pursued by governments determined not to interfere in free-market movements of grain.

Thompson's argument provoked much critical discussion, to which he responded in 1991 with an essay which extended his earlier case over the 'moral economy'.[5] Of particular interest in this later essay is his reply to the comments of Istvan Hont and Michael Ignatieff on his original reading of the passage from Smith. Hont and Ignatieff are themselves good representative proponents of a form of intellectual history which has had a considerable influence since the 1970s in studies of the Scottish Enlightenment and of Scottish political economy, and which has worked to an agenda largely set by the influential studies of J. G. A Pocock. In an extensive research project in the late 1970s and early 1980s Hont and Ignatieff attempted to fill out the intellectual lineage of political economy between 1750 and 1850 by charting the argumentative and discursive legacies of earlier traditions of moral and political discourse, as well as earlier forms of economic analysis, within the new discipline. In their own work on the *Wealth of Nations*[6] they thus debate the relative influence on Smith's arguments of, on the one hand, 'the Renaisssance civic paradigm' (p. 44) described by Pocock,[7] and, on the other, a tradition of writings on natural jurisprudence dating back through Pufendorf and Grotius to Thomas Aquinas; and they conclude that Smith's conception of liberty owed more to the latter tradition, in which the term has connotations of passivity, than it did to the former, in which liberty is an active civic virtue.

Thompson's criticism of Hont and Ignatieff raises interesting questions. He does not accuse them of particular or hostile
ideological engagements in their reading of Smith, in the way
in which, for instance, he suggests of another critic's attack on
his own work that 'There may ... be a little ideological pressure
behind his polemic. When I first published "The Moral
Economy", "the market" was not flying as high in the ideological firmament as it is today' (p. 267). Instead, he makes a point
about the disciplinary constraints that he finds in their
approach: working in the 'detached discipline of political ideas
and rhetoric' (p. 275), and examining Smith's text solely in the
light of its conjectured intellectual lineage, Hont and Ignatieff
and their ilk forget that it was produced and had consequences
in a real social world. In this context 'Intellectual history, like
economic history before it, becomes imperialist and seeks to
over-run all social life. It is necesssary to pause, from time to
time, to recall that how people thought their times need not
have been the same as how those times eventuated' (p. 273).

The relation between intellectual history and textual analysis, on the one hand, and the 'facts' of social-historical actuality, on the other, is, of course, fraught with problems, but the
opposition between the two need not, perhaps, be as absolute
as the examples above suggest. In this volume, for instance,
Kathryn Sutherland investigates another area in which Smith's
paradigms of the economy had a profound influence on the
shaping of later economic discourse, and on the social policies
which governments pursued as a result of working within the
limits of that discourse, but in which those paradigms bear
strikingly little relation to the actualities of economic behaviour
which 'eventuated' in the society in which Smith lived. In tracing the pattern of silences on the subject of female labour in
the *Wealth of Nations*, against the abundant evidence of its
importance in the contemporary economy, she provides a
powerful example of the extent to which the text has functioned as an ideological construct, shaping the world in its
image, rather than offering a 'scientific' analysis of the empirical evidence of that world, as a neutral basis of economic policy
decisions.

The project of abstracting principles from Smith, which Brown calls 'absolutist', underlies those forms of academic economic analysis in which the propositions of Smith are set ahistorically against those of other theorists – Ricardo or Keynes or Marx – in the course of discussion of general points of economic principle – though in this context discussion almost invariably acquires at least an edge of historical perspective. More crudely, particularly in the last fifteen years, the principles that are said to inform Smith's arguments have repeatedly been abstracted from their source by commentators of the new right, and taken as the foundation of general polemics on a variety of social and political issues. In this context, as Heinz Lubasz points out below, Smith's principles have been taken to be those of free-market liberalism and *laissez faire* – a disputed identification which has been at the heart of controversy over his arguments for many twentieth-century commentators. In an historical survey of 1926, for instance, J. M. Keynes writes of the doctrine of *laissez faire* that it is 'just discoverable in Adam Smith', but points out that the term was never used by Smith, Ricardo or Malthus, and that in the eighteenth-century physiocratic writings where it can first be traced it does not have the connotations that it had acquired by the later nineteenth century.[8]

The characteristics of recent new right polemics are brought into sharp relief if they are set against a commentary on the *Wealth of Nations* which appeared at the time of the bicentenary, and which is typical, in its underlying assumptions, of a number produced to mark that occasion. In 'Adam Smith and Laissez Faire Revisited'[9] Nathan Rosenberg acknowledges that later economics largely consists of 'footnotes' to Adam Smith, but suggests that these footnotes are 'getting longer and remoter from the original text' (p. 19). For Rosenberg, *laissez faire* is an historically outmoded doctrine: he assumes that modern commentators have rejected it, but suggests that it is possible to see why, in different historical circumstances, Smith could have found cogent reasons for advocating it. He writes that 'Adam Smith was no capitalist apologist (though it cannot be denied that such apologists have used – and misinterpreted – Adam Smith for their own purposes). On the contrary, his central preoccupation was to prevent businessmen from pursuing their own interests in antisocial ways' (p. 24). Overstating considerably (and tellingly) he none the less identifies an important strand of debate in the *Wealth of Nations* when he suggests that 'Smith's *whole argument* [my italics] is concerned with the need for erecting an institutional order where the businessman pursuing his self-interest will be compelled to advance the public's welfare. This is not something that happens naturally; it has to be carefully arranged and contrived because businessmen tend naturally to work in opposition to the public welfare' (p. 25).

The contrast with the new ideological orthodoxies that have prevailed and influenced government policies since the 1980s could not be more striking. A collection of essays from 1990, entitled *Adam Smith's Legacy: His Thought In Our Time*, published by the Adam Smith Institute,[10] illustrates very clearly not only the economic and political programmes, but also the populist projects and triumphalist tone, of the new right proponents of 'Smithian' doctrine. The editor, Nicholas Elliott, announces that 'The Adam Smith Institute works to apply the principles of Adam Smith to the modern-day political process', in a world marked by the 'demise of socialism' and the 'growing endorsement of markets'. He argues that Smith 'has arguably had more impact on modern economic policy than any other figure in economic history. While the prescriptions of Karl Marx and John Maynard Keynes have not withstood the test of time, the ideas of Smith are still regularly invoked and modern economic policy is measured against his principles' (p. 1). In the light of this claim, his reading of the *Wealth of Nations* is entirely ahistorical: he dwells on what he identifies as 'the timeless parts of Smith's writing', such as 'his explanation of a spontaneous order arising from the market system', which, Elliott suggests, can be drawn on to counter 'the still widespread assumption in some places that planning is better than laissez faire' (pp. 1–3). A similar ahistoricism, identifying Smith simply and unproblematically as a proponent of *laissez faire*, marks many of the later essays. It is clear, for instance, when Leo Rosten writes that Smith 'advocated a new cause, laissez faire (the phrase was Gournay's; oddly enough, Smith never used it)' (p. 6). Gournay's supposedly original deployment of *laissez faire* in relation to reform of eighteenth-century French trade, and Smith's non-deployment of it, are both confidently subsumed into the nineteenth-century liberal usage, with its extended and acquired associations in that period, as the key to reading Smith in the present.

The proselytising mission of the Adam Smith Institute is evident throughout the book, whether in the enthusiasm shown by contributing politicians such as Nicholas Ridley for carrying the message of free enterprise to Eastern Europe, or in the insistence of various contributors on the importance of a general dissemination of Smith's ideas. In this connection, Elliott's claim that 'An appreciation of Adam Smith should not be confined to the realm of academic economics. In his time he was a popular writer and he should remain so today' (p. 3) is backed up by Russell Lewis's suggestion that 'An entirely re-arranged and abridged edition, with different headlines for the main sections, and published in paperback, would do wonders for public enlightenment' (p. 98). Lewis's enthusiasm for such a project contrasts sharply with Leo Rosten's assessment in the same volume of what a large swathe of the public might expect to gain from the book. Rosten's insistence on the credentials necessary to qualify as one of Smith's initiated readers involves the provision of an extraordinary list of groups excluded from understanding his conclusions and from appreciating their inevitability; and in the process Rosten gives those conclusions an almost metaphysical status. When he links the list with an equation between purchasing power and democratic rights which is peculiarly characteristic of the 1980s, he provides a striking example of the terms in which the political and social policies of the decade were justified by their proponents. He thus writes of Smith's advocacy of the free market that

> It is folly to expect the dispossessed, the confused, the unskilled, the foolish, the scorned, the insecure, the jobless, the emotion-ridden, the impatient, the unanalytic, the failures of the world to accept an abstruse, unreachable scheme which they, in fact, blame for undeserved adversity and unjustified defeats. The crucial point about democracy, I think, is that men who feel too poor to cast significant votes in the market-place, do cast very large votes in the polling booths. (p. 14)

As has frequently been pointed out, and as is demonstrated in various ways in the essays in this volume, the version of Adam Smith's economic and social philosophy which has been invoked by proponents such as those in the Adam Smith Insttute has often not been the product of a reading of the whole of the *Wealth of Nations*, but has rested instead on acceptance of the selective reading of parts of the book developed by nineteenth-century market liberals. Even acknowledging this, however, the fact that the book can bear such radically different interpretations as those quoted above is testimony not only to its difficulty, but also to the contradictoriness that marks some of Smith's arguments, and that is particularly clear if the book is considered as a whole. In this regard, the internal conflicts in the text have proved particularly interesting for those whose training has been in literary theory, and who have consequently been particularly aware of the terms in which Smith's arguments are presented – the ways in which they persuade rhetorically, the tropes they deploy, the value judgements they incorporate, the associations they encourage and the conflicts they accommodate. Those involved in developing this approach to the text have drawn usefully on the work of intellectual historians of the Scottish Enlightenment such as those discussed earlier. However, their manner of proceeding is in some ways antithetical to those outlined above, since they do not look for the coherence of logical argument, let alone for the elucidation of consistent principles, but for the inconsistency and contradictoriness that marks rhetorical performance. The divide between this form of textual analysis and other types of historical commentary has in the past seemed unbridgeable, but more recently the mutual advantages of the approaches have increasingly been recognised. A number of contributions to this volume draw on the techniques of literary analysis to a greater or lesser extent. Kurt Heinzelman, for instance, examines the contribution made by the *Wealth of Nations* to 'the kind of storytelling ... appropriate to economics' by tracing an elaborate series of intertextual links back to the 'story about farming' told in a classical poem – Virgil's *Georgics*. Below I want to sketch some of the areas that are highlighted in a detailed, textually aware reading of the *Wealth of Nations*, and suggest the ways in which this form of analysis of the work might complement other historically based approaches.

The complexities of Smith's account of the economy and of society in the *Wealth of Nations* are at their most involved in his representation of the 'naturalness' of the economic behaviour he analyses, whether the term is used to describe the 'natural' propensities motivating human behaviour, or the 'natural' form in which commercial society develops.[11] In a phrase from Ted Benton's essay in this volume, in which he discusses Smithian political economy and the environment, there are marked 'conceptual tensions' in the *Wealth of Nations*, at 'the interface between wealth-creation and its natural conditions'. This level of difficulty is hardly surprising since, as Raymond Williams remarks in *Keywords*, 'Nature is perhaps the most complex word in the language'.[12] In one sense Smith's project is clearly to endorse and naturalise the economic processes of commercial society as he analyses them, by grounding them in generalisations about the defining characteristics of human psychology. The division of labour, and the evolution of the mechanisms of commercial exchange, on which 'the wealth of nations' and 'the progress of society' depend, are thus presented as the un-planned consequences of a fundamental human 'propensity' or 'disposition' 'to truck, barter, and exchange one thing for another' (I.ii.1). Although Smith holds back from deciding whether this is an original feature of human nature, or the first consequence of human culture, for him it is universal, and marks human beings out from the rest of the animal world. As he remarks, in contrast to human beings, 'Nobody ever saw a dog make a fair and deliberate exchange of one bone for another with another dog' (I.ii.2). None the less, although the 'propensity to truck, barter, and exchange one thing for another' (I.ii.1) is said to be univer-sal, and is presented as an overwhelming determinant of behav-iour, Smith's generalisations about it, and analysis of its consequences in society, involve considerable areas of exclusion – such as the participation of women in the commercial econ-omy; and they are extensively qualified at various stages in his argument, in particular in relation to those who can be seen to be distanced in some way from primary economic production –

amongst whom 'the philosopher', the figure sufficiently distanced from the economic workings of society to be able to understand and explain them, might be taken as a prime example.[13]

Contrary to the claims of some later commentators, commercial activity is not unambiguously endorsed in *Wealth of Nations*. Commerce is prone to competing readings deriving from the various vocabularies that Smith deploys in his arguments, whether these are drawn from political arithmetic, physiocratic economic theory, traditional humanist political discourse, jurisprudential writing, Christian moralism, passional psychology, literary sources such as satire or georgic, or indeed proverbial wisdom. The distinct concerns of each retain residual – if sometimes decentred – roles in his arguments, and they are sometimes essential to the persuasive effect of those arguments, even if their consequences are only partially acknowledged.

In part, this complexity results from the characteristic mode in which Enlightenment historical studies such as Smith's are written, as they move between newly 'scientific' forms of descriptive analysis and older forms of exemplary history or moral commentary aimed at offering implicit or explicit prescription and endorsement of social conduct. In the case of the *Wealth of Nations*, actuality and paradigm, description and prescription, generalisation and disabling qualification, are repeatedly, and sometimes bewilderingly, elided in Smith's account of the way in which 'the obvious and simple system of natural liberty establishes itself of its own accord' in commercial economies, and by extension in the societies in which they develop, once 'systems either of preference or of restraint' have been 'taken away' (IV.ix.51). When, for instance, Smith concedes, late on in the book, that 'To expect, indeed, that the freedom of trade should ever be entirely restored in Great Britain, is as absurd as to expect that an Oceana or Utopia should ever be established in it' (IV.ii.43), he retrospectively modifies the status of what had earlier appeared to be descriptive and analytical reports of the actual development and working of this 'freedom of trade', and so undercuts, or at least qualifies, the terms of the arguments which he had previously based on those reports. Similarly, his explanation and endorsement of the benefits of spontaneous self-regulation in the economy and in society, later extended by commentators as the key to his whole programme, is repeatedly qualified in the text of the *Wealth of Nations* with the insistence that these benefits will appear only 'in a well-governed society' (I.i.10) – though, given the general direction of his argument, it is sometimes difficult to imagine how that government might be constituted or conducted, or who in society might be qualified to provide it.

As Hont and Ignatieff and others have pointed out, the terms in which the 'system of liberty' is described in the *Wealth of Nations* are themselves problematic throughout, since Smith deploys distinct (but by no means always differentiated) meanings of 'liberty' in the course of his arguments. The 'liberty' of trade which he advocates is thus not the same as political 'liberty', as it is defined in the civic humanist or jurisprudential traditions: indeed in some respects it is inimical to both, as he acknowledges at various points. None the less, his argument that economic liberty might lead (or might be made to lead) to political liberty is frequently buttressed with the implicit suggestion that the two terms can be elided, or that they can be regarded as synonymous. As Andrew Skinner points out in this volume, the problems in Smith's position in this regard are particularly acute in Books IV and V of the *Wealth of Nations*, in which, having earlier expounded the economic advantages of the division of labour and its consequence in the development of commerce, Smith surveys the cultural cost of that process, and suggests that, without countervening public measures such as the provision of some means of education, the progress of commerce leads to a loss of 'capacity', and consequently to the disablement, of the majority of the members of society – a situation which in turn threatens them with the loss of 'liberty'. As he writes, whereas the different members of primitive societies tend to pursue a range of varied social activities, and so exert their mental capacities in varied ways, 'In the progress of the division of labour, the employment of the far greater part of those who live by labour, that is, of the great body of the people, comes to be confined to a few very simple operations; frequently to one or two'. In this context, the labourer 'naturally loses, therefore, the habit of such exertion, and generally becomes as stupid and ignorant as it is possible for a human

creature to become. ... His dexterity at his own particular trade
seems, in this manner, to be acquired at the expence of his intellectual, social, and martial virtues' (V.i.f.50).

This development produces a situation in which the capabilities of the different members of society appear to be sharply
differentiated, so justifying hierarchic social divisions. Although
these differences are not innate, but the result of habit and
circumstances, their outcome is inevitable, since the circumstances themselves are the inevitable consequence of the
tendencies in human nature that Smith has earlier defined:

> The difference of natural talents in different men is, in reality,
> much less than we are aware of; and the very different genius
> which appears to distinguish men of different professions, when
> grown up to maturity, is not upon many occasions so much the
> cause, as the effect of the division of labour. The difference
> between the most dissimilar characters, between a philosopher
> and a common street porter, for example, seems to arise not so
> much from nature, as from habit, custom, and education. ... [After
> the first few years of life] The difference of talents comes then to
> be taken notice of, and widens by degrees, till at last the vanity
> of the philosopher is willing to acknowledge scarce any resem-
> blance. But without the disposition to truck, barter, and
> exchange, every man must have procured to himself every neces-
> sary and conveniency of life which he wanted. All must have had
> the same duties to perform, and the same work to do, and there
> could have been no such difference of employment as could alone
> give occasion to any great difference of talents. (I.ii.4)

In these circumstances, the privileged members of society are
those such as the philosopher who can afford the time to stand
back from engagement in the economic processes of society in
order to observe them, and who can in consequence preserve their
own capacity and the multiplicity of their mental engagements:

> In a civilised state ... though there is little variety in the occupa-
> tions of the greater part of individuals, there is an almost infinite
> variety in those of the whole society. These varied occupations
> present an almost infinite variety of objects to the contemplation
> to those few, who, being attached to no particular occupation
> themselves, have leisure and inclination to examine the occupa-
> tions of other people. The contemplation of so great a variety of
> objects necessarily exercises their minds in endless comparisons

and combinations, and renders their understandings, in an extra-ordinary degree, both acute and comprehensive. Unless those few, however, happen to be placed in some very particular situations, their great abilities, though honourable to themselves, may contribute very little to the good government or happiness of their society. Notwithstanding the great abilities of those few, all the nobler parts of the human character may be, in a great measure, obliterated and extinguished in the great body of the people. (V.i.f.51)

There is some doubt in this passage as to whether the philosopher who is described can ever have a real rather than an ideal social identity: John Barrell, for example, suggests that Smith

encounters the problem that within a complex, commercial society, there may be no viewing-position from which the organisation of society or the public good can possibly be grasped ... He is reduced to inventing a fictitious and disembodied social spectator, the 'philosophic eye' whose viewpoint and whose breadth and depth of vision no individual can be imagined as possessing';[14]

and Smith is noticeably shy of specifying the 'very particular situations' that the philosopher might occupy in order to promote the public good.

In this and other respects, the cultural analysis offered by Smith in Books IV and V of the *Wealth of Nations* bears strong affinities with the arguments developed by a number of his contemporaries in the Scottish Enlightenment – notably Adam Ferguson, whose *Essay on the History of Civil Society* appeared in 1767. Unsurprisingly, this part of Smith's study was largely ignored by nineteenth-century political economists in favour of his more famous pronouncements in the earlier books about the advantages of commerce, and the later books have been similarly ignored by the twentieth-century legatees of those economists. It is easy to imagine, for instance, which parts of the *Wealth of Nations* would be included and given prominence in Russell Lewis's proposal for a rearranged and retitled paperback edition, and what impression of Smith's arguments this would produce.

In the nineteenth century, critiques of the effects of the division of labour were developed outside political economy by

a sequence of British cultural critics from Hazlitt and Coleridge
to Carlyle and Arnold, who deployed them in their attacks on
contemporary industrial capitalism and the 'dismal science' of
economics which they saw as providing its intellectual rationalisation; more radically, they formed an important element in
the critique of political economy developed by Engels and
Marx. In *Capital*, for example, Marx argues that the 'social
separation of branches of labour' in manufacture 'attacks the individual at the very roots of his life': in the same passage he points
the contrast between Smith and later political economists when
he quotes parallel passages from Smith and Ferguson on the
need for government to compensate for the debilitating effects
of the division of labour by providing what he calls 'prudently
homeopathic doses' of education, and compares them with the
absolute non-interventionism advocated by Smith's early nineteenth-century French translator Germain Garnier.[15] Reaffirming
the importance of the cultural analysis in the *Wealth of Nations*
as a whole has been an important element in re-examining the
historical particularity of Smith's work.

Bearing in mind the strength of the cultural critique developed in the later books of the *Wealth of Nations*, a textually
aware reading of the whole work suggests the extent to which
its earlier and most famous arguments rest on what might be
called strategic imprecisions. At the very start of Book I Smith
proposes that

> The greatest improvement in the productive powers of labour,
> and the greater part of the skill, dexterity, and judgement with
> which it is anywhere directed, or applied, seem to have been the
> effects of the division of labour.
>
> The effects of the division of labour, in the general business of
> society, will be more easily understood, by considering in what
> manner it operates in some particular manufactures. (I.i.1–2)

He then elaborates on the principle in action in relation to the
famous example of 'the trade of a pin-maker', in which the division of labour is, as he argues, clear and much observed, but
not necessarily any more developed than in other manufacturing processes where it is less visible. Already the connections
between Smith's terms are elusive, particularly when he offers
his account of the industrial process of 'pin-making' as a model

of 'the general business of society'. Read narrowly, this model simply relates one manufacture to others in an economic discussion, but it clearly also carries wider connotations. In the late eighteenth century the word 'business' does not necesssarily have the predominant connection with commerce which it later acquires. (In Dr Johnson's *Dictionary* (1755), for example, there is no entry which makes this exclusive connection.) Instead it covers a more general range of areas of 'busy-ness', so that Smith's suggestion seems to be that pin-making provides an appropriate model for a broad range of professional social activities and transactions. In the first part of the book in particular, this claim provides an important foundation for his enumeration of the economic advantages of the division of labour, and for his suggestion that these economic advantages also constitute social advantages. Later, but only later, the reader discovers the extent to which they are countered by cultural disadvantages, and to which, in some areas of social 'business', they do not apply, or apply only with severe qualifications.

In this larger context other of the terms that Smith uses in the opening paragraphs have complex connotations. Taking an example from the passage above, although he argues throughout that increased 'skill' and 'dexterity' are the results of the division of labour, his later concession that these qualities are socially disabling suggests that they are in some ways inimical to the development of 'judgement', in the extended sense in which that term is deployed in other contexts in the book and elsewhere in his work.[16] Inevitably this puts into question the extent to which his claim that these abilities 'are directed' implies internal volition on the part of those engaged in 'labour' – and so acknowledges a capacity in the labourer which renders that volitional action possible, or how far it implies the existence of an external directing agency. Without fully admitting it, Smith introduces one of the most puzzling strands of discussion in the work – the extent to which his 'system of perfect liberty' implicitly incorporates areas of compulsive social regulation; and at the same time he launches into the later fraught debate over the social and cultural consequences of the division of labour.

Further ramifications of these discussions are introduced

when Smith suggests that, although the division of labour seems to have been carried furthest in 'very trifling' manufactures such as pin-making, this is only because it is more readily comprehensible in this context: the same principle applies throughout the economy (I.i.2). Smith's discussion here introduces a further set of relations – between labour and leisure, activity, supervision and knowledge – which are crucial in various guises to the later arguments of the book, implicating its readers in interesting ways in the processes it describes; and with which I will now conclude. In 'pin-making', as it is a small-scale process, 'those employed in every different branch of the work can often be collected into the same workhouse and placed at once under the view of the spectator.' In contrast, in 'great manufactures', 'We can seldom see more, at one time, than those employed in one single branch'.

On one level, the account simply records the process of capitalisation of production, the consequences of which are one of Smith's later subjects. More strikingly, perhaps, it introduces a variety of relations between the 'artisan' and the literal and figurative 'spectator' of his labour. In this connection, the workhouse appears as an economic panopticon, making possible observation of the work disciplines of the artisan, and so boosting economic production by preventing the 'habit of sauntering and of indolent careless application' which Smith later claims infects dispersed, unspecialised and unsupervised labour (I.i.7). By the same token, however, it ensures the progressive disablement of the artisans whose labours are observed. The extension of the image of the spectator of labour thus serves as a figure for what Smith will offer in the ensuing work, which will indeed reveal ramifications of the division of labour invisible to the naked eye at any one site. In doing so, however, it will mark a distinction, implicit for much of the work, explicit at certain moments and in certain respects, between observer and observed, between the material economy in which the activity described happens and the domain of 'science' in which the explanation of the working of that economy is textualised as knowledge.

Notes

1   Margaret Thatcher, 'Progress through Independence', in *Let Our Children Grow Tall: Selected Speeches 1975–1977* (London: Centre for Policy Studies, 1977), p. 15; Hugo Young, *One of Us: A Biography of Margaret Thatcher* (London: Macmillan, 1989), p. 528; Margaret Thatcher, *The Downing Street Years* (London: Harper Collins, 1993), p. 618; Ian Gilmour, *Dancing with Dogma: Britain Under Thatcherism* (London: Simon & Schuster, 1992), p. 185; Martin Holmes, *The First Thatcher Government 1979–1983: Contemporary Conservatism and Economic Change* (Brighton: Harvester, 1985), p. 149. Further examples of identification with Smith, from the USA, are noted in Heinz Lubasz's essay in this volume.

2   John Gray, *Beyond the New Right* (London: Routledge, 1993).

3   Maurice Brown, *Adam Smith's Economics: Its Place in the Development of Economic Thought* (London and New York: Croom Helm, 1988).

4   E. P. Thompson, 'The Moral Economy of the English Crowd in the Eighteenth Century', *Past and Present*, 50 (1971), reprinted in *Customs in Common* (1991; Harmondsworth: Penguin, 1993), pp. 185–258. Page references below cite this volume.

5   E. P. Thompson, 'The Moral Economy Reviewed', in *Customs in Common*, pp. 259–351.

6   'Needs and Justice in the *Wealth of Nations*: An Introductory Essay', in Istvan Hont and Michael Ignatieff, ed., *Wealth and Virtue: The Shaping of Political Economy in the Scottish Enlightenment* (Cambridge: Cambridge University Press, 1983), pp. 1–44.

7   See, in particular, J. G. A. Pocock, *The Machiavellian Moment: Florentine Political Thought and the Atlantic Republican Tradition* (Princeton: Princeton University Press, 1975).

8   J. M. Keynes, 'The End of Laissez Faire' (1926), in *The Collected Writings of John Maynard Keynes* (London and Basingstoke: Macmillan, 1972), vol. 9, pp. 272–94. The origins of the term '*laissez faire*' are much disputed. Keynes suggests Legendre, d'Argenson, Franklin, and the later Bentham as sources, and is sceptical about 'the tradition associating [ideas of *laissez faire*] with the physiocrats, and particularly de Gournay and Quesnay' (p. 278). Leo Rosten (see p. 10 of this volume) confidently asserts that Gournay was the originator of the phrase.

9   Nathan Rosenberg, 'Adam Smith and Laissez Faire Revisited', in Gerald P. O'Driscoll Jr, ed., *Adam Smith and Modern Political Economy: Bicentennial Essays on 'The Wealth of Nations'* (Ames, Iowa: Iowa State University Press, 1976).

10   Nicholas Elliott, ed. *Adam Smith's Legacy: His Thought in our Time* (London: ASI (Research) Limited, 1990).

11   For an extended discussion of one aspect of Smith's use of the term 'natural', see Noel Parker's essay in this volume. For further discussion, see Kathryn Sutherland's introduction to her edition of the *Wealth of*

Nations (Oxford: Oxford University Press, 1993), pp. xvii–xx, and Stephen Copley, 'The "Natural" Economy: A Note on Some Rhetorical Strategies in Political Economy – Adam Smith and Malthus', in Francis Barker *et al.*, ed., *1789: Reading Writing Revolution* (University of Essex, 1982), pp. 160–9.

12 Raymond Williams, *Keywords: A Vocabulary of Culture and Society* (rev. edn, London: Fontana, 1983), p. 219.

13 See, for instance, WN I.x.b.24–5; I.x.c.37–8; V.i.f.1–10; V.i.f.51.

14 John Barrell, 'The Public Prospect and the Private View: The Politics of Taste in Eighteenth-Century Britain', in Simon Pugh, ed., *Reading Landscape: Country – City – Capital* (Manchester: Manchester University Press, 1990), p. 31.

15 Karl Marx, *Capital*, tr. Ben Fowkes, introd. Ernest Mandel (Harmondsworth: Penguin, 1976), vol. 1, pp. 483–5. Garnier's translation of Smith appeared in 1802.

16 See, for instance, Andrew Skinner's comments on *The Theory of Moral Sentiments* at pp. 87–91 of this volume.

2

Natural liberty and *laissez faire*: how Adam Smith became a free trade ideologue

KEITH TRIBE

The principal object of Political Economists is to enlighten mankind, by showing how their wealth and well-being may be most effectually promoted. And this Adam Smith has done better than anyone else. He has shown that, speaking generally, the riches and comforts that are universally desired will be procured with the least difficulty and in the greatest abundance by allowing individuals to pursue their own interest in their own way, subject only to the condition of their carefully respecting the property and rights of others. Nothing of importance has been added to the masterly exposition he has given of the benefits arising from the freedom of industry.[1]

In 1776 Adam Smith published, under the title *An Inquiry into the Nature and Causes of the Wealth of Nations*, the book which was to become, in the course of the nineteenth century, the gospel of free trade and economic liberalism, and the textual symbol of British economic supremacy. Although the work ran through five editions before his death in 1790, attesting to its literary success, direct evidence of the domestic impact of the arguments it put forward is notably scarce. It was not until some time after Smith's death that his reputation as the founder of classical economics took root in Britain;[2] this reputation is thus one largely forged in the nineteenth century, under conditions quite different from those in which the text was originally conceived and published. The *Wealth of Nations* is today generally viewed as a product of the Scottish Enlightenment, and thus related to arguments on the relation of commerce, virtue and civilisation; but in the nineteenth century Smith was re-read as the founder of a new science of political economy, an idea carried forward by writers such as Malthus, Ricardo and John Stuart Mill, and one which had hardened into an ortho-doxy by the time that Karl Marx took up his study of English political economy in 1843.

What was this science, and in what respect was it new? Smith defined the 'wealth' of a nation not as an accumulation of gold, nor as simple populousness, both of which had been commonly argued by previous writers – instead he proposed that the wealth of a nation consisted of the annual produce of its labour. This could be augmented, he went on, through the development of the division of labour; labour could be made more productive by subdividing tasks and rationalising the production process. There were two provisos attached to this: first, that this process of the increasing division of labour had greater potential in manufacture than in agriculture; second, that the degree to which it could develop was limited by the extent of the market. From this it followed that the most rapid increase of national wealth would result from the augmentation and rationalisation of labour applied to manufacturing, within an economy which was both internally and externally freed from impediments to trade.

Underpinning the economic argument of *Wealth of Nations* is Smith's 'system of natural liberty', a system whose princi-ples, if observed, would bring to all wealth and prosperity. 'Natural liberty' relates to Smith's apprehension of human nature and the nature of the civilising process; it does not imply any particular political order, republican or monarchic, and there is in fact no direct argument made by Smith in the *Wealth of Nations* regarding the adequacy of given political structures to the realisation of wealth and welfare. 'Natural liberty' presupposed a condition in which individual agents were free to pursue their own interests: ultimately this was the driving force of commercial development. But this pursuit of self-inter-est was not inimical to welfare, or to civilisation: by pursuing their own interests individuals best served the interests, and welfare, of all, despite their not intending this outcome. In the eighteenth-century context, this paradox was at the root of reflection upon the manner in which commerce might be reconciled with civic virtue: Smith responding to this positively with the arguments of the *Wealth of Nations*, and Ferguson, for example, arguing in his *Essay on the History of Civil Society* (1767) that commerce would undermine civil society, promote corruption and a decline into slavery.

Within the context of the early nineteenth century, and stripped of its wider implications for an understanding of civil society and economy, the *Wealth of Nations* came to be regarded as the oracle of growth based upon free trade, in which a continuous transformation of the British economy rested upon manufacturing innovation combined with an established British pre-eminence in world trade. This was the popular view of Smith adopted in the nineteenth century, by proponents of free trade as well as by those who argued in favour of protection as a path to national economic development. This nineteenth-century re-reading was not therefore one which adopted Smith as the proponent of economic growth and free trade; his arguments were also accessible to, and employed by, quite different tendencies. If we are to understand some of the cross-currents of economic debate in the early nineteenth century we need to take a more considered view of the theses advanced by Adam Smith.

First, it should be noted that while Smith put forward an argument according to which manufacture was elevated above agriculture as a path to national economic growth, his understanding of manufacturing innovation was a very traditional one, involving the subdivision of manual skills and not the substitution of capital for labour. In this respect it is erroneous to associate the *Wealth of Nations* directly with the economic developments of nineteenth-century Europe and America. Second, he was writing in the context of an economy whose structure and rhythms were dominated by agricultural production. This was not only the major economic sector; it was the immediate source of food and was prone to annual fluctuations in output and associated variations in prices. Since foodstuff represented such a major part of expenditures on the part of a majority of the population, the achievement of a low and stable price for grain was a crucial political problem throughout the eighteenth century for European governments.

Broadly speaking, there were two opposed solutions to this question. The first option was to encourage home production of grain by protecting domestic producers: high tariffs on imported grain would prevent the flooding of the market with cheap food in good years, undermining home production which would then be unable to provide adequate supplies whenever the sources of foreign grain diminished, or even dried up altogether. This option therefore secured whatever the level of home produce might be to domestic consumers, albeit at a high price. The second option also encouraged home production, but did so by permitting free import and export of grain. According to this line of argument, the availability of a market greater in extent than that offered by the national economy would stimulate domestic producers, consequently rationalising their activities so that cheap foreign grain would not appear to be such a constant threat to domestic production. This second option proposed that the domestic population would be best served by a supply of cheap food based not upon the protection and control of the home market, but rather upon their access to an international market in foodstuffs. Freedom of trade in grains moderated domestic prices and maximised production, since producers with access to extensive markets could be confident of sales at reasonable prices.

It is of course the latter option that Adam Smith proposed, and a great deal of the *Wealth of Nations* is taken up with his refutation of two versions of the opposing view: that of the 'mercantile school', which he suggested identified the possession of gold with wealth and whose policies were protectionist and restrictive; and that of the French 'economists' or physiocrats who, while arguing for free external trade in grain, identified agriculture, and not labour, as the unique source of national wealth. Although Smith was himself influenced by physiocratic thinking, it was the physiocrats' insistence upon agriculture as the sole net productive employment for labour, and the 'sterility' of manufacturing employment, that marked the principal point of disagreement. For Smith, the distinction between 'productive' and 'unproductive' labour involves not the sector in which labour is expended, but the nature of the product which is produced – is it an object which is itself exchangeable, or does it merely vanish into thin air at the point of production, like the song of an opera singer? Therefore it is possible to extend the argument concerning the most advantageous utilisation of national labour with respect to food supply into a general argument on the international division of labour and the advantages of trade – which was what David Ricardo did some forty years later in his *On the Principles of Political Economy and Taxation* (1817).

This clarifies to some extent some of the economic issues in the political economy advanced by Adam Smith, and the elements of a political argument concerning the role of government are evident. But there is more to Smith's political economy than a simple argument for free trade and economic liberty; what is new in Smith is the proposition that a 'system of liberty' would not only stabilise domestic prices and stimulate trade, it would also permit the inherent self-regulating features of a national economy to function. The 'system of liberty' is not simply a charter for the removal of tariffs and duties, both internally and externally; it proposes that the interaction of individuals, if untrammelled by excessive rules and regulations, would result in an optimum increase of national wealth which was at the same time self-regulating and stable.

It is this idea which is at the heart of Smith's reference to the manner in which economies are, in the absence of serious impediments, regulated by an 'invisible hand' – a phrase that occurs only once in the *Wealth of Nations* and which is only properly developed in the discussion of 'sympathy' and the role of the impartial spectator to be found in *The Theory of Moral Sentiments* (1759). The desire to emulate others and gain what they possess, constrained by awareness of the need to gain the consent of others in making such acquisition, provides a powerful motor of wealth-creation modulated by social cohesion within a differentiated society. It was in this way that Smith was also able to break quite decisively with the established view of acquisitiveness as unworthy, of the world of commerce as antithetical to civilised values. By demonstrating the manner in which the individual disposition to emulation of others created at the same time social order and national wealth Smith was able to forge a new moral basis for commercial society – a society in which the creation of wealth through commercial activity was both virtuous and an enhancement of civilisation.

Although the above is now widely accepted as representing the theoretical core of the *Wealth of Nations*, this general acceptance is comparatively recent. The complex interplay of ethics, economics, commerce, government and civilisation that modern historians discern in Smith was not at the centre of the theoretical interests of those writers who contributed to the construction of the new orthodoxy of classical political economy. For them, the *Wealth of Nations* represented a common basis from which this work of construction began, and to which argument constantly recurred; but in the process this basis was covered over with emphases and reinterpretations which obscured the original intent of the work. Ultimately, the *Wealth of Nations* was reduced to a set of principles culled from its first two books – on the division of labour, money, prices and currency, wages, profits and rent, and the accumulation of capital; with perhaps some recognition of the critique of the mercantile school and the physiocrats to be found in Book IV, and of the discussion of taxation from Book V. In his teaching at the East India College, where for over twenty-five years until his death in 1834 Malthus used the *Wealth of Nations* as his textbook, due attention was paid to the critique of the physiocrats and the principles of taxation;[3] while Ricardo's *On the Principles of Political Economy and Taxation* was organised very much as a chapter-by-chapter critique of Smith, in which of course taxation figured large.[4] But in subsequent writings interest in the physiocrats waned, and taxation became the subject of more specialist writing. Political economy became generally perceived as a science of production, distribution and exchange, with additional remarks perhaps, as with James Mill's *Elements of Political Economy* (1821);[5] but with the tripartite distinction of economic activity united by a conception of value.

More important, Ricardo transformed Smith's somewhat diffuse principles into a system linking production and distri-

bution to free international trade, firmly associating economic
policy with a specific line of economic reasoning. When Marx
refocused attention upon the classical theory of value and
reworked it into the cornerstone of his critique of political economy, this had two notable effects. First, the determinate relationship between free trade and economic growth established
by Ricardo, expressed in terms of an argument for free trade in
grain and the impact that this would have on the maintenance
of the rate of profit in all economic sectors, was obscured by
Marx's fixation upon value. Second, this had the effect of
relaunching the classical theory of value as the centrepiece of a
science of political economy precisely when economic theory
was turning away from classical preoccupations. Although it
would be well into the twentieth century before the full implications of the 'marginal revolution' of the 1870s were absorbed,
by the last quarter of the nineteenth century economists were
increasingly inclined to deal with price as a product of (volatile)
market relationships, rather than as an expression of some
inherent value. Marx's economic system was in this respect
therefore doubly anachronistic, obscuring one of the most
important aspects of Ricardo's work while promoting an
untimely emphasis upon another. The net effect of this was to
recreate the 'Smithian' heritage as one turning upon the concept
of value, rather than as a discourse upon wealth, virtue and
civilisation.

This was, however, but one, English, track along which the
reception of the *Wealth of Nations* ran.[6] It would be mistaken
to suppose that the reception process in Britain substantially
conditioned that which occurred in other countries. In fact, the
Wealth of Nations fared rather better in Continental Europe and
North America than it did at home. L. H. Jakob suggested in
1825 that it was the Germans who had first recast Smith's somewhat disconnected principles as a system of national wealth,
several writers at the turn of the century, Jakob among them,
having contributed to this.[7] In the United States, during the 1780s
and 1790s, the writings of Jefferson, Franklin and Madison
drew freely on Smith's writings; while Alexander Hamilton's
Report on the Subject of Manufactures of 1791 was an extended
commentary and critique of principles exposed in the *Wealth*

of Nations.[8] It was, furthermore, out of this American tradition that Friedrich List's denunciation of Smithian economics as 'cosmopolitical economics' was developed in the later 1820s. Consideration of some aspects of the German and American reception process will shed some light on the manner in which that process transforms the text of a writer into an object of discussion and criticism not necessarily congruent with the original. Moreover, once this process has begun, it is important to distinguish between the manner in which the transformed object is further transmitted and modified, and the function and purpose of appeals to the 'original text', in which it is more than likely that contemporary readings are simply re-read back into an origin.

It cannot reasonably be inferred from this fact − that any text undergoes a complex pattern of reading, re-reading and transmutation − that meaning is therefore not only relative, but open to the choices and understandings of equal readers. This would be a curiously liberalistic conception, in which a literary universal franchise settled issues of meaning by majority vote. This affinity of deconstructionism with Chicago economics generally goes unremarked. The reception process reworks a canonical text, but in historically determinate conditions, and it is these conditions that are of interest here, not the simple fact that readings vary. For the reader is not free to choose; choices are made within definite canons of interpretation and competence − there is no such thing as a literary equivalent to a random walk. Rather than disappearing into a speculative morass of relativism and indeterminacy, the points raised above can be distilled into two clear questions: (1) What makes a text readable/unreadable? (2) Given that 'readability' transforms the object read, what are the conditions under which the object is transmitted? These are essentially historical questions, that is, questions which call for the assembly of relevant evidence, the testing of hypotheses, and the exercise of informed judgement. We can test their utility against the German reception of Smith.

J. F. Schiller's German translation of the *Wealth of Nations* appeared in two parts, the first in 1776 and the second in 1778.[9] Despite a number of reviews in prominent periodicals, little general notice was taken of the book until a second translation, by the popular philosopher Christian Garve, assisted by August Dörrien, appeared in 1794. Scattered references can be found in books and essays concerning the nature of wealth and the division of labour; but Smith's book did not at first prompt any lengthy or systematic response. Indeed, at this time the most cited British economic text was Sir James Steuart's *Inquiry into the Principles of Political Economy* (1767), a work which the *Wealth of Nations* was implicitly designed to supplant.[10] Furthermore, reviewers tended to associate Smith's text with the work of the physiocrats; and even when the second volume of Schiller's translation appeared, including Smith's critique of physiocracy in Book IV, the reviewer argued that this critique was founded upon 'mere logomachy', and that Smith on the whole agreed with the physiocrats.[11]

With the appearance of the first part of Garve and Dörrien's translation in 1794 the reception accorded to Smith changed dramatically. In 1796 Sartorius published a précis of the *Wealth of Nations* based upon his lectures at Göttingen.[12] Roscher[13] describes this *Handbuch* as a summary of the *Wealth of Nations*; but as a summary it has important features. First, Sartorius reduces the sometimes rambling text of the *Wealth of Nations* to sets of theses and propositions; but in so doing he obscures the historical form in which Smith's argument develops. The fact that the *Handbuch* is only 234 pages long does perhaps make drastic simplification inevitable, but there is a second, more obvious, feature of Sartorius's exposition. The *Handbuch* is divided into two parts, in which Part I deals with Books I and II of the *Wealth of Nations*, and Part II with Books III, IV and V. Instead, however, of beginning Part II with a summary of Smith's Book III, Sartorius first interjects a discussion of the nature of *Staatswirthschaft* ('state economy'), which is his own gloss on Smith and corresponds to no passage written by the latter. Book III of the *Wealth of Nations* is then reduced to a set of principles (this the most 'historical' part of the book). The greatest and most significant divergence comes in the treatment of Smith's Book V, marked by a shift from précis to commentary, where the expenses and revenues of the state are assessed with respect to a specific objective of the state, 'the security of all native persons and rightfully established law'.[14] This places the various institutions that appear in Book V of the *Wealth of Nations* with respect to a *Staatszweck* proper to *Polizeiwissenschaft*,[15] but which is not clearly in evidence in Smith's text.

In the early years of the nineteenth century an increasing number of treatises appeared which paid homage to the *Wealth of Nations* as the founding moment in modern economic thinking. One of the first instances of this is Lueder's *Ueber Nationalindustrie und Staatswirthschaft. Nach Adam Smith bearbeitet* (1800–04), which saw in the *Wealth of Nations* a system which could reveal the eternal laws of man's existence, if only the confusion resulting from Smith's method of presentation could be removed.[16] This was to be a common complaint of German writers on Smith. Another example is that of Weber's *Systematisches Handbuch der Staatswirthschaft,* volume I (1804). At first sight this appears to offer a paraphrase of the Introduction to the *Wealth of Nations*, arguing that the property of a state consisted not only of goods and chattels but of the skills of its inhabitants, which combine to meet the needs of the state and its citizens:

> The condition under which this is possible is the application and use of the property of the state; and this can take place only through the labour of the citizen, i.e., through the expenditure of effort which the citizen must make in the utilisation of property. Labour is the immediate fund of all the income of a nation and thereby also all the income of the state, and represents the only resource on which the state can draw. The condition, or the real value of the entire national income constitutes national wealth; whose different levels are dependent upon the various degrees of development and completeness of the labour of the nation. The surest foundation for national wealth, its highest development and most advantageous use must be the goal of the internal administration of the state, and thus of the science concerned with this task, which is the object of our study here.[17]

The language of 'national wealth', labour and income used here draws on that of Smith, although this is ultimately incorporated within a conventional view of the state, rather than civil society, as the agent of regulation and order. Nevertheless, it rapidly became common to adapt Smith in this way, such that, as Jakob noted, by the end of the first decade of the new century Smith's arguments were firmly embedded in German economic argument.

How can we account for this varied pace of reception of a book available in both the original English and German translation from 1776? The initial period of relative neglect has often been put down by commentators to the poor quality of the original translation; with the appearance of a more adept translation, undertaken by a writer familiar with Scottish philosophy, an obstacle to the diffusion of Smith's ideas was removed. This account is not, however, very plausible. For one thing, the reception process fared little better in Smith's native country, where the supposed opacity of a translation could not present a barrier to understanding. Furthermore, the suggestion that Schiller's translation was so poor that it concealed the leading ideas of the *Wealth of Nations* was dealt with by Garve himself, who had first read Smith in the Schiller translation, and found on reading the original that nothing had been concealed from him by the translator. The problem, suggested Garve, lay in the style.[18] Style could well obstruct readability; but it is more likely, given the abrupt change in reception following the appearance of the new translation, that something more substantial than style is involved here.

The new translation was not so much the impulse for a re-reading of Smith as part of a trend in which German intellectual discourse suddenly became more open to the principles of liberty and regulation through self-interest that Smith espoused. When Schiller's translation had appeared, hard on the heels of the original English text, Germany was about to undergo a brief but intense dalliance with physiocratic thinking. It was indeed true that this system was based upon a conception of natural order not far removed from Smith's system of natural liberty; while the conventional German conception of natural order was one which laid far more emphasis upon the work of government, rather than the autonomy of free subjects, in the creation of order. Interest in physiocracy might have led to Smith being treated as a physiocrat, but it did also provide an entry into the literary world. This physiocratic reception was itself chronologically displaced, for it adopted principles and arguments that had been current in France some ten years previously. More important, criticism of physiocratic doctrine came to focus upon the unworkability of its single tax doctrine, and general doubt with respect to the wisdom of describing agricultural labour as uniquely productive. Comparatively little was made of its conception of natural order; and so when, around 1782, the vogue for physiocratic argument receded from coffee shops and local societies, the conventional *Staatswissenschaften* ('sciences of the state') carried on their administrative pedagogy as before, a pedagogy which allowed little space for arguments such as Smith's.

It was another intellectual fashion, for critical philosophy, that permanently established the *Wealth of Nations* as a canonical text in Germany. Kant's conception of reason as located in the individual introduced a new conception of sociability based upon the interests of calculating subjects, all of whom *qua* human beings shared the common property of 'neediness', economic activity being construed as activity directed towards the satisfaction of felt needs. The rationality of action directed towards the satisfaction of need was to be evaluated in terms of the interests of the individual, rather than, as hitherto, in the planful activity of the state. Society was best served by a condition of freedom in which each was able to determine the proper application of his or her own capacities through the exercise of reason; a condition analogous to the system of natural liberty which, according to Smith, would promote the maximum public good. Later in the century German philosophers came to see the principles advanced by Kant and by Smith as complementary aspects of a new liberal programme; but it is more accurate to view the Kantian system as, first, a necessary condition for the acceptance of Smithian economic arguments; and second, a substitute which made it unnecessary for Smith to be understood as a theorist of civilisation. Paradoxically, the association with the vogue for critical philosophy made it feasible for Smith to be understood as the proponent of an economic system, in which the underlying moral and cultural arguments could simply be placed on one side.

This provides some kind of answer to the question posed above concerning successive phases of 'readability' and 'unreadability'. Not the availability of a text, nor even of a good translation, is decisive here; rather, what makes a text readable is the intellectual and cultural context within which such a text appears. In the German case, it is possible to show why there was, first, a delay, and then a rapid and enthusiastic adoption of the *Wealth of Nations* as a canonical text. Some explanation is also thereby provided of the manner in which 'reduction' of the text was effected, involving the erosion of the original scope of Smith's argument and its restatement in a more pliant and comprehensible version. This moves us forward into the second question posed above, concerning the conditions under which a text is reproduced in public discourse, and the work of literary transformation which this effects.

In later eighteenth-century Britain economic argument was a part of a general culture, not requiring any especially arcane knowledge for intelligent participation in debate. Knowledge of its principles was part of the intellectual armoury of the cultured man and, after the efforts of Jane Marcet in the early nineteenth century, of the educated woman (see the essay by Kathryn Sutherland, pp. 116–17 below). In the course of the nineteenth century more abstract treatises appeared, but it was not until the end of the century that the transformation began which was to make economic argument arcane knowledge deriving from a specific educational programme.

In Germany, by contrast, economic argument was by the later eighteenth century primarily a university-based body of knowledge, used in the training of public officials, and embodied in hundreds of dense textbooks which, by no stretch of the imagination could be confused with amusing, diverting or cultivated literature. With the demise of the older cameralistic literature in the late eighteenth century, Smith's *Wealth of Nations* became a key element in the construction of a new *Nationalökonomie* that was founded upon the fact of human need, providing the necessary principles regarding the nature of production, distribution and exchange: the study of the formation and augmentation of national wealth.[19] As an academic text the *Wealth of Nations* was considerably attenuated: little of the material on taxation and government activity survived, and the critique of the mercantile and agricultural schools in Book IV disappeared, as did much of the discussion of currency and money from Book II. What remained was a set of principles on productive and unproductive labour, the relationship between wages, profits and rents, the principle of the division of labour, and of course the general prejudice in favour of economic liberty. The reception in Germany of Smith's *Wealth of Nations* as an academic treatise for use in universities sharpened its reduction to a small number of economic principles; although the prevailing German prejudice in favour of economic regulation did much to temper the more *laissez-faire* aspects of the work. This incarnation of the book came later, with the development of a popular critique of Smithian political economy.

Under both headings the process of reception in the United States took a different course. In the course of the eighteenth century there had developed in America a view of Britain that regarded corruption and degeneracy as necessary corollaries of industrial economic development. Jefferson, in his *Notes on the State of Virginia* (1781), proposed therefore a conception of economic development in which moral virtue was to be preserved by a society formed of independent husbandmen.[20] American demand for finer manufactured goods should be met not by the development of domestic manufactures, but rather by imports. In contrast to the contemporary European emphasis on the benefits of domestic manufacture, Jefferson and others argued for their import, for virtue could only be maintained through the pursuit of agricultural production. It was not possible to postpone the stage of manufacturing permanently; but America was uniquely privileged, through its possession of unsettled lands, to defer the social consequences of industrial economic development. This line of reasoning concurs with that advanced by Smith, in Book III of *Wealth of Nations*, concerning natural and unnatural forms of social and economic development; and this agrarianism could be held to be 'Smithian' in other respects as well – particularly in the relation of trade to the international division of labour.

The War of Independence had at least in part been based on a dissatisfaction with Britain's refusal to recognise the growing significance of America in world trade, and in the course of the Revolution the aspiration arose for a reorganisation of international trade and the displacement of Britain as its dominant power. Hamilton, the first Secretary of the Treasury, perceived, however, that the outcome of such a position would be commercial war with Britain, and since the funding of the debt required trade with Britain, he rejected the agrarian arguments of Jefferson and Madison. His *Report on the Subject of Manufactures* of 1791 advanced 'protectionist' as opposed to 'free trade' arguments, but this did not mean that principles established in the *Wealth of Nations* were thereby necessarily rejected. Hamilton drew directly and extensively on the *Wealth of Nations* for his arguments, and his principal objective – to demonstrate that only on the basis of a flourishing manufacturing industry can a nation increase its wealth – employs a form of reasoning drawn directly from Smith.

First, he uses Smith's arguments against the physiocratic evaluation of agriculture and manufacture,[21] and then Smith's argument that manufacturing is inherently more amenable to enhancement of productivity than agriculture.[22] The *Report* argues that the development of agriculture and manufacture must be joint, but with manufacture taking the leading position in stimulating their mutual development and thereby increasing domestic demand for raw produce. Only in this way, suggests Hamilton, will the 'productive powers' of labour be augmented.[23]

But unless manufacture in the United States were protected, the competition of established manufacturing nations in Europe would endanger such a process of indigenous joint development. Hamilton agrees that the 'system of perfect liberty' is desirable and that, if it prevailed, then agricultural specialisation would not be entirely undesirable for the United States. In the contemporary world, however, perfect liberty did not prevail, and the United States was in danger of being forced into unsuitable specialisation:

> In such a position of things, the United States cannot exchange with Europe on equal terms; and the want of reciprocity would render them the victim of a system, which should induce them to confine their views to Agriculture and refrain from Manufactures.[24]

The argument that Hamilton then went on to develop, and which became the basis of protectionist doctrine, suggested that the only means that a nation like the United States had available to secure the eventual benefits of joint development of agriculture and manufacture was a system of protective tariffs –

protecting the young American manufacturers from the advantages their European counterparts enjoyed by virtue of their
maturity.

The first indigenous American treatise on political economy, Daniel Raymond's *Thoughts on Political Economy* (1820),
adopted an adversarial position with respect to the *Wealth of
Nations*. Much of Raymond's argument is sustained by a diffuse
hostility to the principles advanced in the *Wealth of Nations*:
for example, when discussing the nature of national wealth, he
seeks to distinguish this quite sharply from individual wealth.
The latter is '[t]he possession of property, for the use of which,
the owner can obtain a quantity of the necessaries and comforts
of life';[25] national wealth is on the other hand 'a capacity for
acquiring the necessaries and comforts of life'.[26] Failure to grasp
this fundamental distinction, suggests Raymond, results in the
Smithian error of seeing accumulation as a result of thriftiness,
rather than as a development of resources at a national level.
For Raymond, the nation is an entity distinct from a simple
aggregate of persons; it is, he writes, a 'unity, and possesses all
the properties of unity'.[27] Hence public economy and private
economy are distinct, and the public economy of a nation cannot
be properly assessed by decomposing it into constituent parts.

Raymond's critique of Smith, and this conception of
national economy, was adopted by Friedrich List in constructing one of the most durable early nineteenth-century rebuttals
of 'Smithianism'. List was resident in America during the 1820s
– he later became an American citizen – and it was here that
he developed his 'infant industries' argument for protectionism,
and the critique of 'cosmopolitical economy' that was to inform
his book *The National System* (1841). For the first he borrowed
heavily from Hamilton, and for the second he drew extensively
upon Raymond. As he stated by way of introduction to his first
excursion into economic writing, 'I confine my exertions ...
solely to the refutation of the theory of Adam Smith and Co.
the fundamental errors of which have not yet been understood
so clearly as they ought to be'.[28] He begins by dividing the
component part of political economy into three: individual
economy; national economy; and economy of mankind. On this
basis List then suggests that Smith, while entitling his book the

Wealth of Nations, had failed to deal properly with national economy, the second of the three component parts of political economy:

> his book is a mere treatise on the question: How the economy of the individuals and of mankind would stand, if the human race were not separated into nations, but united by a general law and by an equal culture of mankind?[29]

Contra Adam Smith, argues List, national economy aims to increase not simply wealth, but power, and hence its principles go beyond the economy to the political.[30]

Political economy was redefined by List in terms of his conception of national economy: 'Every nation must follow its own course in developing its productive powers; or, in other words, every nation has its particular *Political Economy*.'[31] This was not to be confused with cosmopolitical economy, which simply became a weapon for older manufacturing countries seeking to prevent the emergence of newer ones. American political economy should focus on its own wants and resources; this would also lend domestic manufactures an ascendancy over their competitors overseas who did not enjoy, as did the Americans, the monopoly of an interior market. Pursuit of free trade would merely support English economic objectives, rather than American; and this applied not only to American manufacturers, but to the producers of grain and cotton as well.[32]

The fact that the main protagonists of cosmopolitical economics based their analysis on the case of England enabled List to argue that it was in Britain's interest to foster free trade as a doctrinal principle, since this was the means by which Britain could ensure world domination. The *Wealth of Nations* played a propagandistic role in this, presenting in the guise of a treatise on the wealth of *nations* a charter for the wealth of one *nation*, Great Britain. 'Smithianism' was, in this view, certainly a system of natural liberty, but this was a matter of British natural liberty, and not one which was directly imitable. In an older and better world, where exchange took place between economic powers on an equal footing, the cosmopolitical principles expounded by Adam Smith would be quite acceptable. In the international order as it existed, however, they were a hindrance to the realisation of world economic development.

There is, then, some conception of economic progress and
the civilising role of commerce in List's writings, but it is one
which is determined exclusively by economic forces. As List
wrote later in his 'Introduction' to the *National System*:

> Civilisation, the political development and power of nations are
> principally determined by their economic circumstances, and vice
> versa. The more a nation's economy is complete and developed,
> the more civilised and powerful is that nation; the more its civil-
> isation and power increases, so much the higher will its political
> development be able to rise.[33]

Nations which are at a much lower level of culture than the
advanced manufacturing nations best develop themselves
initially through free trade with their economic superiors.
Protection is here relevant only at the point at which free trade
begins to limit the market for domestic manufacture. On the
other hand, for countries such as England, free trade is also the
most favourable option, since its power is advanced through
the promotion of cosmopolitan principles.[34]

As we have seen with Alexander Hamilton, it was possible
to use Smithian principles in the construction of a protectionist position; but by the second and third decades of the nineteenth century it was everywhere more usual for protectionist
sentiment to set up Smith as a proponent of free trade, creat-
ing an unambigous and readily identifiable target of criticism
of 'Smithianism'. Indeed, there was a remarkable degree of
agreement here, for free traders simply positively identified the
very same constructions which protectionists criticised – there
was little dispute over exactly what it was that Smith stood for.
In the rhetoric of the movement for the repeal of the Corn Laws
in Britain,[35] Smith's name served as argument enough for the
benefits of free trade. Little disagreement existed in the early
nineteenth century therefore over the status of the *Wealth of
Nations*: it was viewed, by proponents and detractors alike, as
the canonical text of free trade. The 'system of natural liberty'
was reorganised into the core of a new economic liberalism
identified with the term *laissez faire*, in which simple nostrums
concerning minimal government were associated with the opti-
misation of economic progress. In Britain, the abolition of the
Corn Laws in 1846 was followed up by a number of bilateral

treaties, beginning with the Cobden–Chevalier Treaty of 1860, which provided a model for the dismantling of tariff barriers to trade.

The 'system of natural liberty' provided the intellectual foundations for Smith's arguments in the *Wealth of Nations*, and today it forms a central point in our understanding of the originality of the work. By the mid nineteenth century this 'system' had been transmuted into a doctrine of *laissez faire* which had not been part of Smith's original intention, a doctrine which allied simplified principles of free trade to conceptions of minimal government intervention into the economic process. So much is already evident in the epigraph to this essay, taken from McCulloch's influential edition of the *Wealth of Nations*. This in turn echoes the view of Garnier, who, in his own 1802 translation of the *Wealth of Nations*, expressed this idea as follows:

> Let government, then, renounce alike the system of prohibitions and of bounties; let it no longer attempt to impede the efforts of industry by regulations, or to accelerate her progress by rewards; let it leave in the most perfect freedom, the exertions of labour and the employment of capital; let its protecting influence extend only to the removal of such obstacles as avarice or ignorance have raised up to the unlimited liberty of industry and commerce; then capitals will naturally develop themselves by their own movement, in those directions which are at once most agreeable to the private interest of the capitalist, and most favourable to the increase of the national wealth.[36]

This is a somewhat more comprehensive statement of the *laissez-faire* position than we might encounter today; but it is important to recognise that free trade and *laissez faire* are not synonymous. Strictly speaking, they are related but distinct ideas: *laissez faire* refers to freedom to produce what one will, and it is *laissez passer* that denotes freedom of trade, the first dating from the 1680s but elaborated in the 1750s, and the second from the 1760s.[37] Garnier's version, where the self-regulating properties of the economy suffice to produce wealth without intevention from government, represents a further elaboration of these ideas, such that Smith's economic argument is made to imply a political disposition. But this political disposition is one stripped of the original conceptions of the civilising process and the function of commerce, replacing this with an economistic conception of the role of government.

Notes

1 J. R. McCulloch, 'Preface to the Edition of 1828', in his edition of Adam Smith, *An Inquiry into the Nature and Causes of the Wealth of Nations*, new edn (Edinburgh: Adam and Charles Black, 1863), n.p.

2 For a detailed discussion of the domestic and American reception of *Wealth of Nations*, see R. F. Teichgraeber, '"Less Abused than I had reason to expect": the reception of *The Wealth of Nations* in Britain, 1776–90', *Historical Journal*, 30 (1987), pp. 337–66.

3 Malthus had long cherished the ambition of publishing an annotated version of *Wealth of Nations*, but was twice pre-empted: first by the appearance of Playfair's eleventh edition in 1804, and then later by the Buchanan edition of 1814 – although in this context the leisurely pace at which Malthus prosecuted his literary ambitions suggests that he had little ground for complaint when others sought to make Smith's arguments more intelligible to a broad public: see P. James, ed., *The Travel Diaries of Thomas Robert Malthus* (London: Cambridge University Press, 1966), Appendix 3, pp. 299–300.

4 See the concordance of chapters presented by Piero Sraffa in his 'Introduction' to D. Ricardo, *On the Principles of Political Economy and Taxation*, in P. Sraffa and M. H. Dobb, eds, *Works and Correspondence of David Ricardo* (London: Cambridge University Press, 1951), vol. 1, pp. xxiv–xxv.

5 James Mill's *Elements of Political Economy* was based upon the notes made of his father's daily lectures by the thirteen-year-old John Stuart Mill, published first in 1821. In addition to chapters on production, distribution and 'interchange' there is a fourth, on 'consumption', which briefly covers consumption and public finance.

6 As a political economist it should be noted that Marx counts as an Englishman, since his studies in this area were conducted almost exclusively in England during a period from the later 1840s to the 1860s; his acquaintance with contemporary developments in economic writing in his native Germany was extremely limited.

7 L. H. von Jakob, *Grundsätze der National-Oekonomie, oder Theorie des National-Reichthums*, 3rd. rev. edn (Halle: im Kommission bei Friedrich Ruff, 1825), pp. iv–v; the first edition of this work had appeared in 1805.

8 See *The Papers of Alexander Hamilton*, ed. H. C. Syrett (New York: Columbia University Press, 1966), vol. 10, pp. 230–340.

9 A. Smith, *Untersuchung der Natur und Ursachen von Nationalreichtümern* (Leipzig, vol. 1, 1776) Books 1–3; (vol. 2, 1778) Books 4 and 5.

10 Translations of Steuart's book began to appear in Tübingen and Hamburg in 1769. See my discussion of the relationship between Smith and Steuart's work in *Governing Economy: The Reformation of German*

Economic Discourse 1750–1840 (Cambridge: Cambridge University Press, 1988), pp. 136–43.

11 'Kr.', Review of *Untersuchung der Natur und Ursachen von Nationalreichthümern*, vol. 2 (1778), *Allgemeine Deutsche Bibliothek*, vol. 38, 1 (1779), p. 300.

12 G. Sartorius, *Handbuch der Staatswirthschaft zum Gebrauche bey akademische Vorlesungen, nach Adam Smiths Grundsätzen ausgearbeitet* (Berlin, 1796).

13 W. Roscher, *Geschichte der National-Oekonomik in Deutschland* (Munich: R. Oldenbourg, 1874), p. 615.

14 Sartorius, *Handbuch*, p. 153.

15 *Staatszweck* can be translated as the 'aim and purpose of the state'; *Polizeiwissenschaft* was the 'science of police', i.e. a systematic outline of forms of non-juridical regulation.

16 (Berlin, 1800), p. xiii. Lueder had studied at Göttingen, and at the time this text appeared was a councillor to the court of the Duke of Brunswick. In 1810 he became professor of philosophy at Göttingen.

17 F. B. Weber, *Systematisches Handbuch der Staatswirthschaft*, vol. 1, part 1 (Berlin, 1804), p. 4.

18 C. Garve, 'Vorrede des Uebersetzers', to A. Smith, *Untersuchung über die Natur und die Ursachen des Nationalreichthums*, vol. 1 (Breslau, 1794), pp. iv–v. It should be noted that it is indeed possible for translations to be made so poorly that many features of the original text are concealed. My own favourite example is the Signet edition of Gogol's short story 'The Overcoat', which systematically excludes repetitions and prevarications from the translation of the text, presumably on the grounds that they got in the way of the story – which is of course Gogol's point.

19 L. H. Jakob, *Grundsätze der National-Oekonomie oder National-Wirthschaftslehre* (Halle, 1805), p. v.

20 See D. R. McCoy, *The Elusive Republic* (Chapel Hill: University of North Carolina Press, 1980), ch. 1.

21 This appears as a straight paraphrase of Smith – Hamilton, *The Report on the Subject of Manufactures, Papers of Alexander Hamilton*, vol. 10, p. 237.

22 Ibid., pp. 247–9.

23 Ibid., p. 251. List's usage of 'productive powers' in *Outlines* (*Schriften*, vol. 2, pp. 116–7) follows that of Hamilton; it was then translated into German by List as *Produktivkräfte* (i.e. productive forces). See his letter to Ernst Weber, 2 October 1828, F. List, *Schriften/Reden/Briefe* (Berlin: Verlag von Reimar Hobbing, 1927–35), vol. 3.1, p. 116.

24 Hamilton, *Report*, p. 263.

25 Citing from the second edition of *Thoughts*, with the altered title *The Elements of Political Economy* (Baltimore: F. Lucas Jun. and E. J. Coale, 1823), vol. 1, p. 36.

26 Ibid., vol. 1, p. 47.

27 Ibid., vol. 1, p. 35.

28 *Schriften*, vol. 2, p. 99. List's essay was first published in the form of twelve letters to C. J. Ingersoll in Philadelphia, appearing from August to November in the *National Gazette*; they were subsequently repub-

lished as *Outlines of American Political Economy* (Philadelphia, 1827).

29   *Schriften*, vol. 2, p. 101.

30   Ibid., vol. 2, p. 105.

31   Ibid., vol. 2, p. 124.

32   Ibid., vol. 2, pp. 146–7.

33   F. List, *Das nationale System der politischen Oekonomie. Bd.I Der interna-
     tionale Handel, die Handelspolitik und der deutsche Zollverein* (1841),
     Schriften, vol. 6, p. 49.

34   Ibid., vol. 6, pp. 54–6.

35   The regulation of imports and exports of grain by price was the object
     of debate whenever prices moved heavily one way or the other. Ricardo's
     seminal *Essay on the Influence of a Low Price of Corn on the Profits of Stock*
     (1815), *Works and Correspondence of David Ricardo*, vol. 4, pp. 1–41
     addressed this question in the context of the reform to the Laws in 1815.

36   Gerard Garnier, 'A Short View of the Doctrine of Smith, compared with
     that of the French Economists', translated in E. Gibbon Wakefield, ed.,
     An Inquiry into the Nature and Causes of the Wealth of Nations, vol. 1
     (London: Charles Knight and Sons, 1843), p. cxxiii.

37   A. Oncken, *Die maxime laissez faire et laissez passer, ihr Ursprung, ihr
     Werden* (Bern: K. J. Wyss, 1886), pp. 29, 84.

3

Adam Smith and the 'free market'

HEINZ LUBASZ

There's definitely something odd about the way Adam Smith and the *Wealth of Nations* have come into vogue during the past fifteen years or so: partisans of what has come to be known as the 'free market' present themselves as true disciples of Smith – yet they seem to care much more for his image than for his ideas. Take, for example, Ronald Reagan's White House, where in the 1980s the 'free market' was all the rage: the President's aides literally sported ties bearing silhouettes of Adam Smith[1] – probably the first time in history an economic theorist has been turned into a pin-up boy. Or, on a different plane, consider the article written by the late Professor Friedrich von Hayek in *The Daily Telegraph* to mark the two-hundredth anniversary of the publication of the *Wealth of Nations* in 1776. Hayek, an eminent economist and one of the chief champions of the 'free market', promises to convey 'Adam Smith's Message in Today's Language'.[2] But apart from a quotation from one of Smith's *other* books, what the article contains is not Adam Smith's ideas but Hayek's, and the language they're conveyed in is not so much today's plain speech as it is the vocabulary of Hayek's own theories and preoccupations. On a different plane yet again, one could fairly expect the self-named Adam Smith Institute to be devoted to the principles of the august economist whose name it bears, including his well-grounded opposition to monopolies. What one finds instead is an Adam Smith Institute that helps the British government to transform public utilities such as gas, electricity and even water into – private monopolies! The more one thinks about it, the more one feels that such people are simply using Smith as a sort of logo for the 'free market', enhancing the status of their own ideas – how meritorious soever – by invoking his name.

It isn't my business in this essay to say anything about the 'free market' one way or the other. But it is my business to comment on the immense gulf that separates Adam Smith's *magnum opus*, the *Wealth of Nations*, from the 'free-market' doctrines propounded by Professor Hayek and others, and *attributed* to Smith.

What, from a scholarly point of view, makes this late twentieth-century would-be revival of Smith truly remarkable is the very idea of applying an economic theory worked out more than two hundred years ago to the substantially different economic world we now live in. Consider a single though absolutely central example: the nature and role of technology. A man like Smith, for whom the term 'machine' meant such things as the plough, the water mill and the simplest sort of steam engine (WN I.i.8 and n.15), could reasonably believe that in order to produce as much as possible one had to employ as many workers as possible. By contrast, given today's advanced technology, every with-it employer aims to have as many labour-saving devices as he or she can afford, and to employ as few workers as possible: besides costing less in the long run, machines don't ask for a rise in wages and don't go on strike. So while it made very good sense for Smith to say, as he did, that maximising employment was the high road at once to national prosperity (by maximising production) and to the welfare of the labouring population (by maximising employment), no present-day employers in their right minds, for whom reducing the work-force is tantamount to increasing the efficiency (read: profitability) of the business, can agree with him. But this means that today's employer hasn't the slightest use for one of the basic tenets of Smithian economics.

What chiefly attracts Adam Smith's latter-day champions to the *Wealth of Nations* is undoubtedly the concept they call 'the invisible hand of the market', which Smith called simply the 'invisible hand', and which turns out on closer examination of the full text of his book to be the hand not of the market but of nature.[3] The attraction for them is that in the *Wealth of*

Nations the invisible hand has the all-important task of bringing it about that, contrary to what one would expect,[4] the individual pursuit of private self-interest actually promotes instead of hurting the interest of society as a whole. But the Smithian invisible hand cannot function in an advanced technological economy, for the simple reason that its operation crucially depends, as we shall see, on the employment of labour being maximised whereas, for the reason just stated, the modern employer will minimise employment instead of maximising it. There is no magic market – at any rate, no Smithian one.

The revival of a would-be practical (as opposed to a merely historical) interest in Adam Smith is remarkable for another reason: despite the praise heaped on the *Wealth of Nations* by various economists, politicians and publicists, its central doctrines have been largely ignored in both theory and practice, even in the Reagan–Bush United States and in Thatcher–Major Britain. Thus, for instance, where Smith preached free and universal competition, Hayek's theory doesn't object to oligopoly – market domination by a handful of firms – provided only that there is free market entry, meaning that any firm rich and powerful enough is free to join the oligopoly and enjoy the advantages of controlling production and prices (instead of leaving them to the free play of the much-advertised 'market forces').[5] And oligopolies are indeed flourishing, in the real world, not just in Hayek's theory. So are monopolies. Moreover, where Smith was firmly committed to free international trade, tariff barriers are still very much with us, and the economic bastion of the European Common Market is being busily built. All of which is not necessarily to say that such theory and such practices are bad; it is just to say that they are diametrically opposed to what the much-praised Smith stood for.

At this point we may fairly ask: if they either cannot, or will not, apply Smithian principles in theory or in practice, what animates the late twentieth-century acolytes of Adam Smith? Three beliefs, I think, prompt aficionados of the free market to talk about the *Wealth of Nations* as though it were a sort of Bible. The first is the belief that Smith opposed state intervention in the economy because he was a sort of instinctive anti-collectivist-before-his-time; the second, that he conceived of the market much as they themselves do, as a level playing field on which individuals and firms freely pursue their private self-interests; and third, the belief that Smith showed that 'the market', moved by nothing but 'market forces' and the quest for profit, was, thanks to the 'invisible hand', somehow not only good for the profit-makers but good for all.

According to the free marketeers it is thanks to the invisible hand that the market mechanism automatically adjusts both production and distribution. For example, if all that is needed to achieve satisfactory production is, as Professor Hayek held, entrepreneurs who go in pursuit of the greatest possible profits; and if all that is needed to obtain satisfactory distribution is, as he also affirmed, that people get through the market process whatever they happen to get (which may well be nothing); then clearly there is no warrant for government action either to guide production or to adjust distribution (and to Hayek the notion of a fair distribution, not to speak of social justice, was in any case absolutely anathema).[6] 'Trickle-down' will do the trick: feed the horse enough oats and some will pass through on to the road for the sparrows.[7] But, once more, that's Hayek, not Smith – emphatically not Smith.

One reason these twentieth-century notions are so wide of the mark is that most of the people who talk so much about Adam Smith have never read the *Wealth of Nations*. What they *have* read is at most two, by now extremely famous, passages from that exceedingly long and in part pretty boring book. Indeed, the nuggets of 'Smithian' wisdom they are familiar with come to people nowadays not from reading even those passages in their brief entirety, but from the doctored versions and isolated phrases presented in economics texts of one kind or another, in popular articles and political speeches, in conversation. Selected sound-bytes such as 'market', 'invisible hand', 'self-interest' and the like are circulating – sound-bytes that correspond to what we might call 'print-bytes' in the *Wealth of Nations*, though in the context of the text they can be seen to mean something rather different. Wrenched as they have been from the context of the book's rich data and complex reasoning, these few terms and phrases – these word-bytes – are then treated as gospel truth.

That such ignorance can be paraded as knowledge is one mark of the difference between the elite culture in which the *Wealth of Nations* was produced and the mass culture in which it is being consumed. It is one difference between an aristocratic polity in which the landed gentlemen of the governing class could safely be left to wallow in their ignorance, and a democratic culture in which politicians are anxious to convince voters that their policies are sound and attractive. It is one difference between a leisurely culture in which a leading politician interested in Adam Smith's ideas, such as the younger Pitt, could find the time to read and digest the book, and a hectic culture in which most leading politicians are too pressed for time to read anything but what they absolutely have to.

But that such a pseudo-restoration of Adam Smith can occur at all is of course not to be accounted for in terms of cultural differences alone. It also reflects the partisan attachment of some people to the 'gospel truths' in question. Partisans of the free market invoke Adam Smith in order to lend the authority of his name to the case they themselves want to make: for the complete removal of the state from economic enterprise; for the economic sovereignty of the market; and for leaving all questions of production and distribution to the magic of the invisible hand. But the 'presidential acolytes in Mr. Reagan's White House [who] wore neckties bearing the picture of the master'[8] would have promptly taken them off again had they known what Smith really thought. For they would have discovered to their dismay that the reason Adam Smith wanted an end to government intervention in the market was that in his time (in contrast to today) it was only thanks to state intervention that what he called 'the mean rapacity, the monopolising spirit of merchants and manufacturers' (IV.ii.c.9) was able to dominate the economy, to the great detriment of the society as a whole.

One small, partial remedy for this state of ignorance mingled with confusion is to set the two most-quoted passages in the context of the *Wealth of Nations* as a whole and to read them in the light of those of Smith's views that bear most directly on them. It makes sense to begin with the passage in which Smith proposes that the state should relinquish its practice of directing private enterprise, and to examine his reasons for this proposal. Having discussed at length what he called 'the mercantile system' and, more briefly, 'the agricultural systems', all of which he saw as systems which, by means of governmental legislation and policy, imposed restrictions and granted advantages that promoted the private interests of one section of society at the expense of the rest, Smith wrote as follows:

> All systems either of preference or of restraint, therefore, being thus completely taken away, the obvious and simple system of natural liberty establishes itself of its own accord. Every man, as long as he does not violate the laws of justice, is left perfectly free to pursue his own interest his own way, and to bring both his industry and capital into competition with those of any other man, or order of men. The sovereign is completely discharged from a duty, in the attempting to perform which he must always be exposed to innumerable delusions, and for the proper performance of which no human wisdom or knowledge could ever be sufficient; the duty of superintending the industry of private people, and of directing it towards the employments most suitable to the interest of the society. According to the system of natural liberty, the sovereign has only three duties to attend to; three duties of great importance, indeed, but plain and intelligible to common understandings: first, the duty of protecting the society from the violence and invasion of other independent societies; secondly, the duty of protecting, so far as possible, every member of the society from the injustice or oppression of every other member of it, or the duty of establishing an exact administration of justice; and, thirdly, the duty of erecting and maintaining certain publick works and certain publick institutions, which it can never be for the interest of any individual, or small number of individuals, to erect and maintain; because the profit could never repay the expence to any individual or small number of individuals, though it may frequently do much more than repay it to a great society. (IV.ix.51)

Three features of this statement should be carefully noticed: (1) it flows from a concern to be rid of systems of preference and restraint; (2) it assumes that in the system of natural liberty '*every* man' would have a chance to apply 'his' industry and capital; and (3) the sovereign is said to have been concerned so to direct the industry and capital of private people as to further the interest of the whole society.

In order to appreciate the force of the first point, we need to know that Smith was deeply hostile to systems of preference and restraint: the manufacturers and merchants – the great entrepreneurs of his time – had 'extorted from the legislature' (IV.iii.c.9) laws and policies which furthered *their* particular interests to the detriment of the society as a whole. This had to be stopped.

As for the second feature, we need to know that Smith's conception of the market was very different from the one in vogue today. Quite fundamental is the fact that he spoke of market*s* in the plural, not of *the* market in the singular. To Smith, a market was a place or a network specifically of *exchange*. As the term '*the* market' is used today it comprises the whole of economic activity, including *production*, *distribution* and *circulation* as well as *exchange*, plus the individuals and firms that participate in it. This far more comprehensive complex, consisting of people and their various economic activities, Adam Smith called not 'the market' but 'commercial society'. Market*s* interested him for the role they played in such a society. The scope of his vision thus being much wider than that of the free marketeers, he took account of many economically significant features of such a society which the concept of 'the market' hides from view. (Recall that at least one prominent champion of the free market gave it as her considered opinion that there is no such thing as society – there's only the market.) Smith took due account of the role which the private ownership of land and capital plays in commercial society; of the effect differences in class position have on opportunity and on bargaining power; of the question of how well people belonging to different classes actually know their own interests; of the various constituent aspects of self-interest; and of the question of how the interests of the several classes (or 'orders', as he called them) of society related to one another and to the interest of the society as a whole. In short, Smith's concept of a structured commercial society composed of complex human beings is radically different from the present-day concept of the market consisting simply of so many gain-seeking individuals and firms.

Finally, in relation to the third feature of the statement, we need to know that Smith had already, in an earlier chapter,

shown that there is a *natural* force which can direct the industry and capital of private people so as to further the interest of
the whole society, namely, the invisible hand. What he is
proposing in the passage before us is, therefore, not that with
the withdrawal of the sovereign the economy would no longer
be directed towards the promotion of the interest of the society, but that in a system of natural liberty the *natural* directive
power of the invisible hand would take over from the *artificial*
(instituted) directive power of the sovereign the task of making
sure that the private pursuit of self-interest actually did
redound to the interest of the society as a whole. These three
topics are taken up in the three following sections.

To understand the change in economic policy Adam Smith was
recommending – and the *Wealth of Nations* was a policy recommendation as well as a theory – we need to recognise that the
economic system he himself was living under and was vigor-
ously criticising – the 'mercantile system', as he called it – was
itself a market system within a commercial society. In other words,
what the *Wealth of Nations* is all about is not some abstraction
called 'the market', and certainly not some such issue as 'the
market versus the state' (an issue that preoccupies many people
today but simply didn't exist for Smith). What the *Wealth of
Nations* is all about is the difference between one kind of
market system in commercial society and another. It is about
the difference between, on the one hand, a market system dominated by merchants and manufacturers who are able to bend
the government to their will in order to obtain legislation which
makes what is in their private interest the law of the land, and,
on the other, a truly open and competitive – 'natural' – market
system in which everyone who is industrious and/or has any
capital has a fair chance. The withdrawal of the state is not, for
Smith, the removal of government from its role as owner, entrepreneur, economic planner or re-distributor – roles readily
conceivable to all who know of socialism but wholly incon-
ceivable to Adam Smith – but its removal from the role of regu-
lator of private enterprise, a role in which it had long been used
to promote the interests of the merchants and the manufacturers over those of all others.

So many people today are convinced that the prime target of Adam Smith's criticisms in the *Wealth of Nations* was the state and its role in economic life that it is worth quoting a contemporary of Smith's as an example of how he was understood in his own time. Dugald Stewart was one distinguished political economist who saw clearly that the direct object of Smith's attack was not government policy but private vested interest. In 1793, three years after Smith's death, he presented to the Royal Society of Edinburgh an *Account of the Life and Writings of Adam Smith, LL.D.*[9] Speaking of Smith's account of the unnatural and harmful turn which social and economic developments in Europe had taken in recent times, Stewart pointed to Smith's assertion that those developments had taken 'their rise, not from any general scheme of [state] policy, but from the private interests and prejudices of particular orders of men'.[10] In course of time, Stewart continued, these private interests and prejudices had been elevated into a systematic scheme, 'a false system of political economy, propagated by merchants and manufacturers; a class of individuals, whose interest is not always the same with that of the public, and whose professional knowledge gave them many advantages' over those who lacked their knowledge and experience. Indeed, the interest of this class of individuals was advanced while that of the society suffered: 'by means of this system, a new set of obstacles to the progress of national prosperity has been created'.[11]

What, then, was this mercantile system which Stewart as much as Smith judged so pernicious? Briefly put, it consisted of a vast national and international (including colonial) network of legally entrenched regulations – bounties, import duties, exclusive rights and the like – which principally benefited the great manufacturers and merchants at the expense of the small, at the expense of the agrarian sector as well as of the labouring population, indeed at the expense of the nation as a whole. A couple of excerpts from the *Wealth of Nations* will show not only what Smith thought of the system but how strongly he felt about it.

> By extorting from the legislature bounties upon the exportation of their own linen, high duties upon the importation of all foreign linen, and a total prohibition of the home consumption of some

> sorts of French linen, they endeavour to sell their own goods as
> dear as possible. By encouraging the importation of foreign linen
> yarn, and thereby bringing it into competition with that which
> is made by our own people, they endeavour to buy the work of
> the poor spinners as cheap as possible. They are as intent to keep
> down the wages of their own weavers, as the earnings of the poor
> spinners, and it is by no means for the benefit of the workman,
> that they endeavour either to raise the price of the compleat
> work, or to lower that of the rude materials. It is the industry
> which is carried on for the benefit of the rich and the powerful,
> that is principally encouraged by our mercantile system. That
> which is carried on for the benefit of the poor and the indigent,
> is too often, either neglected, or oppressed. (IV.viii.4)

This representative excerpt makes clear enough whom Adam
Smith regarded as the principal villains, the legislators or the
entrepreneurs. The legislators Smith regarded as either naive or
corrupt enough to allow the great entrepreneurs to persuade or
bully them into inscribing the mercantile system into the law
of the land. But the initiators, the instigators of the system were
the great entrepreneurs themselves:

> It cannot be very difficult to determine who have been the
> contrivers of this whole mercantile system; not the consumers, we
> may believe, whose interest has been entirely neglected; but the
> producers whose interest has been so carefully attended to; and
> among this latter class our merchants and manufacturers have
> been by far the principal architects. (IV.viii.54)

Scathing as he was about the domestic machinations of manufacturers and merchants, Smith grew positively bilious when he
came to discuss their international operations in general and
their quest for colonies and colonial trade in particular. Their
immense influence in shaping not only domestic legislation but
foreign policy as well seemed to him perhaps the greatest evil
of the whole mercantile system. And that held not for Britain
alone but for all colonial powers – the French, the Dutch, the
Portuguese, the Spaniards, even the Swedes and the Danes.
Everywhere, the great merchants and manufacturers egged
their sovereigns on to wage war for no better purpose than to
enhance their own profits, and were a greater menace to peace
than governments themselves: 'The capricious ambition of kings

and ministers has not, during the present and the preceding century, been more fatal to the repose of Europe, than the impertinent jealousy of merchants and manufacturers' (IV.iii.c.9). The latter coveted colonies and even empires, not for any good they might do for the people of the colonies or of the mother countries, but for the sake of their own private profit. 'Have the exorbitant profits of the merchants of Cadiz and Lisbon', Smith asks rhetorically, 'augmented the capital of Spain and Portugal? Have they alleviated the poverty, have they promoted the industry of those two beggarly countries?' (IV.vii.c.61).

The full weight of his ire, however, was reserved for a British venture: the subjugation and merciless exploitation of India by and on behalf of merchant monopolists who, to add injury to insult, had become the governors of the very people they were plundering:

> No other sovereigns ever were, or, from the nature of things, ever could be, so perfectly indifferent about the happiness or misery of their subjects, the improvement or waste of their dominions, the glory or disgrace of their administration; as, from irresistible moral causes, the greater part of the proprietors of such a mercantile company are, and necessarily must be. (V.i.e.26)

As Smith said of a similar, Danish, company of monopolists ruling the islands of St Thomas and Santa Cruz: 'The government of an exclusive company of merchants, is, perhaps, the worst of all governments for any country whatever' (IV.vii.b.11). Coming as it did from a man amply familiar with the ancient and modern history of tyranny and exploitation, that was no casual judgement.

Still, most governments are not now, and were not then, composed of mercantile monopolists, however much they might be influenced by big business. In Adam Smith's day the government of Britain under its sovereign, King George III, consisted to a great extent of landed gentlemen and aristocrats and their clients. Mere manufacturers and merchants were a lesser breed. For all that they foisted their commercial interests on the socially greater, the entrepreneurs were no majority in Parliament, had no navy or army of their own. They needed the legislative, diplomatic and military power of the state if their schemes were to become reality, and therefore they had to exert influence on government. And exert it they did. It wasn't the King and his ministers – the government – who had devised the mercantile system Smith so hated. But it was certainly the King and his ministers who made that system a living reality – at immense cost to the people of Britain, and not only in money:

> To found a great empire for the sole purpose of raising up a people of customers, may at first sight appear a project fit only for a nation of shopkeepers. It is, however, a project altogether unfit for a nation of shopkeepers; but extremely fit for a nation whose government is influenced by shopkeepers. Such statesmen, and such statesmen only, are capable of fancying that they will find some advantage in employing the blood and treasure of their fellow citizens, to found and to maintain such an empire. (IV.vii.c.63)

Government gets its share of the blame not as the *source* of policies that are deeply harmful to the society as a whole, but as the *tool* of the commercial and manufacturing interests that bend it to their will.

This brief outline of Smith's condemnation of the way merchants and manufacturers impose on landlord-dominated governments insufficiently sophisticated to counter their arguments allows us, I hope, to read what he says about getting the state out of the job of regulating business and industry in a somewhat different light from that of the naked bulb by which it is usually presented.

Next we need to ask about the significance of Smith's belief that in the system of natural liberty '*every* man' would have a fair chance to apply 'his' industry and capital. Smith holds the furthering of the interest of the society to be the paramount objective of that society's economic activity – and by 'the interest of the society' he means both everyone's private interest and the interest of the whole, the public interest. We have already seen that he condemns preferences and restraints because they promote the interests of the rich and powerful at the expense of the poor and indigent. But the removal of the legislated system of preferences and restraints would not by itself ensure that *everyone*'s interest would be furthered: in commercial society as such, even if shorn of a discriminatory system, the members of the different orders or classes of the society are differently placed, and the interests of these classes differ – indeed, they may conflict with one another, and with the interest of the society as a whole. Since the economic life of society is altogether entwined in its economically rooted social structure, we need to look more closely at what Smith says about that structure.

The *Wealth of Nations* notes the existence of three great classes or orders, which it identifies in terms of their source of income:

> The whole annual produce of the land and labour of every country, or what comes to the same thing, the whole price of that annual produce, naturally divides itself ... into three parts; the rent of land, the wages of labour, and the profits of stock [capital]; and constitutes a revenue to three different orders of people; to those who live by rent, to those who live by wages, and to those who live by profit. These are the three great, original and constituent orders of every civilized society, from whose revenue that of every other order is ultimately derived. (I.xi.p.7)

The mere fact of the existence of different classes – a central fact of economic life so far as Adam Smith is concerned, but one that disappears in the modern concept of 'the market' – complicates the picture of economic society: it introduces the possibility of systemic conflicts of interest, that is to say, conflicts of interest which are not individual or incidental but flow willy-nilly from one's class position in economic society. Besides, as Smith astutely observes, the very capacity to judge what is and what is not in one's best interest also varies from class to class. And so does the ability to act on it. What's more, class interest does not necessarily coincide with the public interest, the interest of the society as a whole. Consequently there are conflicts between one's self-interest as the member of a class and the interest of the society, and between one class and another. In other words, there is nothing simple or straightforward about self-interest. It follows that promoting the public interest is no simple matter either. To talk blithely about the interest of all being best served by everyone's simply pursuing his or her self-interest in 'the market' is a systematically misleading simplification with which Smith would have no truck.

As the *Wealth of Nations* depicts it, members of the first and the third class are intrinsically better off than members of the second in that they enjoy the great benefit of being independent. Those who live by rent have the easiest time of it, and are the most secure: their income 'costs them neither labour nor care, but comes to them, as it were, of its own accord' (I.xi.p.8). Those who live by profit have to make some effort and are less secure: they must exert care, at least, and they run some risk, as their profits vary and may be partly offset by losses. The least secure and the ones who have to make the greatest effort are the wage-workers: they must labour hard and constantly to make a living, and are wholly dependent on being employed by someone belonging to the class of those who live by profit, by a master of some kind – be he farmer, merchant or master manufacturer. (At the time Smith was writing, only 5 per cent of workers, by his reckoning, were still independent artisans; the overwhelming majority were wage-workers (I.viii.10)).

Between individuals who belong to these last two classes there is always, according to Smith, a conflict of interest: the workers' interest is to get as high a wage as possible, the masters' interest to pay as low a wage as possible. (Remember that Smith, in an age of minimal technology, cannot imagine it to be in the employer's interest to hire as few workers as possible.) In this respect workers and masters don't differ from other sellers and buyers in a market. But the buying and selling of labour is no ordinary market transaction. To be sure, labour is a commodity (I.viii.40), and like any other commodity it has to be paid for. But it is a commodity of a peculiar kind. First, a worker (implicitly male) is a human being who sells not a thing but his own labour, and in doing so must lay down a 'portion of his ease, his liberty, and his happiness' (I.v.7). Second and crucially, the bargaining power of the buyers and that of the sellers of labour is very unequal, and that's what makes their relation different from the ordinary relations of exchange. The seller lacks the resources to hold out for a better price, a higher wage; the master's resources, being substantially greater, allow him to wait, and to pay less. Master and workman need each other, which is why this species of exchange takes place. But the master is always at a considerable advantage. 'In the long run the workman may be as necessary to his master as his master is to him, but the necessity is not so immediate' (I.viii.12). Should the conflict of interest between them issue in an open dispute in the work-place there is, owing to the difference in bargaining power, little chance of its being settled fairly: once again, the master can hold out longer than the workmen. And as far as organised action is concerned, the law is on his side, not theirs: workers are forbidden by law to combine, whereas 'masters are always and every where in a sort of tacit, but constant and uniform combination, not to raise the wages of labour above their actual rate' (I.viii.13). Finally, if the dispute should get out of hand, the masters – though not the workmen – can always count on the backing of the state (in the person of the civil magistrate) (I.viii.13).

It's pretty clear from the way Smith depicts this conflict of interest that his sympathy rests rather with the workmen than with the masters. Hence it's not in the least surprising that in the 'system of natural liberty' as he conceives it, *every* man' gets the chance to employ his industry (and capital), or that the invisible hand's basic job is to make sure that the employment of labour is maximised and wages are as high as possible.

But the interests of the several classes are not Smith's only concern. He is concerned also, and even more, with the relationship of the interest of each class to the interest of the society as a whole. The *Wealth of Nations* deals with this relationship on two levels, the first relating to the interests themselves, the second to the knowledge people belonging to the several classes actually have of their own interest.

Smith says that the interest of the first and of the third order are always identical with the interest of the society as a whole, because the augmentation or diminution of each of their incomes – the rent of land, the wages of labour – directly parallels the augmentation or diminution of the whole society's wealth. Regarding the second order, those who live by profit, he has a less sanguine view:

> The plans and projects of the employers of stock regulate and
> direct all the most important operations of labour, and profit is
> the end proposed by all those plans and projects. But the rate of
> profit does not, like rent and wages, rise with the prosperity, and

fall with the declension of the society. On the contrary, it is naturally low in rich, and high in poor countries, and it is always
highest in the countries which are going fastest to ruin. (I.xi.p.10)

Indeed, in their quest for profit, manufacturers and merchants
often act in ways which are *contrary* to the interest of the society. Merchants may, for example, be quite willing to export
grain even at a time of severe grain shortage at home if they
can make a greater profit abroad (IV.v.b.38); or they may
engage in long-distance trade, from which their own profits are
greatest but the returns to the home country are the slowest
and least useful (cf. IV.vii.c.86). The worst offenders of all,
however, are the merchants' and manufacturers' dealers:

> The interest of the dealers ... in any particular branch of trade or
> manufactures, is always in some respects different from, and even
> opposite to, that of the publick. To widen the market and to
> narrow the competition, is always the interest of the dealers. To
> widen the market may frequently be agreeable enough to the
> interest of the publick; but to narrow the competition must
> always be against it, and can serve only to enable the dealers, by
> raising their profits above what they naturally would be, to levy,
> for their own benefit, an absurd tax upon the rest of their fellow-
> citizens. The proposal of any new law or regulation of commerce
> which comes from this order, ought always to be listened to with
> great precaution, and ought never to be adopted till after having
> been long and carefully examined, not only with the most scrupu-
> lous, but with the most suspicious attention. It comes from an
> order of men, whose interest is never exactly the same with that
> of the publick, who have generally an interest to deceive and
> even to oppress the publick, and who accordingly have, upon
> many occasions, both deceived and oppressed it. (I.xi.p.10)

Smith also mistrusted merchants and manufacturers because
he believed them to be better than landowners or workers at
knowing their own interest, and less concerned for the public
interest:

> [T]hough the interest of the labourer is strictly connected with
> that of the society, he is incapable either of comprehending that
> interest, or of understanding its connection with his own. His
> condition leaves him no time to receive the necessary informa-
> tion, and his education and habits are commonly such as to render
> him unfit to judge even though he was fully informed. In the

> publick deliberations, therefore, his voice is little heard and less
> regarded, except upon some particular occasions, when his clam-
> our is animated, set on, and supported by his employers, not for
> his, but for their own particular purposes. (I.xi.p.9)

The landed class was not, of course, in the same pathetic condition, but it, too, was at a disadvantage vis-à-vis the manufacturers and merchants. 'That indolence, which is the natural effect
of the ease and security of their situation, renders them too
often, not only ignorant, but incapable of that application of
mind which is necessary in order to foresee and understand the
consequences of any publick regulation' (I.xi.p.8). By contrast,
the merchants and manufacturers who, of all those who live by
profit, are the ones who employ the largest capitals, are
outstandingly adept at judging where their interest lies and
how to argue their case in public.

> As during their whole lives they are engaged in plans and
> projects, they have frequently more acuteness of understanding
> than the greater part of country gentlemen. As their thoughts,
> however, are commonly exercised rather about the interest of
> their particular branch of business, than about that of the society,
> their judgment, even when given with the greatest candour
> (which it has not been upon every occasion) is much more to be
> depended upon with regard to the former of those two objects,
> than with regard to latter. Their superiority over the country
> gentleman is, not so much in their knowledge of the publick
> interest, as in their having a better knowledge of their own inter-
> est than he has of his. It is by this superior knowledge of their
> own interest that they have frequently imposed upon his generos-
> ity, and persuaded him to give up both his own interest and that
> of the publick, from a very simple but honest conviction, that their
> interest, and not his, was the interest of the publick. (I.xi.p.10)

Plainly, only one of the three classes could be relied on to
know its own interest. Just as plainly, none of them could be
relied on to know, much less to promote, the interest of the
society as a whole. But, as we have already seen, neither could
the sovereign, at least in what concerned the direction of the
economy. Where then could one turn, Smith must have asked
himself at some point, for a reliable force that could and would
so direct the industry of private people as to ensure that the
interest of the society was indeed promoted? His answer, in true

eighteenth-century style, was: nature. 'Projectors [i.e., people with plans and projects, be they entrepreneurs or sovereigns] disturb nature in the course of her operations on human affairs', he said as early as 1749, 'and it requires no more than to leave her alone and give her fair play in the pursuit of her ends that she may establish her own designs.'[12] 'Leave her alone' seems extremely close to *laissez faire*. This difference, however, trivial as it may seem, is absolutely crucial . For, in contrast to what *laissez faire* soon came to mean, in Smith's view what needs to be left alone 'to get on with it' is neither individuals nor the market but nature – the invisible hand of nature.

The invisible hand is unquestionably the best-known ingredient of the *Wealth of Nations*, as well as being the one most beloved of the free marketeers; but it is also the least well understood, and in the course of time it has become the most crassly distorted. Writing in 1793 Dugald Stewart, who still shared the Enlightenment culture's focus on nature, understood Adam Smith's text perfectly: the system of natural liberty relies on the benevolent operations of nature.[13] But as early as the beginning of the nineteenth century Smith was being widely taken to have advocated an ordinary system of *laissez faire*, meaning that private economic activity, so long as it was free from governmental interference, was the high road to national prosperity, no matter how capital was invested, what was produced, how trade was conducted, or how labour was treated.[14] By the second half of the twentieth century, neo-classical economists such as Paul Samuelson, Kenneth Arrow and Frank Hahn had firmly identified the Smithian invisible hand with the market itself ('the market' being understood in the modern sense). In their view, what a more sophisticated economic science can now say is that an ideal market operating under conditions of perfect competition will produce what is wanted most efficiently – and that, in the eyes of the neo-classicals, is all the Smithian 'invisible hand' amounts to.[15]

Hayek, who preferred thinking about real markets with their extremely imperfect competition to thinking about ideal ones with their theoretically perfect competition, severed the last remaining links the invisible hand of the market had retained with Smith's concept. According to him, the invisible hand is nothing but the market's function as a co-ordinator of information conveyed by means of 'prices signals', that is, prices which indicate what is being supplied or demanded, where and when, at what cost and at what likely profit, etc.[16] It hardly needs saying that a hand which does no more than co-ordinate information has nothing in common with a hand that actively promotes the social good. All that the free marketeers' invisible hand of the market does is to enable the go-getters, the heroes of the 'enterprise culture', to pursue the biggest possible profits – let the chips fall where they may, and let the sparrows have whatever they find on the road. With the free marketeers of the end of the twentieth century, 'the culture of contentment', as John Kenneth Galbraith calls it – the affluent man's and woman's equivalent of 'I'm all right, Jack' – has finally made complete nonsense of the Smithian text.

What is puzzling about this progressive attentuation of Adam Smith's meaning is that the distinguished economists who attribute their own concept – 'the invisible hand of the market' – to Smith, citing chapter and verse, have actually read the *Wealth of Nations*, in whole or at least in part. However, they manage to see their own ideas in Smith's text because they read that text in the light of their own theories, not his. And what in Smith's text doesn't fit their ideas they simply edit out.[17] So if we are to rescue Smith's most famous concept from his twentieth-century bowdlerisers, we'll have to read the invisible hand passage in the context of his thinking, not theirs. We shall see that the invisible hand of nature has little to do with perfect competition and even less with the co-ordinating of price signals, but has everything to do with natural human desires and inclinations:

> [T]he annual revenue of every society is always precisely equal to the exchangeable value of the whole annual produce of its industry, or rather is precisely the same thing with that exchangeable value. As every individual, therefore, endeavours as much as he can both to employ his capital in the support of domestick industry, and so to direct that industry that its produce may be of the greatest value; every individual necessarily labours to render the annual revenue of the society as great

as he can. He generally, indeed, neither intends to promote the
publick interest, nor knows how much he is promoting it. By
preferring the support of domestick to that of foreign industry,
he intends only his own security; and by directing that industry
in such a manner as its produce may be of the greatest value, he
intends only his own gain, and he is in this, as in many other
cases, led by an invisible hand to promote an end which was no
part of his intention. Nor is it always the worse for the society
that it was no part of it. By pursuing his own interest he
frequently promotes that of the society more effectually than
when he really intends to promote it. I have never known much
good done by those who affected to trade for the publick good.
It is an affectation, indeed, not very common among merchants,
and very few words need be employed in dissuading them from
it. (IV.ii.9)

Notice (1) that Smith speaks here of at least *two* natural inclinations, both of which are actualisations of self-interest: an
inclination to seek security, and an inclination to seek gain; (2)
that the desire for security is responsible for the all-important
preference for the support of *domestic* industry, that is, the
production carried on in one's own country; and (3) that
because Smith assumes profit to be proportional to total product, the desire for gain necessarily prompts a maximising of
product: the profits reaped depend not on how 'clever' one's
deals are but on how much one's factory or farm produces.
These are the very points overlooked or set aside by those who
claim that Adam Smith's invisible hand is that of the market
itself.

Once more we need to know more than this small bit of text
in order to appreciate what Smith is saying. We need to know
that he had a very clear and definite idea of how the interest
of the society *was* best furthered – an idea nowhere even
mentioned by his modern interpreters. 'The most advantageous
employment of any capital to the country to which it belongs',
says Smith, 'is that which maintains there the greatest quantity
of productive labour, and increases the most the annual
produce of the land and labour of that country' (IV.vii.c.35).
That is Smith's all-important hypothesis, and it forms the basic
premise on which the operations of the invisible hand of nature
depend. If the situation is truly as he supposes, and the interest

of the society is best furthered by the investors investing their-capital as close to home as possible, then the investors' natural interest in security and the society's interest in maximal domestic investment do indeed coincide.

In general, in an eighteenth-century context if not in a twentieth-century one, investors reduce their risks and thus increase their security the closer to home they invest. Moreover, in an eighteenth-century context, investment in home production means primarily investing in labour, not technology. So, thanks to the natural desire for security which operates alongside the equally natural desire for gain, and 'directs' the owners of capital to prefer investing in the labour of their own country, the invisible hand of nature does indeed maximise both a country's employment and its production. For good measure, Smith throws in yet another natural inclination, the desire for ease: the owner of capital prefers investing 'at home', not only because it's safer but also because doing so saves all sorts of trouble and inconvenience (IV.ii.6). Via their interest in security and in ease, nature leads the investors of capital to invest where they will do the society the most good – without consciously intending to do so.

We have already noted, in relation to his discussion of the different classes, that to Adam Smith self-interest was no simple matter. We can now add the further complexity that he saw the individual's self-interest as comprising not only the desire for gain but also the desire for security and for ease, and the desire for, and interest in, freedom and independence. By reducing the complexities of the Smithian concept of self-interest to a single, undifferentiated interest in material gain, modern economists (and by no means the 'free marketeers' alone) make Adam Smith's concept of the invisible hand virtually unintelligible – in the first place to themselves.

Understood in the context of Smith's thinking, the invisible hand of nature succeeds in bringing it about that the interests of all the orders or classes of the society are in fact promoted. The interest of the investors of capital is served directly by their desire to maximise product in order to maximise their – proportional – profit, while it is at the same time restrained from chasing maximal profits for themselves

which do the society little good. The interest of the landowners is promoted by the increase in national prosperity. The
interest of the workers is promoted by the maximisation of
employment, as well as by the high wages that are available
when the society prospers. And the interest of the society as a
whole is advanced by the growth in wealth and the consequent
increase in what Smith called 'the public happiness'. Such are,
in Smith's vision, the redoubtable feats of the invisible hand of
nature.[18]

If we compare this invisible hand with the invisible hand
of the market, we notice that little of Smith remains but the
words 'invisible hand'. All the specifically Smithian features are
gone. The several natural inclinations that motivate human
beings in their economic affairs – the desire for security and
ease as well as for gain – have been reduced to the single quest
for gain. The sovereign hand of nature, working through all of
these motivations to direct investment where it will do the most
good to the most people most of the time by *maximising* both
production and employment, has been replaced by a technically
sophisticated concept of economic *efficiency*. And the Smithian
concept of a country's economy, comprising all those who live
in the society, has given way to the concept of the market,
consisting only of those who actively participate in it: the
unemployed, and what Smith called 'the indigent', vanish from
sight. In a strictly Smithian perspective, the trickle-down
theory of the 'free market', so far from constituting 'Adam
Smith's Message in Today's Language', looks instead like a
return to the very situation so bitterly complained of in the
Wealth of Nations: 'It is the industry which is carried on for
the benefit of the rich and the powerful that is principally
encouraged. ... That which is carried on for the benefit of the
poor and the indigent, is too often, either neglected, or
oppressed' (IV.viii.4).

How best to account for the wayward use of the text of the
Wealth of Nations in the outgoing twentieth century? The general
differences already mentioned between the culture of Smith's
time and ours undoubtedly contribute. His text then lends itself
more easily to misuse by those who have an interest in misus-

ing it. So do the more specific differences between Smith's comprehensive political economy and the modern science of economics, with its increasing abstraction of economic phenomena from social and political ones; its simplification of such central concepts as self-interest to make them calculable, and its application of models of self-regulating mechanisms to the economic life of society, as though it, too, were simply a self-regulating mechanism. Such differences play their part most directly when Smith's text itself is read in abstraction from the economic, social and political realities he had in mind when he composed it. But the deliberate attempt lately made to transform Adam Smith into some sort of popular hero lies well beyond such cultural differences. It owes most to the arsenal of techniques developed by a modern/postmodern cultural tool that didn't exist at all in Smith's time: advertising. The Adam Smith 'everyone' today has at least heard of is largely a projection on the mind's screen, concocted from sound-bytes, messages, slogans, images. And the text of *this* Smith's *Wealth of Nations* now exists as a mere resource to be mined and exploited – on behalf of a cause. Adam Smith and the *Wealth of Nations* have been made part of a sales pitch.

Notes

1 John Kenneth Galbraith, *The Culture of Contentment* (London: Penguin Books, 1993), p. 108.
2 Friedrich von Hayek, 'Adam Smith's Message in Today's Language', *The Daily Telegraph*, London, 9 March 1976, reprinted in F. A. Hayek, *New Studies in Philosophy, Politics, Economics and the History of Ideas* (London: Routledge & Kegan Paul, 1978), pp. 267–9.
3 A fuller treatment of Smith's concept of the invisible hand than can be given here may be found in Heinz Lubasz, 'Adam Smith and the Invisible Hand – of the Market?' in Roy Dilley, ed., *Contesting Markets* (Edinburgh: Edinburgh University Press, 1992), pp. 37–56.
4 A leading article in *The Economist*, London, 14 July 1990, p. 11, goes so far as to speak of 'the *paradox* of private gain yielding social good' (emphasis added). Jerry Z. Muller, in his *Adam Smith in His Time and Ours* (Glencoe, Illinois: The Free Press, 1993), p. 86, says merely that 'the notion that the market bestows positive benefits on society seems contrary to common sense.' Some people even speak of a 'miracle'. Such excitement is unnecessary if one attends to Smith's own explanation of how private good may yield social good. See pp. 56–62, below.
5 Hayek gives reasons for accepting oligopoly and monopoly in, for exam-

ple, his *Law, Legislation and Liberty* (London: Routledge & Kegan Paul, 1982) (three volumes in one), vol. III, pp. 65-7.

6 A clear statement of Hayek's view of the market may be found in his *Law, Legislation and Liberty*, vol. II, ch. 10; of his ideas on distribution and social justice, in ibid., ch. 9.

7 Galbraith, *The Culture of Contentment*, p. 108.

8 Ibid., p. 98.

9 Dugald Stewart, *Account of the Life and Writings of Adam Smith, LL.D.* in Adam Smith, *Essays on Philosophical Subjects* (Oxford: Clarendon Press, 1980), pp. 269–332

10 Ibid., p. 316.

11 Ibid.

12 Quoted in Jacob Viner, *Essays on the Intellectual History of Economics*, ed. Douglas A. Irwin (Princeton: Princeton University Press, 1991), p. 87.

13 Stewart, *Account*, pp. 312–17.

14 See the chapter by Keith Tribe in this volume.

15 Cf. Bruna Ingrao and Giorgio Israel, *The Invisible Hand of the Market: Economic Equilibrium in the History of Science* (Cambridge, Mass.: MIT Press, 1990), p. ix and *passim*.

16 See note 6.

17 A few examples of selective quotation show how eminent economists edit out of the text of the paragraph what doesn't fit in with their own views: (1) 'By directing that industry in such a manner as its produce may be of the greatest possible value, he intends only his own gain, and he is in this, as in many other cases, led by an invisible hand to promote an end which was no part of his intention' (the excerpt includes the next two sentences). Hayek, *Law, Legislation and Liberty*, vol. II, p. 186 (a learned, though accesible, treatise). (2) 'every individual ... neither intends to promote the public interest ... he intends only his own gain, and he is in this, as in many other cases, led by an invisible hand to promote an end which was no part of his intention,' Paul A. Samuelson, *Economics*, eleventh edition (New York: McGraw-Hill, 1980), p. 784 (a standard university text book). (3) '[an individual who] intends only his own gain' is 'led by an invisible hand to promote an end which was no part of his intention' (the excerpt includes the next three sentences), Milton and Rose Friedman, *Free to Choose* (Harmondsworth: Penguin Books, 1980), p. 20 (the popularised version of one 'free market' view). All three of the books, written as they were for quite different readerships, omit any reference to *security* as a factor affecting investment decisions, and the individual's endeavour to invest in *domestic* industry. What the authors take note of is solely the interest in private gain and the lack of intention to promote the public good. Hayek, preoccupied as he is with the making of the biggest possible profits, even *adds* a word: 'greatest gain' becomes 'greatest possible gain'. Hayek, Samuelson, and Milton Friedman were each awarded the Nobel Prize for Economics: even at the 'top' the temptation is great to quote from the text only what supports one's own preconceived ideas. Happily at least one distin-

guished economist, who was also a sensitive and brilliant historian of economic ideas, the late Jacob Viner, understood Adam Smith rather better. See 'Adam Smith and Laissez Faire', in Viner, *Essays*, pp. 85–113.

18 For further discussion of the invisible hand see Noel Parker's chapter, pp. 122–43 below.

4

Adam Smith and the role of the state: education as a public service

ANDREW S. SKINNER

Although Adam Smith has been, and still is, claimed as the author of the doctrine of economic liberalism, many modern scholars have drawn attention to aspects of his position which reflect wider concerns. Donald Winch, in particular, has reminded us that for Smith the modern commercial economy, the so-called fourth economic stage, could be seen to be associated with a particular form of social and political structure which influences the outline of government and the context within which it must function.[1] Smith drew attention, in this connection, to the fact that modern government of the British type was a complex instrument in which politics was a competitive game, with as its object the attainment of 'the great prizes which sometimes come from the wheel of the great state lottery of British politicks' (IV.vii.c.75). He added, in a passage which reflects the psychological assumptions of *The Theory of Moral Sentiments* (I.iii.2, 'Of the origin of Ambition'), that 'men desire to have some share in the management of publick affairs chiefly on account of the importance which it gives them' (IV.vii.c.74).

This point leads to another which was emphasised by Smith, namely that the same economic forces which had served to elevate the House of Commons to a superior degree of influence had also served to make it an important focal point for sectional interests. If Smith was alive to the dangers of collective self-interest, he also noted that governments on the English model were likely to be particularly sensitive to public opinion - and frequently constrained by it. He made much of the point and in a variety of ways. He noted, for example, that even if the British Government of the 1770s had thought it possible voluntarily to withdraw from the current conflict with America it could not pursue this eminently rational course for fear of public discredit (Corr. p. 383).

Smith also gave a great deal of attention to the general problems presented by the confirmed habits and prejudices of a people and to the need to adjust legislation accordingly. For example, he likened the fear of engrossing and forestalling in the corn trade 'to the popular terrors and suspicions of witchcraft' (IV.v.b.26), and described the law dealing with the exportation of wheat as one which 'though not the best in itself, is the best which the interests, prejudices, and temper of the times would admit of'. The reference to the wisdom of Solon in the *Wealth of Nations* (IV.v.b.53) finds an echo in *The Theory of Moral Sentiments* (VI ii.2, 16); a timely reminder to those who are currently determined to export the full apparatus of the exchange economy to cultural environments which may not be, as yet, consistent with it.

Complementing Winch's comments, a second, older, line of interpretation is associated with Jacob Viner, who reminded his auditors on the occasion of the celebrations to mark the one hundred and fiftieth anniversary of the publication of the *Wealth of Nations* that 'Adam Smith was not a doctrinaire advocate of *laissez faire*. He saw a wide and elastic range of activity for government, and he was prepared to extend it further, if government by improving its standards of competence, honesty, and public spirit, showed itself entitled to wider responsibilities.'[2]

In Viner's summary, Smith's list of the functions of government is impressive. For example, Smith was prepared to justify the use of stamps on plate and linen as the most effectual guarantee of quality (I.x.c.13), the compulsory regulation of mortgages (V.ii.h.17), the legal enforcement of contracts (I.ix.16) and government control of the coinage. In addition, he defended the granting of temporary monopolies to mercantile groups on particular occasions, to the inventors of new machines, and, not surprisingly, to the authors of new books (V.i.e.30).

But four broad areas of intervention are of particular interest, in the sense that they involve issues of general principle. First, Smith advised governments that where they were faced with taxes imposed by their competitors in trade, retaliation could be in order, especially if such an action had the effect of ensuring the 'repeal of the high duties or prohibitions complained of'.[3]

Second, Smith advocated the use of taxation, not simply as a means of raising revenue, but as a means of controlling certain activities, and of compensating for what would now be known as a defective telescopic faculty, i.e. a failure to perceive our long-run interest (see V.ii.g.4; V.ii.k.50; V.ii.c.12).

Smith was also well aware, to take a third point, that the modern version of the 'circular flow' depended on paper money and on credit; in effect a system of 'dual circulation' involving a complex of transactions linking producers and merchants, dealers and consumers (II.ii.88); transactions that would involve cash (at the level of the household) and credit (at the level of the firm).[4] It is in this context that Smith advocated control over the rate of interest, set in such a way as to ensure that 'sober people are universally preferred, as borrowers, to prodigals and projectors' (II.iv.15). He was also willing to regulate the small note issue in the interests of a stable banking system. To those who objected to this proposal, he replied that the interests of the community required it, and concluded that 'the obligation of building party walls, in order to prevent the communication of fire, is a violation of natural liberty, exactly of the same kind with the regulations of the banking trade which are here proposed' (II.ii.94).

Although Smith's monetary analysis is not regarded as amongst the strongest of his contributions to economic theory, it should be remembered that the witness of the collapse of major banks in the 1770s was acutely aware of the problems generated by a sophisticated credit structure. It was in this context that Smith articulated a very general principle, namely, that 'those exertions of the natural liberty of a few individuals, which might endanger the security of the whole society, are, and ought to be, restrained by the laws of all governments; of the most free, as well as of the most despotical' (II.ii.94).

Fourth, emphasis should also be given to Smith's contention

that a major responsibility of government must be the provision of certain public works and institutions for facilitating the commerce of the society which were 'of such a nature, that the profit could never repay the expence to any individual or small number of individuals, and which it, therefore, cannot be expected that any individual or small number of individuals should erect or maintain' (V.i.c.1). In short, he was concerned to point out that the state would have to organise public works and services which the profit motive alone could not guarantee; the problem of market as distinct from government failure.⁵ The list of government functions serves to remind the modern reader of two important points. First, Smith's list of recommended policies was longer than some popular assessments suggest. Smith emphatically did not think in terms of 'anarchy plus the constable', to use Carlyle's phrase. Second, it is important to recall the need to distinguish the *principles* which Smith used in justifying intervention (which may be generally valid) and the specific *agenda* which he offered. The agenda may reflect his understanding of the situation which he actually confronted at the time of writing, and the problems which he did not choose to address.⁶ The basic *principles* are open to wide application, notably in the circumstances of a modern (or under-developed) society. This point helps to explain Eric Roll's judgement that Smith and Keynes 'would find much common ground in respect of the broad principles that should guide the management of the economy.'⁷ Smith would surely have had sympathy with Lord Keynes's broad reading of a different situation, which led him to defend an *enlargement* of government activity 'both as the only practicable means of avoiding the destruction of economic forms in their entirety and as the condition of the successful functioning of individual initiative'.⁸

The point highlights E. R. Seligman's warning to readers of the 1910 edition of the *Wealth of Nations*, namely that they must avoid 'absolutism' and respect the point that recent 'investigation has emphasised the changing conditions of time and place and has emphasised the principles of relativity'.⁹ It is not appropriate to translate Smith's policy *prescriptions* uncritically from the eighteenth to the twentieth century – moreover, it is quite inconsistent with Smith's own teaching. Smith's work was marked by relativity of perspective – a dominant feature of the treatment of scientific knowledge in his remarkable essay on the history of astronomy and in the analysis of rules of behaviour in his treatment of ethics and jurisprudence. But this is not to be taken to mean that Smith's discussion of both principles and practice cannot in all cases directly be applied to problems of a contemporary nature. The case chosen here is Smith's treatment of education, with particular reference to the universities, where his views find many echoes in a late twentieth-century environment which is dominated by debates over payment, accountability, sensitivity to market forces and the perceived need for external scrutiny.

In the argument which follows we first review Smith's treatment of the principles of public finance and the ideal organisation of public works and services, before going on to consider the application of these principles to the subject of this chapter.

The treatment of defence is clearly related to the discussion of the stages of history, an important part of the argument being that a gradual change in the economic and social structure had necessitated the formal provision of an army. Thus, for example, in primitive stages, such as that of hunting and pasture, almost the whole male community is fitted and available for war by virtue of their occupations and the mode of subsistence which happens to prevail, while the same is also basically true of the stage of agriculture. In short, the provision of this necessary service is basically costless until the stage of commerce or civilisation is reached. It is in this context that the form of economic organisation, the greater complexity of modern war (V.i.a.9, 10) and the high costs associated with the introduction of firearms lead to a situation where the 'wisdom of the state' (V.i.a.14) must arrange for provision.

Of the options open to government, Smith preferred a standing army to a militia as likely to be more effective. While admitting the political dangers which such armies present, as exemplified by Caesar and Cromwell, Smith noted that

> where the sovereign is himself the general, and the principal
> nobility and gentry of the country the chief officers of the army;

where the military force is placed under the command of those who have the greatest interest in the support of the civil authority, because they have themselves the greatest share of that authority, a standing army can never be dangerous to liberty. (V.i.a.41)

On the contrary, he added, such an army

may in some cases be favourable to liberty. The security which it gives to the sovereign renders unnecessary that troublesome jealousy, which, in some modern republicks, seems to watch over the minutest actions, and to be at all times ready to disturb the peace of every citizen. ... That degree of liberty which approaches to licentiousness can be tolerated only in countries where the sovereign is secured by a well-regulated standing army. It is in such countries only, that the publick safety does not require, that the sovereign should be trusted with any discretionary power, for suppressing even the impertinent wantonness of this licentious liberty. (V.i.a.41)

Having determined the preferred form of organisation, Smith concluded that this essential service would have to be paid for. Since the expense involved was laid out 'for the benefit of the whole society' it ought to be defrayed 'by the general contribution of the whole society, all the different members contributing, as nearly as possible, in proportion to their respective abilities' (V.i.i.1).

As far as the organisation of the essential service of justice is concerned, it was Smith's contention that the separation of powers was a basic prerequisite for effective and equitable provision:

When the judicial is united to the executive power, it is scarce possible that justice should not frequently be sacrificed to, what is vulgarly called, politics. The persons entrusted with the great interests of the state may, even without any corrupt views, sometime imagine it necessary to sacrifice to those interests the rights of a private man. But upon the impartial administration of justice depends the liberty of every individual, the sense which he has of his own security. In order to make every individual feel himself perfectly secure in the possession of every right which belongs to him, it is not only necessary that the judicial should be separated from the executive power, but that it should be rendered as much as possible independent of that power. The judge should not be liable to be removed from his office according to the caprice of that power. The regular payment of his salary should not depend upon the good-will, or even upon the good oeconomy of that power. (V.i.b.25)

As Alan Peacock has pointed out, Smith's efficiency criteria are clearly distinguished from the basic issue of organisation, the argument being, in effect, that the services provided by attorneys, clerks or judges should be paid for in such a way as to encourage productivity.[10] Indeed, Smith ascribed the 'present admirable constitution of the courts of justice in England' to the use of a system of court fees which had served to encourage competition between the Courts of King's Bench, Chancery and Exchequer (V.i.b.20, 21). A further interesting and typical feature of the discussion is found in Smith's argument that although justice is a service to the whole community, none the less, the costs of handling specific causes should be borne by those who give occasion to, or benefit from, them. He therefore concluded that the 'expense of the administration of justice ... may very properly be defrayed by the particular contribution of one or other, or both of those two different sets of persons, according as different occasions may require, that is, by the fees of court' (V.i.i.2), rather than by a charge on the general funds.

Smith also considered that public works such as highways, bridges and canals should be paid for by those who use them and in proportion to the wear and tear occasioned. At the same time, he argued that the consumers who pay the charges generally gain more from the cheapness of carriage than they lose in the charges incurred:

> The person who finally pays this tax, therefore, gains by the application, more than he loses by the payment of it. His payment is exactly in proportion to his gain. It is in reality no more than a part of that gain which he is obliged to give up in order to get the rest. It seems impossible to imagine a more equitable method of raising a tax. (V.i.d.4)

In addition, he suggested that tolls should be higher in the case of luxury goods so that by this means 'the indolence and vanity of the rich is made to contribute in a very easy manner to the relief of the poor, by rendering cheaper the transportation of heavy goods' (V.i.d.5).

Smith also defended the principle of direct payment on the ground of efficiency. Only by this means, he contended, would it be possible to ensure that services are provided where there is a recognisable need. Only in this way, for example, would it be possible to avoid building roads through a desert for the sake of some private interest, and to prevent the construction of a great bridge 'thrown over a river at a place where nobody passes, or merely to embellish the view from the windows of a neighbouring palace: things which sometimes happen, in countries where works of this kind are carried on by any other revenue than that which they themselves are capable of affording' (V.i.d.6).

Smith further argued that while governments must be responsible for establishing major public works, care should be taken to ensure that the services were administered by such bodies, or under such conditions, as made it in the interest of individuals to do so effectively. Smith tirelessly emphasised the point, already noticed in the discussion of justice, that in every trade and profession 'the exertion of the greater part of those who exercise it, is always in proportion to the necessity they are under of making that exertion' (V.i.f.4). On this ground, he approved of the expedient used in France, whereby a construction engineer was made a present of the tolls on a canal for which he had been responsible – thus ensuring that it was in his interest to keep the canal in good repair. In fact, Smith used a number of such devices, advocating, for example, that the administration of roads would have to be handled in a different way from canals because they are passable even when full of holes. Here he suggested that the 'wisdom of parliament' would have to be applied to the appointment of proper persons, with 'proper courts of inspection' for 'controuling their conduct, and for reducing the tolls to what is barely sufficient for executing the work to be done by them' (V.i.d.9).

Smith recognised that such services could not always be paid for by those who used them, arguing that in such cases 'local or provincial expenses of which the benefit is local or provincial' ought, so far as possible, to be no burden on general taxation, it being 'unjust that the whole society should contribute towards an expence of which the benefit is confined to a part of the society' (V.i.i.3). But here again it is argued (in the interest of efficiency) that such services 'are always better maintained by a local or provincial revenue, under the management of a local and provincial administration, than by the general revenue of the state, of which the executive power must always have the management' (V.i.d.18).

It is also worth noting that even where recourse has to be made to general taxation, Smith argued that such taxes should be imposed in accordance with the generally accepted canons of taxation; that so far as possible such taxes should avoid interference with the allocative mechanism, and that they ought not to constitute disincentives to the individual effort on which the working of the system was seen to depend.

It will be apparent that Smith's treatment of public works and services is informed throughout by a particular set of principles of public finance. As we have seen, Smith typically explains the nature of each service and why it is required. He contends that the state will have to ensure provision where market forces would fail to do so, recognising that major public works may well require central funding. He also argues that public services should be paid for by those who benefit from them and organised wherever possible in such a way as to induce efficient delivery. All of these principles were to be deployed in the treatment of education.

'Domestic education is the institution of nature; public education, the contrivance of man. It is surely unnecessary to say, which is likely to be the wisest' (TMS VI.ii.1.10). Smith returned to this theme in the *Wealth of Nations* when he observed that those 'parts of education ... for the teaching of which there are no publick institutions are generally the best taught' (V.i.f.16). He went on to suggest that

> Were there no publick institutions for education, no system, no science would be taught for which there was not some demand; or which the circumstances of the times did not render it, either necessary, or convenient, or at least fashionable to learn. A private teacher could never find his account in teaching, either an exploded and antiquated system of a science acknowledged to be useful, or a science universally believed to be a mere useless and pedantick heap of sophistry and nonsense. (V.i.f.46)

He then proceeded to pose the central question:

> Ought the publick, therefore, to give no attention, it may be
> asked, to the education of the people? Or if it ought to give any,
> what are the different parts of education which it ought to attend
> to in the different orders of the people? and in what manner
> ought it to attend to them? (V.i.48)

The answer was affirmative – there must be a system of public
education – for reasons connected with the probable impact of
the division of labour. Smith observed first, that

> In the progress of the division of labour, the employment of the
> far greater part of those who live by labour, that is, of the great
> body of the people, comes to be confined to a few very simple
> operations; frequently to one or two. But the understandings of
> the greater part of men are necessarily formed by their ordinary
> employments. The man whose whole life is spent in performing
> a few simple operations, of which the effects too are, perhaps,
> always the same, or very nearly the same, has no occasion to exert
> his understanding, or to exercise his invention in finding out
> expedients for removing difficulties which never occur. He natu-
> rally loses, therefore, the habit of such exertion, and generally
> becomes as stupid and ignorant as it is possible for a human crea-
> ture to become. The torpor of his mind renders him, not only
> incapable of relishing or bearing a part in any rational conversa-
> tion, but of conceiving any generous, noble, or tender sentiment,
> and consequently of forming any just judgement concerning
> many even of the ordinary duties of private life. (V.i.f.50)

He added that in every improved and civilised society 'this is
the state into which the labouring poor, that is, the great body
of people, must necessarily fall, unless government takes some
pains to prevent it' (V.i.f.50).

Second, Smith drew attention to the contrast between the
modern commercial stage, where all goods and services
command a price, and the more primitive stages of hunting,
pasture and agriculture. In the latter three cases all male
members of the society were likely to be involved in martial
exercise and in military action whereas the 'number of those
who can go to war, in proportion to the whole number of the
people, is necessarily much smaller in a civilised, than in a rude
state of society' (V.i.a.11). The problem for Smith was that of a
decline in 'martial spirit' in modern society:

a coward, a man incapable either of defending or of revenging himself, evidently wants one of the most essential parts of the character of a man. He is as much mutilated and deformed in his mind, as another is in his body, who is either deprived of some of its most essential members, or has lost the use of them. He is evidently the more wretched and miserable of the two; because happiness and misery, which reside altogether in the mind, must necessarily depend more upon the healthful or unhealthful, the mutilated or entire state of the mind, than upon that of the body. (V.i.f.60)

Third, Smith drew attention to the social problems associated with isolation which could follow from the growth of cities and/or manufactures. In contrast to the man of better condition, whose conduct is exposed to scrutiny by his fellows in the manner suggested by the analysis of *The Theory of Moral Sentiments*,

A man of low condition, on the contrary, is far from being a distinguished member of any great society. While he remains in a country village his conduct may be attended to, and he may be obliged to attend to it himself. In this situation, and in this situation only, he may have what is called a character to lose. But as soon as he comes into a great city, he is sunk in obscurity and darkness. His conduct is observed and attended to by nobody, and he is therefore very likely to neglect it himself, and to abandon himself to every sort of low profligacy and vice. (V.i.g.12)

As Smith noted, one *possible* reaction to the difficulty could be through membership of small societies or religious groups, whose standards of conduct, however, might be disagreeably rigorous and 'unsocial'.

In dealing with the first problem, Smith suggested that, while the relatively poor cannot be as well educated as people of rank and fortune, 'the most essential parts of education, however, to read, write, and account, can be acquired at so early a period of life, that the greater part even of those who are to be bred to the lowest occupations, have time to acquire them before they can be employed in those occupations' (V.i.f.54). He noted that the public could facilitate this process by establishing schools on the Scottish model 'where children may be taught for a reward so moderate, that even a common labourer may afford it', and commented in a characteristic passage, whose implications we shall examine later, that the master should be 'partly, but not wholly paid by the publick; because if he was wholly, or even principally paid by it, he would soon learn to neglect his business' (V.i.f.55).

It is to be noted that Smith advocated a policy which would encourage the poor to send their children to school, but also that he supported *compulsion*:

> The publick can impose upon almost the whole body of the people the necessity of acquiring those most essential parts of education, by obliging every man to undergo an examination or probation in them before he can obtain the freedom in any corporation, or be allowed to set up any trade either in a village or town corporate. (V.i.f.57)

It is also to be noted that the poor were to be compelled to act in this way since they typically lacked either incentive or inclination to provide an education for their children. The poor, he observed, have little time to spare for education; as soon as children 'are able to work, they must apply to some trade by which they can earn their subsistence' (V.i.f.53). In a telling passage in the *Lectures on Jurisprudence* Smith noted that 'a boy of six or seven years of age at Birmingham can gain his threepence or sixpence a day, and parents find it to be in their interest to set them soon to work. Thus their education is neglected' (LJ (B) 329–30).

Second, Smith advocated compulsory military exercises as a means of offsetting the problem of a decline in martial spirit. While he recognised that a people trained in the martial arts could be useful for the purposes of defence, he supported the policy largely on welfare grounds:

> Even though the martial spirit of the people were of no use towards the defence of the society, yet to prevent that sort of mental mutilation, deformity and wretchedness, which cowardice necessarily involves in it, from spreading themselves through the great body of the people, would still deserve the most serious attention of government; in the same manner as it would deserve its most serious attention to prevent a leprosy or any other loathsome and offensive disease, though neither mortal nor dangerous, from spreading itself among them; though, perhaps, no other

publick good might result from such attention besides the prevention of so great a publick evil. (V.i.f.60)

Finally, Smith argued that the problems presented by the disagreeable and unsocial morals often associated with small, and especially religious, sects could be offset by two remedies:

> The first of those remedies is the study of science and philosophy, which the state might render almost universal among all people of middling or more than middling rank and fortune; not by giving salaries to teachers in order to make them negligent and idle, but by instituting some sort of probation, even in the higher and more difficult sciences, to be undergone by every person before he was permitted to exercise any liberal profession, or before he could be received as a candidate for any honourable office of trust or profit. ... Science is the great antidote to the poison of enthusiasm and superstition; and where all the superior ranks of people were secured from it, the inferior ranks could not be much exposed to it. (V.i.g.14)

In this connection, Smith's preference was probably for the classical programme of physics, moral philosophy and logic (V.i.f.23). The second of Smith's remedies was found in the frequency and gaiety of public diversions:

> The state, by encouraging, that is by giving entire liberty to all those who for their own interest would attempt, without scandal or indecency, to amuse and divert the people by painting, poetry, musick, dancing; by all sorts of dramatic representations and exhibitions, would easily dissipate, in the greater part of them, that melancholy and gloomy humour which is almost always the nurse of popular superstition and enthusiasm. Publick diversions have always been the objects of dread and hatred, to all the fanatical promoters of those popular frenzies. The gaiety and good humour which those diversions inspire were altogether inconsistent with that temper of mind, which was fittest for their purpose, or which they could best work upon. Dramatick representations besides, frequently exposing their artifices to publick ridicule, and sometimes even to publick execration, were upon that account, more than all other diversions, the objects of their peculiar abhorrence. (V.i.g.15)

Some passages cited in this section have encouraged those with an eye to the role of the state to identify support for national health and perhaps something akin to an Arts Council among Adam Smith's recommendations. But it is more important for our present purpose to note Smith's advocacy of a *compulsory* programme of higher education. It is also significant that Smith's advocacy of such a programme was rooted in a perceived need to offset the social costs of the division of labour and that in particular the programme was intended not only to preserve a capacity for moral judgement, but also to support individuals in their roles as citizens:

> Though the state was to derive no advantage from the instruction of the inferior ranks of people, it would still deserve its attention that they should not be altogether uninstructed. The state, however, derives no inconsiderable advantage from their instruction. The more they are instructed, the less liable they are to the delusions of enthusiasm and superstition, which, among ignorant nations, frequently occasion the most dreadful disorders. An instructed and intelligent people besides are always more decent and orderly than an ignorant and stupid one. They feel themselves, each individually, more respectable, and more likely to obtain the respect of their lawful superiors, and they are therefore more disposed to respect those superiors. They are more disposed to examine, and more capable of seeing through, the interested complaints of faction and sedition, and they are, upon that account, less apt to be misled into any wanton or unnecessary opposition to the measures of government. In free countries, where the safety of government depends very much upon the favourable judgment which the people may form of its conduct, it must surely be of the highest importance that they should not be disposed to judge rashly or capriciously concerning it. (V.i.f.61)[11]

As to the organisation of educational provision, Smith's analysis of principles which are of general application refers primarily to the universities and may well reflect the content of a letter which he wrote to William Cullen in September 1774. Cullen had written to Smith seeking his opinion on proposals from the Royal College of Physicians of Edinburgh. The petition suggested that doctors should be graduates, that they should have attended university for at least two years and that they should present themselves for examination. The proposals from the College followed a scandal which revealed the laxity of some

Scottish medical schools; a matter which was brought to a head
by the dismissal of an Edinburgh graduate from his post at the
London Hospital.

While confirming his view that in 'the present state of the
Scotch universities I do most sincerely look upon them as, in
spite of their faults, without exception the best seminaries of
learning that are to be found anywhere in Europe', Smith none
the less rejected the proposals from the Royal College. As he
wrote to Cullen: 'There never was, and I will venture to say
there never will be, a University from which a degree could
give any tolerable security, that the person upon whom it had
been conferred, was fit to practise physic' (Corr. p. 176). But
the most telling argument was based on the advantage of
competition:

> You propose, I observe, that no person should be admitted to
> examination for his degrees unless he brought a certificate of his
> having studied at least two years in some University. Would not
> such a regulation be oppressive upon all private teachers, such as
> the Hunters, Hewson, Fordyce, etc.? The scholars of such teach-
> ers surely merit whatever honour or advantage a degree can
> confer, much more than the greater part of those who have spent
> many years in some Universities, where the different branches of
> medical knowledge are either not taught at all, or are taught so
> superficially that they had as well not be taught at all. When a
> man has learnt his lesson very well, it surely can be of little
> importance where or from whom he has learnt it. (Corr. p. 174)

While the reaction of Dr Cullen may be imagined, the letter is
an important document, since it may well form the basis of that
section in the *Wealth of Nations* where Smith examined issues
of a more general nature. The key question Smith addressed was
this: if universities are appropriate agencies for the provision
of higher education, then what conditions have to be met if efficiency is to be assured? The answers emerge in the course of
Smith's critique of the contemporary situation.

One problem of fundamental importance identified by
Smith refers to the supply of talent to the universities:

> In countries where church benefices are the greater part of them
> very moderate, a chair in a university is generally a better estab-
> lishment than a church benefice. The universities have, in this

case, the picking and chusing of their members from all the
churchmen of the country, who, in every country, constitute by
far the most numerous class of men of letters. Where church
benefices, on the contrary, are many of them very considerable,
the church naturally draws from the universities the greater part
of their eminent men of letters. (V.i.g.39)

Thus, Smith argued, we can explain the lack of eminent teachers, especially on the arts side, in Roman Catholic countries and
in England, while in Protestant countries such as Germany,
Holland, Sweden and Scotland 'the most eminent men of letters
whom those countries have produced, have, not all indeed, but
the far greater part of them, been professors in universities'
(V.i.g.39).

But even where the universities can attract professors of
quality it is necessary to provide appropriate stimuli on the
ground that it 'is the interest of every man to live as much at
his ease as he can' (V.i.f.7). Smith objected to a situation where
high salaries might be paid irrespective of competence or industry. As he observed, in some universities 'the teacher is prohib-
ited from receiving any honorary or fee from his pupils, and
his salary constitutes the whole of the revenue which he derives
from his office. His interest is, in this case, set as directly in
opposition to his duty as it is possible to set it' (V.i.g.39)..

There were other problems which could affect academic
efficiency. Smith objected to the fact that the privileges of grad-
uation 'necessarily force a certain number of students to [attend
some] universities, independent of the merit or reputation of
the teachers' (V.i.f.11), while in addition specific endowments
often force students to attend particular colleges. He added:

> If in each college the tutor or teacher, who was to instruct each
> student in all arts and sciences, should not be voluntarily chosen
> by the student, but appointed by the head of the college; and if,
> in case of neglect, inability, or bad usage, the student should not
> be allowed to change him for another, without leave first asked
> and obtained; such a regulation would not only tend very much
> to extinguish all emulation among the different tutors of the same
> college, but to diminish very much in all of them the necessity
> of diligence and of attention to their respective pupils. (V.i.f.13)

Institutional structures which did not provide adequate stimuli to the academic could, Smith argued, also have adverse effects on the quality and the content of what was taught:

> several of those learned societies have chosen to remain, for a long time, the sanctuaries in which exploded systems and obsolete prejudices found shelter and protection, after they had been hunted out of every other corner of the world. In general, the richest and best endowed universities have been the slowest in adopting ... improvements, and the most averse to permit any considerable change in the established plan of education ... improvements were more easily introduced into some of the poorer universities, in which the teachers, depending upon their reputation for the greater part of their subsistence, were obliged to pay more attention to the current opinions of the world. (V.i.f.34)

Smith drew attention to a further point of an organisational nature. He was conscious of the fact that there were dangers in the privilege of self-government. In referring to the behaviour of the individual academic, he noted that

> If the authority to which he is subject resides in the body corporate, the college, or university, of which he himself is a member, and in which the greater part of the other members are, like himself, persons who either are, or ought to be teachers; they are likely to make a common cause, to be all very indulgent to one another, and every man to consent that his neighbour may neglect his duty, provided he himself is allowed to neglect his own. In the university of Oxford, the greater part of the publick professors have, for these many years, given up altogether even the pretence of teaching. (V.i.f.8)

In sum, an efficient system of higher education requires: a state of free competition between established institutions and private teachers; a capacity effectively to compete in the labour market for men of letters; a situation whereby the teacher's income is related to his capacity to attract and to sustain student numbers; freedom of choice for the student as between teachers, courses, colleges or schools; and the capacity to be competitive and sensitive to market forces, even if these forces are not always of themselves sufficient to ensure the provision of the basic infrastructure.

A number of points might be made in support of the assertion that Smith's treatment of education is of direct interest to the modern reader. First, it is worth emphasising that Smith supported *compulsory* education for particular groups in society. Education at the level of the school is to be regarded as compulsory for *all* members of society, although Smith offered an implicit distinction between vocationally orientated instruction for the lower orders, and university education for all those who aspired to an honourable office of trust or of profit. Compulsion of this sort would seem to indicate a major modification to the claim to individual freedom, although it must be remembered that Smith's discussion of education in general is to be seen against the background of his analysis of the social consequences of the division of labour. The real significance of what Robert Heilbroner has called the 'dark side' of the *Wealth of Nations* can be fully appreciated only when seen against the background of Smith's ethics.[12] Readers of *The Theory of Moral Sentiments* will be familiar with the argument that a capacity for moral *judgement* requires the exercise of faculties and propensities such as imagination, sympathy and reflection – qualities of mind which are likely to be eroded in the context of the modern economy unless preventative steps are taken.

Smith's concern with isolation and mental mutilation can be interpreted as part of another contemporary debate, to do with the ideals of civic humanism and the extent to which modern 'men' could attain something approaching the classical concept of citizenship.[13] But we are also reminded of the revision of liberalism undertaken by the Oxford idealists in the nineteenth century, and of T. H. Green's distinction between negative and positive freedom. In a lecture delivered in 1880 on the subject of 'Liberal Legislation and Freedom of Contract', Green defined negative freedom as freedom from restraint, and positive freedom as a 'power or capacity of doing or enjoying something worth doing or enjoying',[14] recognising that the condition of positive freedom could only be attained with the assistance of the state.

Second, the modern reader will recognise the central importance of *choice and* the emphasis which Smith gave to *freedom of choice*. To make choice of educational services effective we require information about the range and quality of provision available in particular institutions, so that Smith's position would be entirely consistent with the publication of tables (if not *league* tables) which provide information as to performance and range.

Smith's basic principles of public finance also suggest that the beneficiary of a service should pay for it whenever possible – the outstanding exceptions being some local services and national defence, where the whole society must pay through a system of taxation which is organised in such a way as to respect the canons of taxation. In the case of education, Smith recognised that there is a benefit to the individual, but also to the state, where the latter is expressed in terms of investment in human capital and in terms of the capacity of the individual to act as a responsible citizen. Smith's position was thus somewhat ambiguous:

> The expence of the institutions for education and religious instruction, is ... beneficial to the whole society, and may, therefore, without injustice, be defrayed by the general contribution of the whole society. This expence, however, might perhaps with equal propriety, and even with some advantage, be defrayed altogether by those who receive the immediate benefit of such education and instruction, or by the voluntary contribution of those who think they have occasion for either the one or the other. (V.i.i.5)

It seems likely that Smith would have supported the arrangements which he envisaged for elementary education where there is a combination of modest private, and a more significant public, contribution. Of the modern alternatives of student loans and the graduate tax, his treatment of taxation might suggest support for the latter on the ground that it minimises the disincentive effects – where the amount is modest and related to the actual capacity to pay.

But in many ways the most intriguing aspects of Smith's argument relate to his treatment of the performance of the academic, especially since he offers us an implicit distinction between research and teaching:

> To excel in any profession, in which but few arrive at mediocrity, is the most decisive mark of what is called genius or superior talents. The publick admiration which attends upon such distinguished abilities, makes always a part of their reward; a

greater or smaller in proportion as it is higher or lower in degree. It makes a considerable part of that reward in the profession of physick; a still greater perhaps in that of law; in poetry and philosophy it makes almost the whole. (I.x.b.24)

Public admiration may be taken to refer to literary or scientific reputation, and here Smith had some interesting observations to make in *The Theory of Moral Sentiments*:

> There are some very noble and beautiful arts, in which the degree of excellence can be determined only by a certain nicety of taste, of which the decisions, however, appear always, in some measure, uncertain. There are others, in which the success admits, either of clear demonstration, or very satisfactory proof. Among the candidates for excellence in those different arts, the anxiety about the public opinion is always much greater in the former than in the latter. (TMS III.2.18)

The contrast is between the poet, or philosopher, uncertain of his reception, and the great mathematician who is confident of his results.[15] Yet both are 'candidates for excellence' and both are likely to be conscious of literary or scientific reputation as a source of social distinction and influence. As Smith remarked, when the opinions of another person

> not only coincide with our own, but lead and direct our own; when in forming them he appears to have attended to many things which we had overlooked, and to have adjusted them to all the various circumstances of their objects; we not only approve of them, but wonder and are surprised at their uncommon and unexpected acuteness and comprehensiveness, and he appears to deserve a very high degree of admiration and applause. For approbation heightened by wonder and surprise, constitutes the sentiment which is properly called admiration, and of which applause is the natural expression. (TMS, I.i.4.3)

The pursuit of public reputation is entirely consistent with competition and emulation; a point which Smith made quite forcefully in the *Wealth of Nations*:

> The greatness of the objects which are to be acquired by success in some particular professions may, no doubt, sometimes animate the exertion of a few men of extraordinary spirit and ambition.

But, he added,

Great objects, however, are evidently not necessary in order to occasion the greatest exertions. Rivalship and emulation render excellency, even in mean professions, an object of ambition, and frequently occasion the very greatest exertions. Great objects, on the contrary, alone and unsupported by the necessity of application, have seldom been sufficient to occasion any considerable exertion.(V.i.f.4)

Rivalship, emulation and the pursuit of professional standing undoubtedly are, as they always have been, at least part of the explanation for academic research effort. But if the mechanism is inadequate in some or many cases, then Smith's treatment of the principles of public works could be used to justify the introduction of other measures – for instance, those which are represented by the modern interest in the Research Assessment Exercise, an example of what Smith would have called an 'extraneous jurisdiction'.

Smith also had a number of points to make regarding the provision of *teaching*, which is in fact the main focus of attention in his discussion of universities in the *Wealth of Nations*. He noted, for example, that the work of the teacher provides the individual with an 'education which is most likely to render him a man of solid learning and knowledge', and that to 'impose upon any man the necessity of teaching, year after year, any particular branch of science, seems, in reality, to be the most effectual method for rendering him compleatly master of it' (V.i.g.40). In a further, telling passage, he observed:

In some universities the salary makes but a part, and frequently but a small part of the emoluments of the teacher, of which the greater part arises from the honoraries or fees of his pupils. The necessity of application, though always more or less diminished, is not in this case entirely taken away. Reputation in his profession is still of some importance to him, and he still has some dependency upon the affection, gratitude, and favourable report of those who have attended upon his instructions; and these favourable sentiments he is likely to gain in no way so well as by deserving them, that is, by the abilities and diligence with which he discharges every part of his duty. (V.i.f.6)

This is an interesting statement when we consider the emphasis which Smith gave to the point that all our actions are subject to the scrutiny of our fellows, together with the stress which he placed (in *The Theory of Moral Sentiments*) on our natural desire not just to be praised, but to be *praiseworthy*. However, as the statement just quoted, and indeed the whole tenor of the discussion, suggests, Smith believed that the diligence of the teacher can be *relied* on only where the stated efficiency criteria are met. The argument may simply represent Smith's attempt to be logically rigorous; but, on the other hand, his bleak conclusion seems to have been arrived at after careful consideration. As Smith remarked to Cullen, 'I have thought a great deal upon this subject, and have inquired very carefully into the constitution and history of several of the principal Universities of Europe.' If the Scottish Universities were among the best, this was only because 'the salaries of the Professors are insignificant. There are few or no bursaries or exhibitions, and their monopoly of degrees is broken in upon by all other Universities, foreign or domestic.' In speaking of the Edinburgh medical school in particular, he concluded, 'I require no other explication of its present acknowledged superiority over every other society of the same kind in Europe.' (Corr. pp. 174–5)

There are further aspects of the argument which are likely to be of contemporary interest. As we noted in dealing with the subject of public works, Smith was willing to consider a variety of ways in which the effective delivery of a service may be assured. If the universities cannot be rendered capable of self-regulation as a result of meeting his stated efficiency criteria, the implication would again seem to be that the 'wisdom of Parliament' would have to be deployed in setting up 'proper courts of inspection' for 'controuling their conduct' (V.i.d.9) – as in the case of public roads, which is hardly a flattering comparison.

There is nothing in Smith's position that would suggest rejection of the contemporary interest in quality assessment at least in *principle* (as distinct from current *practice*). It is not only Cullen who might feel tempted to 'box Smith's ears' for what he had written (Corr. p. 179 and n). However, while not denying that external scrutiny, in the form of a visitation, could on occasion be necessary and desirable, Smith advised Cullen to be cautious, especially in the case of the Scottish universities:

Before any wise man, however, would apply for the appointment
of so arbitrary a tribunal, in order to improve what is already,
upon the whole, very well, he ought certainly to know with some
degree of certainty, first, who are likely to be appointed visitors,
and secondly, what plan of reformation these visitors are likely
to follow. (Corr. pp. 173–4)

If Smith seems to suggest that there should be an opportunity
for serious dialogue between the 'visitors' and those institutions
which are to be visited, he also warned his readers of the
dangers of 'extraneous jurisdictions'. As he remarked,

The person subject to such jurisdiction is necessarily degraded
by it, and, instead of being one of the most respectable, is
rendered one of the meanest and most contemptible persons in
the society. It is by powerful protection only that he can effectually guard himself against the bad usage to which he is at all
times exposed; and this protection he is most likely to gain, not
by ability or diligence in his profession, but by obsequiousness
to the will of his superiors, and by being ready, at all times, to
sacrifice to that will the rights, the interest, and the honour of
the body corporate of which he is a member. (V.i.f.9)

It will be noted that much of this discussion is related to consideration of the *supply* side of the equation. From the standpoint of *demand*, it was Smith's contention, as we have seen, that
when 'a man has learned his lesson very well, it surely can be
of little importance where or from whom he has learnt it'. But
if Smith thought that the 'Scotch' universities in general, and
the University of Glasgow in particular, satisfied this criterion,
not everyone agreed. University education at the time provoked
an adverse reaction from those who were concerned with the
need to introduce cheap courses in science to a wider public.
The spirit of this criticism is neatly caught in the title of a work
by William Thom, Minister of Govan, and an arch-critic of
Smith's university, in a *Letter to J .... M .... Esq., on the Defects
of an University Education and its unsuitableness to a Commercial
People: with the Expediency and Necessity of Erecting at Glasgow
an Academy for the Instruction of Youth*. Thom was apparently
convinced that university education was insufficiently 'voca-
tional', and that they could be forced to move in this direction
through competition to be provided by alternative academies.[16]

In dealing with public works, Adam Smith's preference was undoubtedly for a competitive environment, so structured as to ensure that the efficiency criteria which he identified could be met. Where market forces work effectively, his position suggests that there will be no need for further (external) scrutiny. But where the market for educational services either fails, or operates only partially, as a result of inability to introduce or to sustain *all* of the arrangements needed to ensure efficient delivery, then, as we have seen, Smith's argument may be interpreted to suggest the need for steps to be taken, which could involve the introduction of other control mechanisms.

This line of interpretation may also apply to Smith's wider views on the functions of the state, as noted in the first section of this chapter. At a *theoretical* level, Smith's analysis of the operation of the exchange economy helps to explain Lord Robbins's contention that Smith bequeathed to his successors in the classical school the belief that 'central authority was incompetent to decide on a proper distribution of resources'; the belief that economic freedom 'rested on a two-fold basis: belief in the desireability of freedom of choice for the consumer and belief in the effectiveness, in meeting this choice, of freedom on the part of the producers'.[17] But Smith's position was also *practical* and was made abundantly clear in his discussion of the Corn Laws when he remarked:

> That security which the laws in Great Britain give to every man that he shall enjoy the fruits of his own labour, is alone sufficient to make any country flourish, notwithstanding these and twenty other absurd regulations of commerce; and this security was perfected by the revolution, much about the same time that the bounty was established. The natural effort of every individual to better his own condition, when suffered to exert itself with freedom and security, is so powerful a principle, that it is alone, and without any assistance, not only capable of carrying on the society to wealth and prosperity, but of surmounting a hundred impertinent obstructions with which the folly of human laws too often incumbers its operations. (IV.v.b.43)

Smith's splendid and eloquent dismissals of the 'impertinent obstructions' to human endeavour in contemporary Britain are among the best known and best loved passages in the book. For Smith, a major task of government was to ensure that the conditions of economic freedom are satisfied in *fact* by removing any institutional impediments to it. Broadly speaking these impediments can be reduced to four main categories. First, there is the problem that in every society subject to a process of transition, 'Laws frequently continue in force long after the circumstances, which first gave occasion to them, and which could alone render them reasonable, are no more' (III.ii.4). In such cases Smith suggested that arrangements which were once appropriate but are now no longer so should be removed, citing as examples the laws of succession and entail, laws which had been appropriate to the feudal period but which currently had the effect of limiting the sale and improvement of land. Second, he objected to institutions which had their origin in the past, which still commanded contemporary support, and which adversely affected the operation of the market mechanism. Smith summarised his appeal to government (the British government) in these terms:

> break down the exclusive privileges of corporations, and repeal the statute of apprenticeship, both which are real encroachments upon natural liberty, and add to these the repeal of the law of settlements, so that a poor workman, when thrown out of employment either in one trade or in one place, may seek for it in another trade or in another place, without the fear either of a prosecution or of a removal ... (IV.ii.42)

Third, Smith objected to positions of privilege, such as monopoly powers, which he regarded as essentially creatures of the civil law. The institution is again represented as impolitic and unjust: unjust in that a monopoly position was one of privilege and advantage, and therefore 'contrary to that justice and equality of treatment which the sovereign owes to all the different orders of his subjects' (IV.viii.30); impolitic in that the prices at which goods so controlled are sold are 'upon every occasion the highest that can be got'. Finally, we may usefully distinguish Smith's objection to monopoly in general from his criticism of one expression of it; namely, the mercantile system, which he described as the 'modern system', of policy, best understood 'in our own country and in our own times' (IV.2).

In particular, Smith insisted that mercantile controls were open to 'that general objection which may be made to all the different expedients of the mercantile system; the objection of forcing some part of the industry of the country into a channel less advantageous than that in which it would run of its own accord' (IV.v.a.24).

The reforms for which Smith called may be impeded by particular interests, but they are identifiable and attainable. What is perhaps of even greater interest for the modern reader is the fact that Smith identified additional principles which justify intervention; a point which returns us to the topics touched upon at the outset of this chapter. Smith, in effect, identified the need to act in ways which reflect the existence of certain imperfections which are *inherent* in the economic system. As noted earlier, Smith suggests that the state should regulate activity to compensate for the imperfect knowledge of individuals. It is the state which must continuously scrutinise the relevance of particular laws and institutions; the state which has the duty to regulate and control the activities of individuals which might otherwise prove damaging to the interests of society at large; and the state which must make adequate provision for public works and services (including education) in cases where the profit motive is likely to prove inadequate. The state, arguably, also has a duty to control the organisation of public services where the efficiency criteria cannot be met. If the key principle is that intervention is a function of market imperfection it is little wonder that Professor Macfie could remark that the strategies which can be culled from the *Wealth of Nations* could be interpreted to 'suggest a formidable state autocracy; a socialist spread of controls that would make some modern socialists' eyes pop'.[18] Alec Macfie was, of course, indulging his dry, Glasgow, humour.

Notes

1 Donald Winch, *Adam Smith's Politics : An Essay in Historiographical Revision* (Cambridge: Cambridge University Press, 1978).

2 Jacob Viner, 'Adam Smith and Laissez Faire', *Journal of Political Economy*, 35 (1927), reprinted in *Adam Smith: Critical Assessments*, ed. J. C. Wood (Beckenham: Croom Helm, 1984), vol. 1, pp. 143–67.

3 Donald Winch, 'Science and the Legislator: Adam Smith and After', *Economic Journal*, 93 (1983), p. 509.

4 See Franco Zallio, 'Adam Smith's Dual Circulation Framework', *Royal Bank of Scotland Review*, 166 (1990), pp. 34–43.

5 See, for example, Edwin G. West, 'Adam Smith's Economics of Politics', *History of Political Economy*, 8 (1976), in Wood, *Adam Smith*, vol. 1, pp. 581–600.

6 See, for example, Andrew Skinner, 'Sir James Steuart: The Market and the State', *History of Economic Ideas*, 1 (1993), pp. 1–42.

7 Eric Roll, '*The Wealth of Nations*, 1776–1976', *Lloyds Bank Review*, 119 (1976), reprinted in Wood, *Adam Smith*, vol. 2, pp. 146–55.

8 John Maynard Keynes, *The General Theory of Employment Interest and Money* (London: Macmillan, 1936), p. 380.

9 E. R. A. Seligman, ed., *The Wealth of Nations* (London: Dent, 1910), p. xv.

10 Alan Peacock, 'The Treatment of the Principles of Public Finance in the *Wealth of Nations*', in *Essays on Adam Smith,* ed. Andrew Skinner and Thomas Wilson (Oxford: Oxford University Press, 1975), pp. 553–67.

11 Of the voluminous literature on the problems associated with the division of labour, see Winch, *Adam Smith's Politics*; Robert Heilbroner, 'The Paradox of Progress: Decline and Decay in the *Wealth of Nations*', in *Essays on Adam Smith*, ed. Skinner and Wilson, pp. 524—39; Robert Lamb, 'Adam Smith's Concept of Alienation', *Oxford Economic Papers*, 25 (1973), in Wood, *Adam Smith*, vol. 2, pp. 478–88; Nathan Rosenberg, 'Adam Smith on the Division of Labour: Two Views or One?' *Economica*, 32 (1965), in Wood, *Adam Smith*, vol. 3, pp. 171–83; E. G. West, 'Adam Smith's Two Views on the Division of Labour', *Economica*, 31 (1964), in Wood, *Adam Smith*, vol. 3, pp. 162–70. See also Maurice Brown, *Adam Smith's Economics: Its Place in the Development of Economic Thought* (London and New York: Croom-Helm, 1988).

12 See Heilbroner, 'Paradox of Progress'.

13 See Winch, *Adam Smith's Politics*; Istvan Hont and Michael Ignatieff, ed., *Wealth and Virtue: The Shaping of Political Economy in the Scottish Enlightentment*, (Cambridge: Cambridge University Press, 1983).

14 T. H. Green, *Works*, ed. R .L. Nettleship (London: Longman, 1885–), vol. 3, pp. 370–1.

15 See TMS III.2.20–3.

16 See Donald Withrington, 'Education and Society in the Eighteenth century', in *Scotland and the Age of Improvement*, ed. Nicholas T. Phillipson and Rosalind Mitchison (Edinburgh: Edinburgh University Press, 1970).

17 Lionel Robbins, *The Theory of Economic Policy in English Classical Economy* (London: Macmillan, 1953), p. 12.

18 Alec L. Macfie, 'The Moral Justification of Free Enterprise: A Lay Sermon on an Adam Smith Text', *Scottish Journal of Political Economy*, 14 (1967), reprinted in Wood, *Adam Smith*, vol. 1, p. 164.

5

Adam Smith's master narrative: women and the *Wealth of Nations*

KATHRYN SUTHERLAND

There are various concealed and apparent gender positions inherent in the Smithian economic model. Its definitions of labour and its naturalisation of an absent female economy have proved prescriptive in shaping the narrative of commercial and industrial society from the late eighteenth century. More decisively than the writings of his contemporary economists James Steuart and Josiah Tucker, Smith's account of those joined psychological and technological considerations, which together define progress as the generation of wealth, entailed at the level of language and ideology an influential redescription of the sexual division of labour. This served to suppress the female contribution and to categorise work as a male preserve. Yet recently social and economic historians have begun to show how women's active engagement at this time in labour outside the home – in workshops and factories, in textile industries and down mines – provided a major boost to the consumer revolution and to proto-industrialisation. How do we explain this real/theoretic distinction? Beyond this, if certain interests (not least those of the developing discipline of political economy) are served by hiding the female links in the economy, it is also paradoxically evident that women emerge from the late eighteenth century as the ablest interpreters of the Smithian narrative to a general public. Important in forging connections between the (older) 'moral' and (newer) 'political' economies and in sustaining a tradition of 'readable' economics, the work of early female commentators – Priscilla Wakefield, Hannah More, Jane Marcet, Harriet Martineau – also disputes what it communicates, the exclusively masculine ground of work and the narrative of work. These points will be returned to, but the bulk of this essay will concentrate on the source of the problem – in the *Wealth of Nations* itself.

Where are the women in the *Wealth of Nations*, and where are the women in the wealth of nations? While it would be false to suggest that a female contribution to labour is not assumed in the panorama of human activities which constitutes Smith's productive nation, it is nevertheless true that the exemplars and standards of labour in terms of which his narrative progresses are predominantly male. There are perhaps three explicit references in the whole text to women's participation in market or industrial activity or to women's wage-earning capacity. At Book I.viii, 'Of the Wages of Labour', a calculation of subsistence wages for 'the lowest species of common labourers' assumes a family unit in which the wage earning capacities of husband and wife are together essential for their larger survival, though the exact proportion of the wife's paid contribution to the household will clearly be limited, it is suggested, by her further (and unpaid) employment in the rearing of children. Visible only in relation to the family which attaches to the male labourer, the female worker is nevertheless supposed to be at least capable of earning 'sufficient to provide for herself' within its dependent context. Smith speculates:

> Thus far at least seems certain, that, in order to bring up a family, the labour of the husband and wife together must, even in the lowest species of common labour, be able to earn something more than what is precisely necessary for their own maintenance; but in what proportion ... I shall not take upon me to determine. (I.viii.15)

The statement comes at the end of a paragraph which shifts interestingly from the gendered declaration that '[a] man must always live by his work' to the implied distinction between the necessarily waged and unwaged aspects of female labour: only sometimes will a woman live by her work.

Further, if the initial truism about a man's labour is

extended to include the occasional necessity of others living also 'by his work' –

> and his wages must at least be sufficient to maintain him. They must even upon most occasions be somewhat more; otherwise it would be impossible for him to bring up a family, and the race of such workmen could not last beyond the first generation

– then the desirable expansion of the workforce proceeds in terms of woman's unrecompensed labour, which is nothing less than her capability to increase the productive capacity of the workforce itself. Within the early capitalist economy woman's use in the creation of new workers, a use recognised in man's higher wages, is of greater value than her use as a worker in paid employment. Man's labour has built into it a recompense beyond his immediate needs, while woman's essential labour, though directly augmenting the fixed capital of society, generates for her no immediate reward. The foundation of the productive economy, her labour is placed decisively outside the economic order. Though the need for an expanding supply of labour is no longer a feature of the labour market, this male–female differential has remained established. In Britain only in the late twentieth century, and through the relocation of funds from tax concessions (payable to the wage-earning husband) to increased family allowances, has it been recognised that women need to be imbursed directly for rearing children.[1]

Later in this same chapter Smith turns briefly to consider women who return from service in 'cheap years' (years of declining prosperity) to live with their parents and find employment in the home. These women 'commonly spin in order to make cloaths for themselves and their families'. Such labour, he observes, 'never enters the publick registers of manufactures' (I.viii.51). Though such women produce a vendible commodity, the productive nature of their labour, like their status as workers, is concealed within the economics of the home and thus functions as part of an 'informal' economy.

The only other clear reference to a female wage-earner occurs at Book I.x, where Smith notes the contribution to the precarious cottager economy throughout Scotland of the woman's spinning, a grossly underpaid employment:

The produce of such labour comes frequently cheaper to market than would otherwise be suitable to its nature. Stockings in many parts of Scotland are knit much cheaper than they can any-where be wrought upon the loom. They are the work of servants and labourers, who derive the principal part of their subsistence from some other employment ...

The spinning of linen yarn is carried on in Scotland nearly in the same way as the knitting of stockings, by servants who are chiefly hired for other purposes. They earn but a very scanty subsistence, who endeavour to get their whole livelihood by either of those trades. In most parts of Scotland she is a good spinner who can earn twenty-pence a week. (I.x.b.50–1)

In Book IV this picture is glossed: 'but our spinners are poor people, women commonly, scattered about in all different parts of the country, without support or protection' (IV.viii.4).

Spinning (on the distaff) long remained a female and home-based occupation, even after the introduction of technology, in the form of spinning wheels and spinning jennies, in the late eighteenth century. The extremely low pay attached to the work, not only in Scotland but throughout Britain, reflected the assumption that women could attend to it alongside or in the intervals from other labours. As late as 1823 Hugh Miller observed of women's roles in the harsh economy of the Scottish Highlands:

for here (shall I venture the expression?) as in all semi-barbarous countries, the woman seems to be regarded rather as the drudge than the companion of the man. It is the part of the husband to turn up the land and sow it; the wife conveys the manure to it in a square creel with a slip bottom, tends the corn, reaps it, hoes the potatoes, digs them up, and carries the whole home on her back. When bearing the creel she is also engaged in spinning with the distaff and spindle. I wish you but saw with what patience these poor females continue thus dumbly employed, for the greater part of a long summer's day.[2]

The economy of the Scottish cotter or farming subtenant depended on such self-exploitation within the family. As Smith notes, the spinning and knitting of stockings, more cheaply by hand than with machines, is built on the assumption that such labour, however arduous, is only supplementary. If it were undertaken in workshops, the cost would be higher; as it is, costs are kept low by association with the land and with the family, both of which serve to categorise labour as unspecialised, cheap, and often female.

These female workers form a hidden under-class whose employment might be compared with that of late twentieth-century 'homeworkers' or outworkers, who earn below minimum agreed wages by stuffing envelopes, making fishing flies, etc. Such women need (because of other aspects of their unpaid labour) to be at home, and so they take on such work, but they do not appear in statistics about the workforce. Smith's low estimate of twenty pence a week as the wage of a good woman spinner is to be compared with his earlier estimate of eightpence a day as 'the most usual wages of common labour' in the Scottish Lowlands (I.viii.34).

These passing remarks are Smith's only specific references to female workers. Nowhere in his extended discussion of the division of labour does he attend to the shifts in the sexual division of labour within the eighteenth-century labour market; yet implied by its absence as contemporary description is a far-reaching prescriptive assumption concerning the gendered nature of work at a time when women's labour outside the home was an important contribution to the proto-industrialisation of Britain. Employed in increasing numbers in the manufacture of commodities like pottery, kitchen utensils, cutlery and textiles, and influential as domestic purchasers on the expanding markets, women were complexly involved in the production and consumption of goods at all levels. It has even been suggested that the market for mass-consumer goods, which represents the beginnings of the industrial revolution, 'took much of its impetus to consume from the earnings of women and children'.[3] The humble pin, on which Smith's sophisticated economic model turns, is in its bold triviality a feminised example: pins being commonly manufactured at this time with as well as for female labour.[4]

Nail-making, according to Smith's own observation 'by no means one of the simplest operations' (I.i.6), was undertaken by women in the West Midlands, as the erotically charged account of one male spectator records:

In some of these shops I observed one, or more females, stript of
their upper garments, and not overcharged with their lower,
wielding the hammer with all the grace of the sex. The beauties
of their face were rather eclipsed by the smut of the anvil; or in
poetical phrase, the tincture of the forge had taken possession of
those lips, which might have been taken by the kiss. Struck with
the novelty, I enquired, 'whether the ladies of this county shod
horses?' but was answered, with a smile, 'they are nailers.'

A fire without heat, a nailer of a fair complexion, or one who
despises the tankard, are equally rare among them.[5]

The account is William Hutton's, from his travels as a young
man in 1741, and we find in it a response which develops in
terms of a perceived transgression of acceptable sexual boundaries. By their work, the women nailers are at once unsexed
('the beauties of their face were rather eclipsed') and exces-
sively sexed ('a fire without heat' is 'rare among them'). The
male spectator's fascinated interest constructs as sexual loose-
ness or unfixity the determining circumstances of female
labour: in the Black Country women worked regularly alongside men in all forms of heavy industry because there was no
lighter alternative paid occupation. It is worth noting that in
Smith's eye-witness account of nail-making (at I.i.6) the work
is undertaken exclusively by men and boys.

In his discussion of the wages of labour and the conditions
of employment (Book I.viii, ix and x), Smith advocates a high
wage/high productivity economy which, in the interest of the
freedom of trade, should be as little encumbered as possible by
apprenticeship regulations and the exclusive privileges of trade
corporations to control labour conditions. In many trades
ancient usage protected the rates for the job. Tailoring and
wheelmaking were covered by the Elizabethan Statute of
Artificers of 1563; that is, they restricted entry, upheld apprenticeships, and by-laws made established rates of pay and terms
of work enforceable by magistrates. Such rules gave qualified
journeymen a property in their trade and a strong position for
collective bargaining. In London, journeymen tailors and stay-
makers (exclusively masculine trades) were the most powerful
combinations in the later eighteenth century. However, in
rapidly expanding industries and in unincorporated or newer
towns like Birmingham (uncontrolled by craft organisations or

guilds), apprenticeship took on a more flexible shape or lapsed altogether, as cheap labour replaced formal training.[6] Workers in towns (not yet a large percentage of the workforce) were sometimes better placed to combine against exploitation, but those in dispersed domestic industries, the victims of monopolistic practices or of rigid polarisations between masters and workers, were open to great abuse. Domestic nail-makers were notoriously exploited by the ironmongers who held them in debt and controlled their wages. Spinners, often housewives in the countryside, had no organisation for resistance when their wage rates fell, as they very often did.

Smith's argument (at I.viii.28–30), that the wages of labourers are 'in the present times' more than sufficient for subsistence, is based only on the irregular evidence that such wages are frequently higher in the summer than the winter (when need is greater) and that there has been little rise in the money price of labour despite rises in food prices.[7] Moreover, he persistently assumes the male identity of his typical worker. But as Dorothy George concludes from the case of three women found dead from starvation in 1763 in an empty house in Stonecutter Street, London: 'It is significant that all the victims should have been women; there can be little doubt that the hardships of the age bore with especial weight upon them. Social conditions tended to produce a high proportion of widows, deserted wives, and unmarried mothers, while women's occupations were over-stocked, ill-paid, and irregular.'[8] By ignoring throughout the female contribution to the flourishing commercial society, Smith severely distorts the inequalities which existed in wage rates between the sexes, across trades and in different areas of the country.

Traditionally, apprenticeships were open to women as well as men in a wide range of trades from weaving to blacksmith's work; early apprenticeship records suggest no fixed conception of appropriate female labour. But in the course of the later eighteenth century, rapid expansion undermined the powers of corporations to control labour conditions, and it was to the advantage of employers to take on women and children as cheaper, unskilled labour. In the long term, the consequence was to deny women the security of decent wages and skilled

employment and to erode their rights (always fragile) to apprenticeships.[9] In the interest of the freedom of trade, Smith calls for
the abolition of the statute of apprenticeship and exclusive
privileges, arguing that these are 'real encroachments upon
natural liberty' (IV.ii.42). In retrospect, at least, it would seem
that the absence of labour protection which such liberty entails
worked to widen the gap between workers (now often mere
labourers) and employers, who had most to gain from the freedom, and between male and female labour. The history of
employment over the last two hundred years confirms women's
limited access to skilled work because of their usefulness in
times of need (war, for example); but such access can be quickly
withdrawn in harsher times, when women fall quickly to the
bottom of the employment ladder, being always in any case on
a lower rung than their male counterparts.

In 1798 Priscilla Wakefield published *Reflections on the
Present Condition of the Female Sex; with suggestions for its
improvement*, in which she directly criticised Smith's free enterprise economy as itself an encroachment on the liberty of
women, who are denied access to dignified and well paid work,
and pushed out into poverty and enforced prostitution by male
workers within the new economic order. Part of her argument
is for the return of exclusive privileges in the interests of a more
generally productive economy of women as well as men. She
would, for example, have male workers excluded from certain
markets and functions – like midwifery and shop work, where
the goods for sale target female purchasers. She writes:

> It is asserted by Doctor Adam Smith, that every individual is a
> burthen upon the society to which he belongs, who does not
> contribute his share of productive labour for the good of the
> whole. The Doctor, when he lays down this principle, speaks in
> general terms of man, as a being capable of forming a social
> compact for mutual defence, and the advantage of the community
> at large. He does not absolutely specify, that both sexes, in order
> to render themselves beneficial members of society, are equally
> required to comply with these terms; but since the female sex is
> included in the idea of the species, and as women possess the
> same qualities as men, though perhaps in a different degree, their
> sex cannot free them from the claim of the public for their propor-
> tion of usefulness. ...

Men monopolize not only the most advantageous employments, and such as exclude women from the exercise of them, by the publicity of their nature, or the extensive knowledge they require, but even many of those, which are consistent with the female character. Another heavy discouragement to the industry of women, is the inequality of the reward of their labour, compared with that of men, an injustice which pervades every species of employment performed by both sexes. ...

In employments which depend upon bodily strength the distinction is just; for it cannot be pretended that the generality of women can earn as much as men, where the produce of their labour is the result of corporeal exertion; but it is a subject of great regret, that this inequality should prevail, even where an equal share of skill and application are exerted. Male stay-makers, mantua-makers, and hair-dressers are better paid than female artists of the same professions; but surely it will never be urged as an apology for this disproportion, that women are not as capable of making stays, gowns, dressing hair, and similar arts, as men; if they are not superior to them, it can only be accounted for upon this principle, that the prices they receive for their labour are not sufficient to repay them for the expence of qualifying themselves for their business, and that they sink under the mortification of being regarded as artizans of inferior estimation, whilst the men, who supplant them, receive all the encouragement of large profits and full employment, which is ensured to them by the folly of fashion.[10]

While a case can be made (and Wakefield makes it powerfully) for an influential women's market with purchasing power in the hands of the female in the new manufacturing household, it is nevertheless true that as wage-earners women were grossly exploited in the late eighteenth century. Their employment came to depend on the low status of their labour and their lack of rights as a work force. As cheap labour came to play a crucial part in the industrialising process, women were employed in large numbers, but often as the means to drive down the rates for a job and to bypass orthodox training customs. Hence, they were as readily laid off as engaged by employers. Adam Smith is not, of course, directly responsible for this inequality, but his exposition of the conditions for national wealth remains influential through its determining concealment of society's reliance upon women's active contribution to the production of value.

Over two hundred years later and seemingly at the end of the European commercial narrative which Smith celebrated, Britain's post-productive economy is in the hands of a largely unvocal and unacknowledged female workforce. Since 1970 women have taken almost ninety per cent of new British jobs, but the gap between male and female wages is one of Europe's largest. The abolition of the remaining wages councils, argued by the Conservative government as necessary for the creation of new jobs, and taking effect from 30 August 1993, further boosts female employment, but at the expense of training, job security and investment in workers' well-being. Wages councils set minimum rates for 2.4 million workers, eighty per cent of whom are women, including many from ethnic minorities, working in the hotel and catering trade, hairdressing and other traditionally low-paid and 'female' areas of the economy. Established in 1909 by Winston Churchill, then President of the Board of Trade in Asquith's Liberal administration, wages councils (originally boards) set the demands of the market against the demands of conscience. During the second reading of the Trade Boards Bill, as it was known, Churchill expressed these anti-Smithian sentiments:

> But where you have what we call sweated trades, you have no organisation, no parity of bargaining, the good employer is undercut by the bad, and the bad employer is undercut by the worst; the worker, whose whole livelihood depends upon the industry, is undersold by the worker who only takes the trade up as a second string, his feebleness and ignorance generally renders the worker an easy prey to the tyranny of the masters and middle-men, only a step higher up the ladder than the worker, and held in the same relentless grip of forces – where those conditions prevail you have not a condition of progress, but a condition of progressive degeneration ... In the case of any great staple trade in this country, if the rate of wages became unnaturally low and the workers could not raise it by any pressure on their part, the new generation at any rate would exercise a preference for better pay and more attractive forms of industry. The gradual correction over large periods of time is thus provided for, but in these sweated industries it is not the new generation who came to the fore; it is a particular class which has been constituted of the widow, the women folk of the poorer class labourer,

the broken, the weak, the struggling, those are the people who largely depend upon these trades, and they have not the same nobility of choice, exerted, it is true, by the second generation, but which is undoubtedly operative as to the great staple trades of the country.[11]

Smith's gendered narrative, like the late manifestation of the free market in labour in the 1990s, assumes no inherent conflict between the market operations and society's ethical relations. In both cases women, the invisible workforce, are the losers.

The modern term 'economics' did not exist in Smith's time to describe the collectivity of writings on money, trade, manufacture, etc. which documents the wealth of nations. Throughout the eighteenth century, the unattributed term 'oeconomy' (subsequently 'economy', from the Greek *oikonomia*) retained as its primary significance 'the management of a house' or 'domestic regulation', as in this passage from Dr Johnson's travels in the Scottish Highlands: 'When we entered, we found an old woman boiling goats-flesh in a kettle ... she was willing enough to display her whole system of economy.'[12] 'Political oeconomy' is cited in the *Oxford English Dictionary* from 1767, from James Steuart's *Inquiry into the Principles of Political Oeconomy*, though it can be found in English in the late seventeenth century. In Steuart, Smith's contemporary, 'political oeconomy' is an extension from the domestic context, from a system of house-holding, and refers to arguments concerning the laws and management of a national economy, or the formulation of the economy as an aspect of the state. Steuart writes: 'Oeconomy in general is the art of providing for all the wants of a family, with prudence and frugality ... What oeconomy is in a family, political oeconomy is in a state.'[13] Behind Steuart lies a system of thinking about the state's role in the management of the economy which runs back through Hume and Cantillon in the eighteenth century, to Petty, Child and North in the seventeenth, and ultimately to Aristotle. It is this connection which Smith is by agreement considered to have loosened. Whether legitimately or by distortion, the *Wealth of Nations* is seen as a point of departure, a key moment in the development of economic discourse. Involved in this redescription is the severing of the epistemological link of household and economy at a national level.[14]

But if Smith is credited with rejecting the 'as in a household, so in a nation' analogy and thereby inaugurating the self-regulating discourse of modern economics, the unadopted term 'economy' as used in the *Wealth of Nations* (still 'oeconomy' in the early editions) continues to retain the domestic as its primary significance. Furthermore and complicatingly, while Steuart's domestic household is a patriarchal institution, with a 'lord and steward' at its head, Smith's usage of the term 'oeconomy'/'oeconomist' implies, both literally and ideologically, a feminised space within an unappropriating and unappropriated larger narrative. Not only, then, does Smith reject the older analogy, he might be said effectively to disempower it by regendering it.

At Book III.ii Smith explains why '[i]t seldom happens ... that a great proprietor is a great improver' of land. If, as was frequently the case, the landowner lived beyond his means, then there was no renewable fund on which he might draw to pay for developments. But '[i]f he was an oeconomist, he generally found it more profitable to employ his annual savings in new purchases, than in the improvement of his old estate' (III.ii.7). In Smith's example, the traditional patriarchal householder, the nobleman on his estate, forfeits his title to be a model manager of resources by virtue of a congenital predisposition to value novelty and show. (The passage continues: 'The situation of such a person naturally disposes him to attend rather to ornament which pleases his fancy, than to profit for which he has so little occasion. The elegance of his dress, of his equipage, of his house, and houshold furniture, are objects which from his infancy he has been accustomed to have some anxiety about.') Character and training unfit him for the truly commercial spirit, which is 'an exact attention to small savings and small gains', necessary for all forms of improvement. If within Smith's larger narrative the desirable distinction of male and female is guaranteed by man's confident property in his labour, his self-creation through industry, then the landowner's gratification through consumption alone threatens to 'unman' him, by rendering him the objective exemplification of value,

its reproducer rather than its producer. In this case his claim to
be an 'oeconomist' can be seen to be dangerously feminising.

Later, at Book V.i, however, Smith provides a picture of the
woman as oeconomist which appears to revise earlier sexually
constructed assumptions in her favour. His concern here is
education and the role of the state in its provision. He writes:

> There are no publick institutions for the education of women, and
> there is accordingly nothing useless, absurd, or fantastical in the
> common course of their education. They are taught what their
> parents or guardians judge it necessary or useful for them to
> learn; and they are taught nothing else. Every part of their educa-
> tion tends evidently to some useful purpose; either to improve
> the natural attractions of their person, or to form their mind to
> reserve, to modesty, to chastity, and to oeconomy: to render them
> both likely to become the mistresses of a family, and to behave
> properly when they have become such. In every part of her life
> a woman feels some conveniency or advantage from every part
> of her education. It seldom happens that a man, in any part of
> his life, derives any conveniency or advantage from some of the
> most laborious and troublesome parts of his education. (V.i.f.47)

This is a curious argument, characterised by that perverse and
expedient logic which we find in other areas of Smith's analysis. (See, for example, his explanation of the 'bad economics' of
slavery at III.ii.9 and IV.ix.47.) Women were throughout the
eighteenth century educated within the home and exclusively
for the performance of domestic duties; very few benefited from
organised schooling, and though some received irregular scholarly education from male relatives, all higher institutions of
learning were closed to them. To view this as cause for social
congratulation requires us to consider only the efficiency of the
provision (or lack of it) and not its justice; nor, having criticised elsewhere in this chapter what he sees as the failure of
the higher reaches of education, does Smith regard this as an
argument for reassessing educational and career opportunities
and women's rights to them as several women commentators
were soon to do, notably Mary Wollstonecraft, in *A Vindication
of the Rights of Woman* (1792). What in fact occurs in the
passage is a further marginalisation of the traditional manager-
ial functions of the household as national economic paradigm.

As household oeconomist, the female is conditioned by her limited, practical perspective; there is nothing redundant (but also nothing surplus to immediate requirements, nothing which resonates in a larger context) in the effort expended on her education and the returns it brings.

The expanding commercial interests of eighteenth-century Britain entailed a more thorough regrouping of the divisions in society than ever before, and in particular a widening of the influence of a middle ground of citizen-producers. The obvious hero of Smith's narrative of wealth accumulation is the capital-ist – the merchant, the entrepreneur or master-manufacturer. He it is whose morally disencumbered energies epitomise the competitive drive which provides the key to the general char-acter of a modern commercial society. The manufacturer belongs to 'an order of men, whose interest is never exactly the same with that of the publick, who have generally an interest to deceive and even to oppress the publick, and who accord-ingly have, upon many occasions, both deceived and oppressed it' (I.xi.p.10). Against the manufacturer stands tradition in the form of the country gentleman, the proprietor of land, whose indolence and security render him 'incapable of that applica-tion of mind' (I.xi.p.8) which constitutes the manufacturer's advantage. Within Smith's thesis of the determining power of productive activities in history the country gentleman and the manufacturer each expresses a significant psycho-economic configuration.

The problem, as Smith and others saw it, was how might a progressive commercial society preserve its institutional stabil-ity and the 'virtue' of its members while at the same time stim-ulating wants and extending prosperity (as the success of the commercial model dictated that it must) even down to its lowest ranks. The classical political derivation of virtue as martial virtue, as represented to later ages by the independent warrior-citizen of the Graeco-Roman city republics, was clearly stretched beyond its limits in the context of an eighteenth-century consumer society. This older ideal assumed a restricted propertied elite and a concept of citizenship which was exclu-sively aristocratic, male, and undivided, in so far as the landowning householder would also be the lawgiver and the soldier. The newer model, on the other hand, assumed the unfixing of the distinctions of rich and poor and of male and female, a steady democratisation through consumption, the progressive subdivision of labour and delegation of civic duties, and in consequence the erosion of courage, integrity and an older collectivity of attributes by convention styled 'manliness'.

The standard modern account of commercial 'feminisation', as it has come to be described, is that by J. G. A. Pocock, whose analysis has been influential across a range of readings of eighteenth-century man;[15] but neither he nor subsequent exponents has considered how this so-called feminisation of man impinges upon the constructions of woman in the same period. Clearly, in the context of social description, terms like 'feminisation' and 'manliness' imply an instability which obtains at the level of representation and lexis only. Clearly, too, this instability does not necessarily include a renegotiation of the social or ideological categories of 'men' and 'women' and their relations to power. In fact, the burden of my argument is that, 'feminised' or 'unfeminised', men retain their social, political and economic ascendancy. Rather, what is confirmed in the course of the eighteenth-century redescription of the economy, a redescription which the *Wealth of Nations* has come to symbolise so powerfully, is the traditional opposition between 'woman' and 'authority'. If woman's undifferentiated labour facilitated Britain's proto-industrialisation, her differentiated capacity to represent the ideal of leisure supplied its justification. The formula is an economically serviceable fiction and a morally precarious trap: woman as the 'other' of man's self-realisation via production. In so far as she monitors society's consumer appetites, woman embodies prudent domestic good and steady national advancement; but she also isolates in her sex the basest and most irregular aspects of consumerism as excessive luxury or 'effeminacy'.

The word 'luxury', which in eighteenth-century usage can encompass a range of moral and political evils,[16] usually denotes in the *Wealth of Nations* no more than a particular kind of economic expenditure, even in an apparently loaded phrase like 'wanton luxury' (I.vii.9). In an interesting passage at Book I.viii, however, two forms of expansion and productivity appear to contend for the feminine ground of the market, and women are seen to exist at the intersection of two incompatible notions of productivity, or rather of reproductivity. Smith's subject is the familiar eighteenth-century obsession, population:

> Poverty, though it no doubt discourages, does not always prevent marriage. It seems even to be favourable to generation. A half-starved Highland woman frequently bears more than twenty children, while a pampered fine lady is often incapable of bearing any, and is generally exhausted by two or three. Barrenness, so frequent among women of fashion, is very rare among those of inferior station. Luxury in the fair sex, while it enflames perhaps the passion for enjoyment, seems always to weaken, and frequently to destroy altogether, the powers of generation. (I.viii.37)

While 'the passion for enjoyment' (and here women are by convention appealed to as major consumers) stimulates the economy and employs productively an expanding workforce, it can also, paradoxically, affect the national stock detrimentally: the association of female luxury and consequent infertility being something of a moral and medical commonplace at the time. In a high-employment economy, such as Smith envisages, population growth is synonymous not just with national power but with further commercial progress; failure to procreate is a source of socio-economic failure and of individual guilt.[17]

The consumer economy which Smith celebrates declares at once the feminising properties of commodities and the strict masculine preserve of commercial activity. Establishing the ascendancy of the market place within a progressive society involved therefore both its redescription as feminine space and its appropriation as the primary ground for the construction of male subjectivity in the person of the master-manufacturer. Although the concept of the market does not correspond in any direct or simple way to an existing (eighteenth- or twentieth-century) social reality, it has nevertheless been prescriptive in the construction of our modern understanding of gender and of the divided spheres within which male and female supposedly operate: the public as against the private; the commercial as against the domestic; the worker as against the nurturer; the independent as against the dependent sphere; the productive as against the reproductive agent. Furthermore, as feminist theorists point out, 'the male/female distinction itself has operated not as a straightforwardly descriptive principle of classification, but as an expression of values'.[18] And values are inescapably contingent upon economic systems, however we constitute those economies – as personal or market economies, each being in any case implicated in and dependent on the other's construction.[19]

It could be argued that the value which Smith, together with other eighteenth-century social commentators, places on woman's diverse reproductive capabilities (from procreation to luxury purchasing) signals her importance in maximising the wealth of nations. But the corresponding sense we gain from Smith's text of the marginalisation of women's *productive* activity is better explained in terms of the kind of scientific description of the economy which the *Wealth of Nations* inaugurates. We can now see that one consequence of Smith's method was to be the professionalisation of the discourse of the economist. By rendering the disciplinary model more exclusive at a theoretic and analytical level, he refines the social model which he purports to describe. Editing out of account women's waged labour as it contributed to the nascent commercial economy both vindicates that economy's ideological extension (the division of public from private interests) and is a necessary stage towards the establishment of the serious (manly) study of economics itself.

In a significant sense Smith is his own hero, the master-manufacturer of a master narrative of the national economy. Against the contained portrait of the female oeconomist, the domestic manager, we need to set another description from Book V, that of the newly authorised, public economist. Smith writes:

> In a civilized state ... though there is little variety in the occupations of the greater part of individuals, there is an almost infinite variety in those of the whole society. These varied occupations present an almost infinite variety of objects to the contemplation of those few, who, being attached to no particular occupation themselves, have leisure and inclination to examine the occupations of other people. The contemplation of so great a variety of objects necessarily exercises their minds in endless comparisons and combinations, and renders their understandings, in an extraordinary degree, both acute and comprehensive. (V.i.f.51)

Where the female oeconomist is conditioned to a life of usefulness by the contracted limits of her training, the untrained
(male?) economist commands the apparently limitless prospects
of the synthesising spectator, set above the world of subdivided
production rather than in the Hegelian 'nether world' of the
family. The comparison is rich in contradictions whose para-
doxical nature serves merely to enforce the gendered opposi-
tions of the underlying economic model: against the busy
female is set the detached and uninvolved spectator; against
every woman's informal and unfashioning labour is set the
assimilative and formalising energy of 'those few'.

In line with his self-definition as the spectatorial economist,
Smith shapes a master narrative which has always already posi-
tioned other narratives within itself, exerting a force which
denies the possibility of establishing alternative tellings. Behind
the master narrative is an ur-narrative. In the case of the
Smithian narrative this is a deterministic vision of history as
progress – the stadial theory (familiar in French and Scottish
writings of the Enlightenment) of social and economic organisation.[20] According to this theory, all societies will in due course
advance, in fixed order, through four (sometimes three) stages
– the hunting, shepherd, farming and commercial economies –
and to each of these stages certain social, legal and political
institutions, as well as psychological traits, will appertain.
Importantly and at each stage, sexual relations (and therefore
women) provide the primary evidence of a society's development. As argued by John Millar, Smith's pupil and a leading
exponent of the Scottish version of this 'scientific' narrative of
civil society,

> Of all our passions, it should seem that those which unite the
> sexes are most easily affected by the peculiar circumstances in
> which we are placed, and most liable to be influenced by the
> power of habit and education. Upon this account they exhibit the
> most wonderful variety of appearances, and, in different ages and
> countries, have produced the greatest diversity of manners and
> customs.[21]

But to define sexual relations (and therefore women) as a
function of progress in history is to establish a narrative which
will be inflexible to alternative forms of evidence. At the

commercial (and final?) stage of history, it is women's duty to reproduce the products of an exclusive male industry within a domestic context of family order. Again Millar provides the definitive pre-Victorian formulation of a sexual division of labour which is still ideologically powerful today:

> when [men] have made some progress in arts, and have attained to a proportional degree of refinement, they are necessarily led to set a value upon those female accomplishments and virtues which have so much influence upon every species of improvement, and which contribute in so many different ways to multiply the comforts of life. ... Loaded by nature with the first and most immediate concern in rearing and maintaining the children, she is endowed with such dispositions as fit her for the discharge of this important duty, and is at the same time particularly quali-fied for all such employments as require skill and dexterity more than strength, which are so necessary in the internal management of the family. Possessed of peculiar delicacy, and sensibility, whether derived from original constitution, or from her way of life, she is capable of securing the esteem and affection of her husband, by dividing his cares, by sharing his joys, and by sooth-ing his misfortunes.
>
> ... Being respected upon account of their diligence and profi-ciency in the various branches of domestic economy, [women] naturally endeavour to improve and extend those valuable qual-ifications. They are taught to apply with assiduity to those occu-pations which fall under their province, and to look upon idleness as the greatest blemish in the female character. They are instructed betimes in whatever will qualify them for the duties of their station, and is thought conducive to the ornament of private life.[22]

The problem with this speculative narrative of sexual commerce is that, like all master narratives, it denies the value of the rela-tive and the contingent: it disallows the contributory insights of the impaired point of view. In this case, and with peculiarly ironic effect, what is denied are the particularised details of female *and* historical reality themselves, those details which manifest history's contradictoriness to laws and the disjunction between woman as ideal construct and the evidence of her disorderly 'real' existence. The circumstances of women's lives, like the circumstances of history, exist in tension with the idealising strategies of master narratives, of which that paradox the Enlightenment scientific or theoretic history is one.

It has been argued that the grand project of the *Wealth of Nations*, Smith's combining of economics, politics and a history of civil society, represents the high point of a Scottish philosophical synthesis which also 'contains the seeds of its own disaggregation'. After Smith and as a consequence of Smith, such 'system-building' becomes compartmentalised, as separate, specialised treatises on 'scientific' economics and with a resultant marginalisation of the moral critique of commercial society.[23] There is much evidence, from Horner and Mill and on to Ricardo, to support such a bifurcated reading of social explanation. But the thesis becomes less clear if we turn to the 'unofficial' tradition of women's economic writings which begins to emerge from the late eighteenth century. In the 1790s commentators like Hannah More, Priscilla Wakefield and Mary Ann Radcliffe revive old links between civic virtue and national regulation as part of a case for the reabsorption of a moralised critique into the economic description of commercial society.[24] The public and private anxieties which attend even the relatively optimistic male understanding of commercial advancement can be resolved, they argue, only through women's more active involvement in the production of value. Their discussions assume the contextualisation of economic factors within larger debates concerning the nature and membership of the state, patriotism and social ethics. Grounded in the immediate political crises of the 1790s, their arguments are sharpened by what they see as women's contribution to Britain at war. In this context, they are concerned to establish a more inclusive view of society and to reintroduce a moralised agenda to deal with those problems which seem to them to be disregarded in the narrow focus on the workings of the market – in particular, the problems of women and the poor. As we have seen, Wakefield's definition of female value (as opposed to Smith's) represents a less mediated engagement with the productive base of commercial society. She argues from a sexually undifferentiated moral code for an equality of right to engage in economic production.

A little later, in the early nineteenth century, two women, Jane Marcet and Harriet Martineau, became the successful expounders of Smith's doctrines to a popular audience – in Marcet's case, 'young persons of either sex'; and in Martineau's, 'the great mass of the people'.[25] In recognising the significance of economic discourse to the description of modern society, both propose to convert its expert unreadability into a language of female articulacy. As Martineau observes, not without condescension, of the *Wealth of Nations*, '[i]t is natural that the first eminent book on this new science should be very long, in some parts exceedingly difficult, and, however wonderful and beautiful as a whole, not so clear and precise in its arrangement as it might be'.[26] And as Mrs B, Marcet's fictional instructress, informs her female pupil: 'In short, my dear, so many things are more or less connected with the science of political economy, that if you persevere in your resolution [not to understand it], you might almost as well condemn yourself to perpetual silence.'[27] Marcet and Martineau depend heavily on the *Wealth of Nations*, not only for the framework and arguments, but also for the examples in terms of which their expositions develop. Beyond this, however, the dialogic models by which they proceed have the effect of editing back in the female contribution to labour and to value. Interestingly, too, both women 'misinterpret' political economy as *household economy* on a national scale. Marcet even manipulates a male authority into providing her with this explanation when Mrs B informs her pupil: 'I once heard a lady ask a philosopher to tell her in a few words what is meant by political economy. Madam, replied he, you understand perfectly what is meant by household economy; you need only extend your idea of a family to that of a whole people – of a nation, and you will have some comprehension of the nature of political economy.'[28] In the context of Smith's masterly redefinition and the exclusive feminisation of the domestic sphere from the late eighteenth century, this misreading is significant.

In so far as it refuses or conceals the female contribution to the economy, Smith's narrative of proto-industrial society continues to exert a masterly authority over our understanding of the relation between women and work. Informalising women's labour as extrinsic to the formal structures of its argument, it powerfully mystifies the relationship between a market economy and the total economy of human existence at the same time as it confuses the dynamics of its telling with the dynamics of a material world of production. Value, which Smith defines as having 'two different meanings' – 'value in use' and 'value in exchange' (I.iv.13) – undergoes a further, unacknowledged refinement in the transformation of economic value into narrative value. Smith's apparent purpose, to describe how things are in an unhindered free market, becomes by its strategies of exclusion a prescriptive formula whose narrative can be invoked to justify further acts of exclusion. Over two hundred years later, the question remains – where are the women in the wealth of nations?

Notes

1 Cf. Carole Pateman, *The Disorder of Women: Democracy, Feminism and Political Theory* (Oxford: Polity Press, 1989), pp. 179–209, on the patriarchal welfare state, esp. pp. 192–5.

2 From *The Life and Letters of Hugh Miller* (1871), cited in Eric Richards, 'Women in the British Economy since about 1700: An Interpretation', *History*, 59 (1974), p. 341.

3 Neil McKendrick, 'Home Demand and Economic Growth: A New View of the Role of Women and Children in the Industrial Revolution', in *Historical Perspectives: Studies in English Thought and Society, in Honour of J. H. Plumb*, ed. Neil McKendrick (London: Europa Publications Ltd, 1974), p. 172. On the increase in job opportunities for women and the lucrative exploitation of female labour in the later eighteenth century, see Maxine Berg, *The Age of Manufactures, 1700–1820* (London: Fontana Press, 1985), pp. 129–75.

4 See Ivy Pinchbeck, *Women Workers and the Industrial Revolution 1750–1850* (1930; repr. London: Virago, 1981), pp. 276–7.

5 From William Hutton, *History of Birmingham* (1781), cited in Berg, *The Age of Manufactures*, p. 312.

6 According to Berg, '[o]f 108 buttonmakers in Birmingham in 1767 only 18 took indentured apprentices or had themselves served as apprentices', *The Age of Manufactures*, p. 306; and see John Rule, *The Experience of Labour in Eighteenth-Century Industry* (London: Croom Helm, 1981).

7 According to Campbell and Skinner, in some cases 'Smith may overestimate the wage rates slightly' (*An Inquiry into the Nature and Causes of the Wealth of Nations*, ed. R. H. Campbell, A. S. Skinner and W. B. Todd, 2 vol. (Oxford: Clarendon Press, 1976), vol. I, p. 92 note 25).

8 M. Dorothy George, *London Life in the Eighteenth Century* (1925; Harmondsworth: Penguin, 1966), p. 174.

9 See Alice Clark, *Working Life of Women in the Seventeenth Century* (1919; 3rd edn, London: Routledge, 1992), p. 299: 'Capitalistic organisation

tended therefore to deprive women of opportunities for sharing in the more profitable forms of production, confining them as wage-earners to the unprotected trades'; and Jane Rendall, *Women in an Industrialising Society: England 1750–1880* (Oxford: Blackwell, 1990). Clark's pioneering account of women's working lives in history needs, however, to be read with caution. Her confused gesturing to industrialism (machine production, the factory system) and capitalism (private ownership, wage labour) in relation to the decline in women's status has been much criticised – by, for instance, Harriet Bradley, *Men's Work, Women's Work: A Sociological History of the Sexual Division of Labour in Employment* (Oxford: Polity Press, 1989), pp. 33–42.

10 Priscilla Wakefield, *Reflections on the Present Condition of the Female Sex; with suggestions for its improvement* (London, 1798), pp. 1–2; 150–3.

11 From the second reading of the Trade Boards Bill (28 April 1909), *Parliamentary Debates (Official Report)* (1909), vol. IV, pp. 388–9.

12 Samuel Johnson, *A Journey to the Western Islands of Scotland* (1775), ed. J. D. Fleeman (Oxford: Clarendon Press, 1985), p. 24.

13 James Steuart, *An Inquiry into the Principles of Political Oeconomy: Being an Essay on the Science of Domestic Policy in Free Nations*, 2 vol. (London, 1767), vol. I, pp. 1–2.

14 See Keith Tribe, *Land, Labour, and Economic Discourse* (London: Routledge & Kegan Paul, 1978), pp. 80–109, for a discussion of the formation of a discursive space called 'political oeconomy'.

15 See, for example, J. G. A. Pocock, 'The Mobility of Property and the Rise of Eighteenth-Century Sociology', in *Virtue, Commerce and History* (Cambridge: Cambridge University Press, 1985), p. 114, where it is argued that '[e]conomic man as masculine conquering hero is a fantasy of nineteenth-century industrialisation ... His eighteenth-century predecessor was seen as on the whole a feminised, even an effeminate being.'

16 See John Sekora, *Luxury: The Concept in Western Thought, Eden to Smollett* (Baltimore and London: Johns Hopkins University Press, 1977), esp. pp. 63–109, for eighteenth-century conceptions of luxury.

17 The restriction of female sexuality to motherhood is dedicated to economic expansionism in a remarkable range of eighteenth-century texts, by women as well as by men. Writing in 1726 in *Some Considerations upon Street-Walkers with a Proposal for lessening the present Number of them*, Defoe observed: 'The great Use of Women in a Community, is to supply it with Members that may be serviceable, and keep up a Succession' (in *Women in the Eighteenth Century: Constructions of Femininity*, ed. Vivien Jones (London: Routledge, 1990), p. 69). In other writers, the association of female luxury and infertility is treated in overt terms of moral condemnation. See, for example, the complicated denunciation in Mary Wollstonecraft, *A Vindication of the Rights of Woman* (1792), where it is argued: 'Luxury has introduced a refinement in eating, that destroys the constitution ... The depravity of the appetite which brings the sexes together, has had a still more fatal effect. Nature must ever be the standard of taste, the gauge of appetite – yet how grossly is nature insulted by the voluptuary. ... Women becoming ... weaker, in

mind and body, than they ought to be, were one of the grand ends of
their being taken into the account, that of bearing and nursing children,
have not sufficient strength to discharge the first duty of a mother ...
The weak enervated women ... are unfit to be mothers, though they may
conceive ...' (ed. Miriam Kramnick (Harmondsworth: Penguin, 1975), pp.
247–9). In Martha Mears's *Pupil of Nature* (1797), a manual of midwifery,
a description of female health during pregnancy reappropriates to the
personal economy of the body an earlier borrowing into the language of
political economy: the link between the circulation of blood, the body
itself as a circulatory system, and wealth as a further circulatory system
was consciously exploited in economic writings from the seventeenth
century. Advising 'ladies of fortune' of the dangers of luxury and indolence during pregnancy, Mears observes, '[t]hey both produce nearly the
same effects: they tend to increase, in a state of pregnancy, the natural
disposition to fulness: the system is loaded: the blood loiters in its course:
the juices, retarded in their circulation, stagnate and grow foul: the
whole body becomes languid and inactive: the powers of the womb in
particular are enfeebled or perverted; and various disorders, abortion, or
long, severe, and dangerous labours are the usual consequences' (in
Women in the Eighteenth Century, ed. Jones, p. 96).

18 Genevieve Lloyd, *The Man of Reason: 'Male' and 'Female' in Western
    Philosophy* (London: Methuen, 1984), p. 103. See, too, Jane Rendall,
    'Virtue and Commerce: Women in the Making of Adam Smith's Political
    Economy', in *Women in Western Political Philosophy*, ed. Ellen Kennedy
    and Susan Mendus (Brighton: Harvester Wheatsheaf, 1987), p. 45: 'Adam
    Smith's writing on natural jurisprudence, on moral philosophy and on
    political economy was structured throughout by a sense of this critical
    transition, in which both public and private spheres received new defi-
    nitions, dividing the commercial world of the market economy, from the
    domestic morality of the family.'

19 See the argument by Barbara Herrnstein Smith, *Contingencies of Value:
    Alternative Perspectives for Critical Theory* (Cambridge, Mass.: Harvard
    University Press, 1988), pp. 30–1.

20 Versions of the stadial theory were propounded in France by Anne-
    Robert-Jacques Turgot; in Scotland by Lord Kames, Adam Ferguson and
    Smith. For a discussion of the theory in relation to Smith's economic
    contribution, see Ronald L. Meek, *Social Science and the Ignoble Savage*
    (Cambridge: Cambridge University Press, 1976), pp. 116–30.

21 John Millar, *The Origin of the Distinctions of Ranks; or, An Inquiry into
    the Circumstances which give rise to Influence and Authority in the Different
    Members of Society* (3rd edn, revised, London, 1781), p. 17.

22 Ibid., pp. 108–10.

23 Michael Ignatieff, 'John Millar and Individualism', in *Wealth and Virtue:
    The Shaping of Political Economy in the Scottish Enlightenment*, ed. Istvan
    Hont and Michael Ignatieff (Cambridge: Cambridge University Press,
    1983), p. 343.

24 Hannah More, *Strictures on the Modern System of Female Education* (1799);
    Wakefield, *Reflections on the Present Condition of the Female Sex* (1798);

and Mary Ann Radcliffe, *Female Advocate; or, An Attempt to Recover the Rights of Women from Male Usurpation* (1799).

25 [Jane Marcet], *Conversations on Political Economy; in which the Elements of that Science are Familiarly Explained* (London, 1816), p. vi; Harriet Martineau, *Illustrations of Political Economy* (3rd edn, London, 1832), p. x.

26 Ibid.

27 Marcet, *Conversations on Political Economy*, p. 8.

28 Ibid., pp. 17–18; cf. Martineau, *Illustrations of Political Economy*, p. viii.

6

Look, no hidden hands: how Smith understands historical progress and societal values

NOEL PARKER

To us the *Wealth of Nations* is so obviously the first ever book of economics that it is natural to go through trying to pick 'the economics' out of it and forget the rest. But, of course, to Smith and his age it was something quite different: a book of *political* economy. That is to say, it is an economics book only in the sense that it sets out the position that government, under the guidance of enlightened opinion, should adopt towards what we have since come to call 'the economy'. But the economy only acquired an identity, and a name *subsequently* – and that precisely because books such as the *Wealth of Nations* constituted it as an object of the attention of governments.

Because Smith was engaged in constituting the economy before the very existence of the economic had been worked out, the *Wealth of Nation* drew on numerous extra-economic dimensions of the evolution of social life, which are referred to both within the book and elsewhere in Smith's work. For this reason, if for no other, we should be wary of reading it with the famous 'hidden hand' of popular economics and right-wing ideologues in mind. But, in addition, we should be wary of the hidden hand because it is the magic in the economy: that element which makes things work out all right in a pure market, without extraneous factors to explain them.

As I will show, whatever Smith believed about the market

and hidden hands,[1] he certainly did not – and could not – consistently maintain that 'commercial society' was a naturally occurring form of life requiring no further supports and no further explanation. For Smith, such a society arises in very particular ways in the course of the progressive historical evolution of societies and their values; and, as Andrew Skinner has put it, in this process, 'the motivation behind many of the most important changes is political, rather than simply economic'.[2] For commercial society, as for other forms of society, values must match the advance of history: a contingent process of enculturation is vital.

Hence, this chapter focuses upon a particular dimension of the *Wealth of Nations*. Partly in order to underpin his pro-commercial prescriptions for government, Smith tried to understand how the societies he knew of (especially contemporary commercial ones) develop – values and all. His notion of historical progress was imbued with the optimism of Enlightenment thinking, and took for granted the special, and specially favourable, qualities of contemporary European society. These are the qualities which we would today think of as belonging to modernity. But vital elements to account for historical progress are drawn from outside the strictly economic field.

The stages leading to commercial society

Smith conceptualised the overall shape of historical progress through an idea of successive stages of social development, which was in due course to become the marxist theory of modes of production. Various other writers had pursued this approach and various earlier versions of the sequence of stages had been put forward.[3] In general it was taken to involve a progress from hunter-gatherer to pastoral, to agrarian and finally to commercial society.

Naturally, the most interesting step in this sequence is that which leads to modern, commercial society, since that is the one which contemporary Europe was actually experiencing and which it ought, in Smith's view, to be encouraging. In pursuing the question of how commercial society arose in Europe, Smith is following both the method and the issue established by Montesquieu. Like Montesquieu, Smith was confronted by the peculiarity of Europe's history in this regard: in particular, the way that commercial society reappeared, in a new form, after the fall of Rome and the feudal period.[4] So Smith's broad, speculative model of stages is overlaid by an interpretation of the more particular recent history of Europe. This creates a major fault line within history as expounded in the *Wealth of Nations*, between the progressive dynamic inherent in the abstract conception of the four stages and more complex possible interpretations of the process of change in modern Europe. In Book III, which I discuss below, Smith explores the context of the historical transition which either made or prevented the commercialisation of European societies.

In the early parts of the first chapter of Book V, the *Wealth of Nations* contains some references to the stages through which societies evolve. The subject is the growth of the defence and justice elements of government, and Smith makes various comparisons between the viability of government and its apparatus at different stages. But for a full exploration of Smith's view of the stages through which societies evolve, we have to look to *Lectures on Jurisprudence*. Although these are notes of the lectures he gave at Glasgow University in 1762–64, their correspondences with the structure of, and topics treated in, the *Wealth of Nations*[5] make them a reliable guide to the thinking behind the later work. In the *Lectures*, Smith identifies four 'stages of society': hunting, pasturage (i.e. nomadic shepherds), agriculture (both pastoral and arable) and commerce (LJ (A) i.27; LJ (B) 149–50). Each stage is accounted for in terms of its utility as the previous society confronts increasing population. At each stage, distinct and more complex societal values, laws and jurisprudence, which are the subject of the *Lectures*, are called for.[6] The sequence described, then, involves an even, rational ascent towards increasing complexity matched by increasing utility. Onto this sequence, however, has to be mapped the chequered history of agricultural society in Europe, where progress is plainly ruptured by the collapse of the classical world. For Europe, then, Smith includes two, more plainly historical, sub-categories that occur within the agricultural phase, immediately prior to commerce: feudalism and allodial agriculture. The latter, a stage of large, autarchic estates, precedes the more familiar feudal stage (LJ (A) i.116–125; LJ (B) 50–52).

Allodial 'government' is something of a misnomer, since Smith argues that such a situation, dominated by more or less equal, armed landowning families, is pretty well inimical to good order. By comparison, then, feudal government represents an advance upon the lawlessness of baronial lawlords. The difference between the allodial system and feudal government is significant for Smith's overall historical-explanatory scheme. Conversely, according to the historical story of Book III of the *Wealth of Nations*, feudalism made a space for the slowly building strength of the boroughs, allied to the power of the monarchy, which would in due course bring about the passage from feudalism to modern, 'improved' society. Thus it was that the bourgeoisie acquired the new, distinguished place in history, which was to be echoed by many others in the eighteenth and nineteenth centuries.

Smith's history of improvement in Europe

In Book III of the *Wealth of Nations*, Smith begins the history of Europe's improvement with the fall of Rome. It emerges that progress from then on has been a rather chancy business. Only with difficulty can Smith make it conform to his theoretical pattern.

Allodial land holdings served to create some zones of security in the general breakdown of civil order following the fall of Rome. But the privilege of uninhibited power within a large demesne produced a situation of low production and economic stagnation (WN III.ii.7–13; LJ (B) 289–93). The power-holders had no need or motive to improve the productivity of their lands since they either had access to all the produce they could feel the need of, or could extract more by simple force. For their part, the subject farmers, with no power or security against the barons' demands, could not expect to retain the benefits of any improvement they might initiate.

In spite of some differences, the overall structure of this stagnation is, in fact, exactly the same as arose in Rome itself and in all other ancient civilisations. The key to the structure is the position of the slave or subject and the absence of security in independence for those on whom falls all the burden of productive labour. The slave/subject has no autonomy and no expectation of reward for invention; hence, no reason to improve the productivity of his ways of working. Smith conveys this interpretation of the economic effects of slavery and like situations in a number of places:[7] by doing so, he suggests the need for its opposite; that is, personal autonomy and security for the economically productive agents.[8] Nevertheless, given the frequency in known history of the inertia produced by stable, slavery-type patterns of power, it is they, rather than autonomy and improvement, that might appear to be the norm.

The concurrent appearance of feudalism and of the first towns conspired to produce the first chink in this stable, depressed condition of society. Under feudalism, the barons found themselves nominally under the tutelage of a monarch (WN III.iv.9) who was, however, without the power to enforce his rule. Because the towns had most to fear from the barons, 'Mutual interest ... disposed them to support the king, and the king to support them against the lords' (III.iii.8). As a counter-balance to the landed classes, the king granted to towns a special tax status and rights of representation.

Smith makes clear that the new townspeople were quite different from the land-owning citizens and slaves of earlier history. They had nothing but their autonomy and freedom to trade (III.iii.1–2); but out of that they would develop in due course the force that would undermine the entire economically stagnant edifice of the landed aristocracy. Guaranteed the continued possession of whatever gains they might make by their own initiative, they at last had the motive to improve the productivity of their labour: 'That industry, therefore, which aims at something more than necessary subsistence, was established in cities long before it was commonly practised by the occupiers of land in the country' (III.iii.12).

The entrepreneurship of the cities then placed imported and manufactured goods before the eyes of the great proprietors. A new taste for such things pushed aside the nobility's traditional practice of unconsidered spending on hospitality and retainers (III.iv.10–16). But this had been the basis of both their military power and the clientelist social structure in which they wielded influence. They were now spending on themselves, rather than on their clients. They let go their retainers, who had provided their private coercive resources, and they could no longer obstruct the workings of justice. In order to realise disposable cash income in their land, they rationalised the allocation of it to tenants, shaking out surplus labour and agreeing to regular leases. The tenants thus had reason to improve their productivity and could afford higher rents. In short, the landed nobility accepted the role of landlord in a newly commercialised agricultural structure.

The conditions for 'improvement' and bourgeois society

At this point in the story, near the end of Book III, Smith draws the strands together. His text contains a classic formulation of those utterances which could be summed up in the claim that he believes in a 'hidden hand' working in market society:

> A revolution of the greatest importance to the publick happiness, was in this manner brought about by two different orders of people, who had not the least intention to serve the publick. To gratify the most childish vanity was the sole motive of the great proprietors. The merchants and artificers, much less ridiculous, acted merely from a view to their own interest, and in pursuit of their own pedlar principle of turning a penny wherever a penny was to be got. Neither of them had either knowledge or foresight of that great revolution which the folly of the one, and the industry of the other, was gradually bringing about. (III.iv.17)

A number of striking aspects of this history need to be borne in mind in evaluating these concluding remarks. First, to repeat a point already made, the historical sequence of events is not automatic: indeed, the advent of improvement runs against the grain of the historical development that Smith recounts elsewhere in the *Wealth of Nations* and in *Lectures on Jurisprudence*. Usually, one stable but economically unproductive set-up has been followed by another. Second, consistent with that, a delicate, quite unexpected balance between the interests of the players (kings, landowners and townspeople) is required if personal autonomy and its consequence, the self-interested effort to improve productivity, are to appear. Hence, third, the end of feudalism and the beginnings of improvement appear to arise from a chancy coalition of circumstances. Finally, and in consequence, the association Smith draws between the bourgeoisie and the spirit of justice and good government (repeated more than once: see, for instance, III.iii.12, V.iii.7) is less reliable, and more flattering to the bourgeoisie's role in history, than might be justified. There is no deliberate intention to produce justice: it too is a side-effect of coincidences and narrow motives.

Before leaping to conclusions about the meaning of the classic passage quoted above and about the hidden hand metaphor,[9] we should note how little the passage says: it merely states that no part of this 'great revolution' was the result of deliberate intention on the part of any of the social actors involved, who produced a beneficial outcome over and above anything they had in mind. There is no omnipresent, benign hidden process at work; rather, very particular circumstances have stimulated behaviour with unanticipated blessings. In a word, this is an eighteenth-century optimist's version of the objectivity of the social scientist. Social science examines social interactions for global outcomes beyond the awareness of those involved. In Smith's optimistic perception, such outcomes are usually good.

A further difficulty about Smith's history of improvement in Europe is that it runs counter to the straightforward dynamic of the development of the market as he understands it. Normally, for Smith, the prime mover should be the market in agricultural goods,[10] not in luxuries. This makes matters awkward for him, as can be seen from the way his account proceeds from the end of Book III, and from the tone of the passage that immediately follows the outburst of optimistic progressivism above:

> It is thus that through the greater part of Europe the commerce and manufactures of cities, instead of being the effect, have been the cause and occasion of the improvement and cultivation of the country.
>
> This order, however, being *contrary to the natural course of things*, is necessarily both slow and uncertain. Compare the slow progress of those European countries of which the wealth depends very much upon their commerce and manufactures, with the rapid advance of our North American colonies, of which the

wealth is founded altogether in agriculture. (III.iv.18–19 – my emphasis)

In keeping with this half-hearted acknowledgement of his own historical findings, Smith feels called upon, at the end of Book III, to insist (as he had at the start) on a 'natural' course towards improvement which is drastically different from the one he sets out in the body of the book. In the 'natural' course of things, efforts to increase productivity start with those resources that are nearest to hand, and are extended as the spread of market relations increases the scope for specialisation and the division of labour. 'The cultivation and improvement of the country ... must, *necessarily*, be prior to the increase of the town' (III.i.2 – my emphasis). The artisanal and trading activities of towns are then drawn into the market created by commercial agriculture, because 'the cultivation of land cannot be carried on' without 'the assistance of some artificers' (III.i.4). Hence, in Smith's normal course of developments, 'the progressive wealth and increase of the towns would ... be consequential, and in proportion to the improvement and cultivation of the ... country'.

The only case Smith can adduce for what he calls 'the natural course of things' (III.iv.19) is North America, which he refers to in Book III chapters i and iv. He claims that improvement there is proceeding apace thanks to legal and trading conditions that make it a commercial proposition to improve one's land. The subsequent course of the birth of American industry in the nineteenth century, or the growth of American agribusiness in the twentieth, have not exactly borne him out, of course. But even without the benefit of our historical vantage point, we can ask how Smith can be content to counter all the evidence of the past with one barely started historical instance.

I suggest three reasons why Smith might allow the 'natural' course of improvement to override the evidence of difficulties standing in the way of its articulation in the actual course of history. First, the 'natural' route offers modernisation without tears: improvement along 'natural' lines would proceed without much deliberate political intervention or excessive conflict – and rapidly (III.iv.19). In this connection, Smith speaks reassuringly of how the 'inhabitants of the town and those of the country are mutually the servants of one another' (III.i.4). Second, the natural order of improvement is grounded on a small number of pre-conditions that can be easily stated and commended: a well-informed motivation towards profit on the part of individuals, growing communications and security of ownership. Together Smith's pre-conditions for improvement make an elegant case for liberal policy prescriptions which would appear both convincing and agreeable to urban intellectuals like himself, and which would appeal to the cultivated bourgeois circles of the rising towns. Finally, Smith's natural course of improvement reflects that optimistic impression of the rising bourgeoisie which Smith and his fellows felt – and which they were, as Keith Tribe explains in this volume, to convey to their nineteenth-century posterity:

> Whoever has had the fortune to live in a mercantile town situated in an unimproved country [such as the Scottish towns in the late eighteenth century], must have frequently observed how much more spirited the operations of merchants were ... than those of mere country gentlemen. The habits ... of order, economy and attention, to which mercantile business naturally forms a merchant render him fitter to execute, with profit and success, any project of improvement. (III.i.3)

Thus it is that Book III's discussion of history sandwiches a lengthy exploration of the complex and chancy appearance of commercial modernisation between over-hasty statements of the true, 'natural' course of development. As Smith himself acknowledges, 'this natural order of things ... has, in all the modern states of Europe, been ... entirely inverted' (III.i.9). Accordingly, he is inclined to take swipes at the actual course of Europe's economic and social history, insisting that it was 'contrary to the natural course of things ... necessarily both slow and uncertain', and suggesting that it only happened because 'human institutions ...disturbed the natural course of things' (III.i.4).

The importance of societal values

The shakiest of the pre-conditions for improvement as set out above is the motivation of the individuals involved. Well-informed *homo economicus*, as has been many times observed, can be hard to find in real societies. So, though communications and liberal laws are easy to describe, the commercial spirit is diverse and unpredictable. Yet, impressed as Smith may have been by the commercial spirit he found around him, the broader lines of his thought suggest an awareness that the values of commercial society are not only weakly rooted but also contradictory.

Let us consider the argument of Books I and II of the *Wealth of Nations*. Book I is an exposition of the abstract principles underlying a successful commercial nation. Three chapters describe the division of labour, its benefits and the factors (such as limits on the range of the market) which impede it. Eight chapters then consider the behaviour of money in a market, arriving finally at the three different forms in which money is realised: wages, profits and rents.

Now, crucially, as Book I closes, it moves away from an abstract model of the market. By being divided into these three forms, Smith tells us, the wealth (or 'annual produce') of a nation

> constitutes a revenue to three different orders of people; to those who live by rent, to those who live by wages, and to those who live by profit. These are the three great, original and constituent orders of every civilized society, from whose revenue that of every other order is ultimately derived. (I.xi.p.7)

Smith has abandoned abstraction and turned to identifying specific social groups because he has reached the limits of what can be said without embracing something more; namely, specific social mechanisms.

One pressing issue for a political economy, immediately taken up in the conclusion of the last chapter of Book I, is the relative political potential of the different classes. That affects how, or rather by whom, the nation's annual produce is to be managed. Smith evaluates how each of the classes will pursue its interests (I.xi.p.8–10). In the course of the chapter, he has argued that the value of rents is in direct proportion to the wealth of society as a whole. So, assuming (as is not always the case) that the landed, rent-drawing class 'have any tolerable knowledge of that interest', they have both the knowledge and the leisure for rule. Those who live by wages have the same interest in the overall wealth of society, but lack the leisure for understanding. As well as lacking the leisure, the class who live

by profits, on the other hand, inveterately have the wrong
interests and values.

> The interest of the dealers ... in any particular branch of trade
> or manufactures, is always in some respects different from, and
> even opposite to, that of the publick. To widen the market and
> to narrow the competition, is always the interest of the publick;
> but to narrow the competition must always be against it, and can
> serve only to enable the dealers, by raising their profits ... to
> levy, for their own benefit, an absurd tax upon the rest of their
> fellow-citizens. (I.xi.p.10)

The commercial classes are, Smith concludes, 'an order of men,
whose interest is never exactly the same with that of the
publick, who have generally an interest to deceive and even to
oppress the publick' (I.xi.p.10). As regards the issue of distrib-
uting power, then, Smith suggests the wisdom of a set-up –
much as would have been claimed for late eighteenth-century
Britain – where the so-called 'landed interest' held a responsible monopoly of political power.[11] The basis of his case is in
societal values.

Another problem of values appears in Book II: it is that of
the differing socialisation of participants in the market. The
subject of this book is what affects the size of a nation's overall stock. At the start, Smith categorises the different kinds of
stock (capital used in transport, farming, manufacture, interest-
bearing loans, etc.), and considers which of those uses are most
likely to increase the total. In principle, he is inclined to think
agricultural investment the most productive, but in the end he
has to acknowledge (once more) that the evidence of Europe is
against him (II.iv.37).

He considers the choice to be made between capital-increas-
ing 'productive' uses of wealth and 'unproductive' ones, such
as wages for personal servants (II.iii). Here we see the other side
of the coin to the political potential of the different classes. For,
while the wage-earner has little income to divert in any direction, productive or otherwise, the landlord drawing rents or the
man in public life have much income and a tendency to spend
it in unproductive uses. On the other hand, the widespread
parsimony, or frugality, of the members of the commercial class
prompts them to productive uses for their income:

> Parsimony, by increasing the fund which is destined for the main-
> tenance of productive hands, tends to increase the number of
> those hands whose labour adds to the value of the subject upon
> which it is bestowed. It tends therefore to increase the exchange-
> able values of the annual produce of the land and labour of the
> country. It puts in motion an additional quantity of industry,
> which gives an additional value to the annual produce.
>   ... By what a frugal man annually saves, he not only affords
> maintenance to an additional number of productive hands, for
> that or the ensuing year, but ... he establishes as it were a perpet-
> ual fund for the maintenance of an equal number in all times to
> come. (II.ii.17, 19)

That is how Smith accounts for greater real prosperity in commercial towns such as Glasgow, London or Vienna, as against
towns with a sumptuous court or expensive state apparatus
(II.iii.12).

His earlier pejorative remarks indicate that Smith was not
really as impressed by the new commercial classes as he
suggested at other times. But the point is not simply that Smith
could cast a jaundiced eye on the commercial classes' values.
Rather it is that he realised how all social practices, those of
commercial society included, develop paradoxically, uncertainly
and with a vital role to be supplied by societal values. That
element of his thinking about society, both commercial and
non-commercial, is far more apparent in the analysis of *Lectures
on Jurisprudence*, since they take as their subject the foundation
of justice and the evolution of society more generally.

From the *Lectures* we learn that Smith does not regard even
respect for contract – surely a fundamental value of any
commercial society – as natural. Quite the contrary. 'Breach of
contract is *naturally* the slightest of injuries', he tells us in LJ
(B) 176–8 (my emphasis), because it involves an immaterial loss:
of something promised rather than possessed in good and
earnest. As Smith describes things, the idea that breaches of
contract matter could only dawn on people in various stages,
through the process by which losses less directly connected
with material objects came to be recognised as real losses. This
archetypal element of the market as a form of social behaviour
could be established, then, only through a complex process
which developed the necessary values.

Again in the *Lectures*, Smith's later section on 'police'[12] (LJ
(B) 203-333), provides further examples. As we would expect,
Smith places the greatest emphasis on purely economic conditions of a proper social order, itemising numerous impediments
to the division of labour and the market, and rehearsing the
difficulties occasioned by excessive taxation and public debt.
But interspersed in that analysis are considerations about the
development of societal values, which it is equally necessary to
take into account. These tendencies, too, can have the force of
'nature' behind them.

One value, prevalent in pre-modern societies and antipa-
thetic to commercial society, is a high esteem for military deeds
and a low esteem for economic ones. Smith views this as a
particular instance of our natural distaste for self-interested
action, even where (as in a well-functioning market) it actually
contributes to overall well-being:

> In a rude society nothing is honourable but war. ... We may
> observe that these principles of the human mind which are most
> beneficial to society are by no means marked by nature as the
> most honourable. ... To perform any thing, or to give any thing,
> without a reward is always generous and noble, but to barter one
> thing for another is mean. The plain reason for this is that these
> principles are so strongly implanted by *nature* that they have no
> occasion for that additional force which the weaker principles
> need. (LJ (B) 300–1 – my emphasis)

In the light of that thought, Smith closes his section on police
with remarks (LJ (B) 326–33) about 'the influence of commerce
on the manners of the people'. It is here that, in a manner
echoed in the *Wealth of Nations* and treated elsewhere in this
volume,[13] he describes how commerce and the division of
labour narrow the human spirit. Yet the story is of a mutual
interplay of factors, social practices and societal values developing in tandem. One value in particular is crucial – as we shall
see. The need to deal repeatedly with the same fellow players
in the market puts a value upon reputation ('character', as
Smith calls it) and engenders in commerce scruples which
constrain the urge to seek ruthlessly the immediate satisfaction
of one's self-interest (LJ (B) 326–7).

It is in keeping with this attitude of mind for Smith to

detail, as he often does in the *Lectures*, the evolution of societal values for different historical forms of society. Thus, the transition from allodial to feudal society itself (LJ (B) 53) occurs through the evolution of values. In order to enlist their vassals in their forces, allodial warlords were obliged to grant parcels of land both to the vassals and, in case they should not themselves survive, to their families. In due course, a more natural sympathy imposed itself in cases where the vassals were too old to fight: thus the lands, first granted in return for support, become life long, hereditary possessions.

The interplay that he looks for in passing between forms of society, Smith can trace as well in the development of elements present in all societies. Property, for example, is a recognition of the right to possession common to all forms of society, which grows into different versions according to the specific type (LJ (B) 149–71): of little moment amongst hunters, except in so far as there may be disputes about the possession of a kill, it is greatly extended and complicated in arable societies, where the importance of peaceful, continued possession of the land can easily be agreed upon, and so on. Another example is the institution of punishment (LJ (B) 182–201). It develops out of the natural human sentiment of 'resentment', introjected from those who suffer the injury of crime, and it is then transformed by the existence of public authority which has the burden of keeping order between criminal and victim.

Of course, Smith's view places him firmly in the line of Montesquieu, whose voice can be most plainly heard when the values prevalent in monarchies and in republics are being discussed (LJ (B) 93). The assumption underlying this discussion is that there are different values which arise in, or which have to be encouraged to assist the good ordering of, the different types of society. Smith adopts this presupposition again and again, in accounting for the right to assassinate tyrants (LJ (B) 79), for example, or in describing differing criteria of citizenship (LJ (B) 88). This is not a surprising style of analysis for an Enlightenment thinker to pursue; but it is at odds with a simple-minded view that any form of society – the commercial market included – occurs naturally in the mere absence of external impediments or stimulants.

The theme of the interplay between values and economic-legal structures, which runs through the *Lectures*, can be formulated in terms of two modes of acquiring values: 'authority' and 'utility'. This distinction appears late on in Smith's first version of his course of lectures, conveying a distinctly Humean respect for established conventions (LJ (A) v.119–20). But by the time of the second series, its scope has been broadened, and it appears near the start (LJ (B) 12–14). For fuller explanation of authority and utility, Smith points us to his *Theory of Moral Sentiments*. 'Authority' amounts to the principle behind any adoption of values from outside; that is, where the individual is impressed by those virtues in others: 'utility', on the other hand, designates the principle which leads individuals to adopt values that appear useful to those individuals themselves. Authority is more manifest in monarchical societies than in republican ones, for social superiority is more evident there (LJ (B) 93). But the principle is by no means confined to such societies, or to their hierarchies of prestige and wealth: Smith happily uses the term 'authority' to refer to the impression that any outstanding virtues can make on others (e.g. TMS VI.iii.28). In practice, that is, in the social world as Smith analysed it, both modes of acquisition of values are brought into play without sharp opposition.

Psychological mechanisms to develop societal values

Though *The Theory of Moral Sentiments* was first published in 1759, before Smith began work for the *Lectures* and *Wealth of Nations*, it remained sufficiently part of a single enterprise for him to produce substantial amplifications in the edition that appeared shortly before his death. *The Theory of Moral Sentiments* is an exposition of the philosophy of moral sense, developed by Francis Hutcheson, one of Smith's predecessors in the Glasgow chair of moral philosophy. The agenda of moral sense philosophy was the growth of moral inclinations and judgements out of intuition and other natural sentiments. In pursuing that agenda, Smith describes the development, on the basis of simple natural sentiments, of ever more ramified societal values.

In Smith's case, the origin of moral sentiments is 'sympathy', a term he took over from Hume's *Treatise on Human Nature*. What Smith calls 'sympathy' we would probably call 'empathy'. It is a disposition to experience feelings, values included, in parallel with other people with whom we are in some kind of contact. Sympathy *tout court* achieves an immediate communication of people's feelings. Even in its simplest form, the transfer of feelings is bolstered by the usefulness attributed to the feelings in question (TMS I.i.4.4). 'Authority' and 'utility' interlock, that is to say, even in Smith's original, most general version of the processes conveying societal values.

In Smith's hands, this version is confined within the framework of enlightened sociability that the cultivated society of his day would have admired: this involves primarily moderate, 'social' forms and degrees of passion. Paradigm instances, for example, are generosity, sensitivity and 'self-command' (I.i.5), whereas anger and resentment are less readily communicated (I.i.5 and I.ii.3–4). Similarly, the process of communicating a feeling occasions one party to raise, and the other to lower, the degree of passion felt, so that both gravitate towards a moderate intensity of feeling (I.i.4.8). Evidently, although sympathy must operate in all societies (monarchical and republican included), some features of the less enlightened, more hierarchical ones militate against it. Responding more easily to the feelings of good fortune occasioned in the rich and powerful, we sympathise with their higher standing and accept their rank and their moral leadership. Yet though this is useful and necessary to the social order, it is harmful if hierarchy biases our responses to the extent of barring sympathy with those of lowly station (I.i.2-3).

Those preliminaries once established, the main business of *The Theory of Moral Sentiments* is to explore the transfers and transformations through which, on the basis of sympathy, all the necessary societal values are built up. The merit of good deeds is conveyed to us as we assimilate the benevolence of those who do them and the gratitude of those who benefit from them: and, likewise, the demerit of bad deeds is marked by the ill-will on one side and the resentment on the other (II.i.1–4). In sympathising with the anger of injured parties, we acquire a sense of justice (II.ii). We learn the sentiments of successful, respected people to the extent that their sentiments serve them in their good fortune (TII.iii). We internalise the moral sentiments above; develop self-approbation where we are praiseworthy, self-disapprobation where blameworthy; and then acquire an abiding internal judge of praise and blame, conscience (III.iii.1-3). Finally, the rules of duty serve to guard us against self-delusion in interpreting the voice of conscience (III.iii.4).

At each stage of Smith's account, the generation of feelings out of sympathy is bolstered by the personal and/or social utility of the resulting moral make-up. As Smith puts it in connection with the sentiment of justice,

> It is thus that man, who can subsist only in society, was fitted by nature to that situation for which he was made. All the members of human society stand in need of each others' assistance, and are likewise exposed to mutual injuries. ...
>
> Society ... cannot subsist among those who are at all times ready to hurt and injure one another.
>
> ... In order to enforce the observation of justice, therefore, Nature has implanted in the human breast that consciousness of ill-desert, those terrors of merited punishment which attend upon its violations, as the great safe-guards of the association of mankind, to protect the weak, to curb the violent, and to chastise the guilty. (II.ii.3.1–4).

In short, what we find in *The Theory of Moral Sentiments* is an account of socialisation, the spread of societal values through social processes. In the terms used in *Lectures on Jurisprudence*, this is a process that mixes lateral transmission by 'authority' (from person to person) with adoption on grounds of (often unwitting) 'utility'.

Mostly, Smith presents this socialisation in uniform terms, as a process valid for all societies. However, differences have already been noted between the mode of articulation of 'authority' in societies where ranks are marked and those where they are not, and these suggest that Smith's version of socialisation is open to the claims of historical specificity and change. That aspect of his argument is made all the clearer when, in Part V of *The Theory of Moral Sentiments*, Smith considers the effects of custom and fashion on the process of socialisation. Some of these effects of this are trivial modulations. Others are adaptations of societal values sustained by transmission within a given social group or by the utility of particular values in that group (V.2). This applies, Smith argues (V.4-6), in the case of different professions and ranks: in confirmation, he cites the gravity expected in the clergy, whose calling entails frequent reflection upon death,[14] and likewise the heedlessness of the officer class.

But socialisation also varies according to different stages of society:

> Among civilised nations, the virtues which are founded upon humanity, are more cultivated than those founded upon self-denial. ... The general security and happiness which prevail in ages of civility and politeness, afford little exercise to the contempt of danger, to patience in enduring labour, hunger, and pain. Poverty may be easily avoided, and the contempt of it therefore almost ceases to be a virtue. The abstinence from pleasure becomes less necessary, and the mind is more at liberty to unbend itself, and to indulge its natural inclinations in all those particular respects. (V.2.8)

So Smith's is a theory of enculturation, of the growth and transmission of values particular to the given historical society. The above remarks, towards the end of Part V, indicate as well the historically specific agenda for enculturation propounded in *The Theory of Moral Sentiments*. For they suggest what societal values are essential and particular to the new commercial society. The last substantive part of the book, Part VI, addresses that issue squarely in an assessment of four components of virtue: justice, benevolence, prudence and self-restraint ('self-command').

Nothing new of weight is said about the processes that engender justice, that part of virtue which restrains harm done to individuals by others. As for beneficence, that part which positively addresses the welfare of others, it receives a somewhat despairing consideration. Smith finds that in normal persons it is limited to the immediate family, group, class or nation (VI.ii.1), and then he doubts the sincerity of ordinary humans who claim to exercise it at any higher plane (VI.ii.2–3). Clearly, Smith has the traditional figures of authority in his sights here: of those proclaiming their wide-reaching benevolence, he adds that 'political speculators and sovereign princes are by far the most dangerous' (VI.ii.2.18). Thus far, then, moral sentiments on a higher plane are suspect and virtue seems trapped in the narrowness of vision of the ordinary classes of commercial society.

Prudence and self-command suggest another story, however, because they are both laudable and historically practicable components of virtue for the present age. The prudent look to the health of the body, fortune and reputation; they are serious, earnest, honest, modest and judicious; they confine themselves to their own affairs and duties, without interfering in those of others (VI.i). They enshrine

> the steadiness of ... industry and frugality ... steadily sacrificing the ease and enjoyment of the present moment for the probable expectation of the still greater ease and enjoyment of a more distant but more lasting period of time. (VI.i.11)

These are plainly the virtues of the new urban commercial classes – which is perhaps why prudence is treated, as John Robertson has remarked,[15] with particularly revealing eloquence. Virtues such as prudence are at the centre of Smith's hopes for an enculturation of values well adapted to the new commercial age.

Smith's account of prudence as a virtue tries to skew it towards steadier and longer-term rewards than it would embrace *prima facie*. There is a clear hint of rewards in heaven in the passage quoted above, for example. And Smith envisions a 'superior prudence ... carried to the highest degree of perfection', which inspires 'the most perfect propriety in every possible circumstance and situation' (VI.i.15). Yet prudence at this level is barely to be expected in ordinary men, since 'it supposes the utmost perfection of all the intellectual and of all the moral virtues' (VI.i.15)

Finally, Smith finds in prudence a crucial point of connection with two important strands in his thought. On the one hand, it contains a contemporary form of the Epicurean and Stoic virtues of self-restraint, where Smith drew on classical sources for a morality for his own day.[16] On the other hand, reputation, as I noted above, is a product of socialisation in commercial society: it is in the interests of the individual practising in commerce to court the high regard of others. For Smith, prudence entails the pursuit of reputation, and so forms a bridge between the values drawn from 'utility' and those drawn from 'authority'. The level of virtue required to obtain a good character in the eyes of others is naturally the highest object that will be aimed at by the prudence of ordinary men in commercial society.

Conclusion

I can now retrace the steps of my argument. Smith sometimes talks, in admiring tones, as though the appearance of commercial society and bourgeois sociability are straightforward and natural. But, as he accounts for it, their historical development is in fact haphazard and exceptional. They require a number of circumstances to come together, both to create the initial historical conditions and to sustain the necessary societal values. *Lectures on Jurisprudence* spell out the historical circumstances and the values; *The Theory of Moral Sentiments* constructs the theoretical framework for the processes of enculturation which that entails, and commends the best version Smith can imagine for the society which he sees emerging.

Smith's enterprise was to explain the rise of commerce and the market, and to defend their existence on the grounds of their various benefits. But his analysis does not entitle him to say – as he usually avoids doing – that they are natural, the greatest possible manifestation of human progress, or the normal state of human affairs against which all others must be judged as forced and inferior. It is only ideologically misled epigones and disciples who do that. Instead, Smith examines the processes through which enculturation of societal values occurs, in order to discover (sometimes hoping against hope) how the values of the new urban bourgeoisie may measure up to their role in the coming commercial society.

Notes

1 Smith favoured the word 'invisible' rather than the familiar 'hidden'. The occasions on which he actually used the idea will be examined in

the section on 'The Conditions of Improvement' and note 9 below.

2 Andrew S. Skinner, 'Historical Theory', in *A System of Social Science: Papers relating to Adam Smith* (Oxford: Clarendon Press, 1979), p. 88.

3 The lineage of the stages has been traced to an unpublished essay of 1750 by Turgot (R. L. Meek, 'Smith, Turgot and the Four Stages Theory', in *History of Political Economy*, 3 (1971), pp. 9–27). Amongst the thinkers who constituted Smith's intellectual environment, many speculated about how material and moral/legal aspects of society evolved together: Montesquieu; Rousseau (in the *Discourse on the Origin of Inequality* (1755)); the Scottish judge and sometime sponsor of Smith's lectures, Lord Kames (in his *Law Tracts* 1 and 2); James Steuart (in his *Principles of Political Economy* (1767)); and John Millar (in *The Origin of the Distinction of Ranks* (1771)).

4 See *The Spirit of the Laws*, Books 20–2.

5 Explored by the first editor of the *Lectures*, in Edwin Cannan (ed.) *Lectures on Justice, Police, Revenue and Arms, delivered in the University of Glasgow by Adam Smith* (Oxford, 1896), pp. xxxv–xli

6 Smith's so-called 'stadial' history of social transformations is discussed at more length in Skinner, 'Historical Theory'; in D. A. Reisman, *Adam Smith's Sociological Economics* (London: Croom Helm, 1976); and in D. D. Raphael, *Adam Smith* (Oxford: Oxford University Press, 1985).

7 See WN IV.ix.47, LJ(A) iii.111–14, iii.123–4, LJ(B) 139, 290–1, 299–300.

8 A broad connection between personal liberty and the progress of a society was, of course, drawn by many Enlightenment thinkers: Montesquieu, for example, or Smith's contemporary and fellow Scot, Adam Ferguson.

9 The occasions on which Smith uses the metaphor are, in fact, three, of which only one connects it with the commercial market. In an early essay on 'The Principles which lead and direct Philosophical Inquiries, illustrated by the History of Astronomy' (EPS III, 1–5), he writes that primitive peoples, uncurious and uninformed about the 'hidden chains of events' in nature, are unaware of how influences such as 'the invisible hand of Jupiter' (that is, gravity) are at work. Second, in *The Theory of Moral Sentiments* (IV.i.9–10), there is an argument to the effect that, in *any* society, the wealthy, incapable of ingesting physically all the great excess over their poorer fellows which their wealth has acquired them, 'are led by an invisible hand' to distribute it amongst the less fortunate. Finally, at WN IV.ii.9, Smith does tie the invisible hand to the market, observing that anyone who, for security's sake, invests his capital near to home is 'led by an invisible hand to promote an end that is no part of his intention'. See also A. L. Macfie, 'The Invisible Hand of Jupiter', *Journal of the History of Ideas*, 32 (1971), pp. 595–9, for the case for taking the phrase as nothing more than stylistic continuity.

10 The proper management of that market was the primary concern of Smith's 'physiocrat' fellow political economists in France, where the problem of avoiding famine (and riot!) was as preoccupying for government as anywhere in Europe. In the last chapter of Book IV, Smith himself devotes much attention to the problem, condemning their

account of the basis of wealth but advocating the same liberal remedies as they.

11 As Donald Winch has shown, the politics that Smith could envisage was also founded on a broader maintenance, by the political system, of some elements of republican virtue (*Adam Smith's Politics: An Essay in Historiographic Revision*, (Cambridge: Cambridge University Press, 1978)). Winch updates and defends his position in 'Adam Smith and the Liberal Tradition', in K. Haakonssen ed., *Traditions of Liberalism: Essays on John Locke, Adam Smith and John Stuart Mill* (St Leonards, New South Wales: Centre for Independent Studies, 1988).

12 At this time, 'police' means something like the well-ordering of society.

13 See WN V.i.f., esp. 50 & 53, and Andrew Skinner's chapter in this volume, pp. 70–96.

14 That is at least, one supposes, the appropriate character for the clergy as thought of amongst eighteenth-century Scottish Presbyterians.

15 John Robertson, 'Adam Smith', in *Political Thought from Plato to Nato*, with an introduction by Brian Redhead (London: British Broadcasting Corporation/Ariel Books, 1984), p. 141.

16 Jerry Z. Muller, *Adam Smith in his Time and Ours: Designing the Decent Society* (New York and Oxford: The Free Press, 1993), provides a full account of how Smith, drawing extensively on these classical traditions, contributed to the line of thought which led to the acceptance of new values of 'opulence', etc, and hence permitted the rising benefits of social progress in the eighteenth century.

7

Adam Smith and the limits to growth

TED BENTON

Introduction

Adam Smith begins his *Wealth of Nations* with what will be the central thesis of the book – that it is the 'annual labour of every nation' which is the source of 'all the necessaries and conveniencies of life which it annually consumes' (WN I.1). Labour is not merely a necessary condition for the meeting of human needs and desires, but 'is alone the ultimate and real standard by which the value of all commodities can at all times and places be estimated and compared' (I.v.7). However, Smith also commonly speaks of wealth as the annual produce of 'land and labour', and, when discussing the consequences of the accumulation of capital, he says: 'Hence arises a demand for every sort of material which human invention can employ, either usefully or ornamentally, in building, dress, equipage, or houshold furniture; for the fossils and minerals contained in the bowels of the earth; the precious metals, and the precious stones' (I.xi.c.7). On the one hand, what Smith calls 'the spontaneous productions of nature' can meet no human need or desire unless some human labour is performed, if only to reach out and collect them. On the other, he seems to acknowledge that labour could of itself meet no need unless it had some material or being provided by nature to serve as its object – as that which it collects or 'works up' into an object of use or ornament, or a commodity which can be exchanged for such.

The 'labour-thesis' is, among other things, Smith's key to the dynamic character of wealth-creation, of the progress from a 'rude' and 'uncivilized' to an 'improved', cultivated and thriving state of society. It explains how a people may remain poor, their social development arrested, though their soil is fertile, their climate favourable and their land well supplied with precious metals. Equally, it explains why a nation may attain great wealth without such natural advantages. In addition, for Smith, as for the classical tradition of political economy, the major social classes are defined through their relation to the total labouring activity of society.

Though Smith was writing in the context of a growing commercialisation of economic life, the great technological transformations of nineteenth-century industrialism were yet to come. The *Wealth of Nations* was written on the verge of a thoroughgoing 'disembedding' of wealth-production from its specific ecological conditions and contexts. The emergence of forms of calculation which acknowledge only quantitative considerations of monetary cost and benefit is clearly signalled in Smith's economic discourse, but the modernising delusion of emancipation from natural constraints has not yet taken hold within it. In his commitment to the labour thesis, in the central place he gives to a certain model of economic rationality, and in his overriding concern with the legal and political restraints on freedom of trade, Smith speaks the language of an economy whose natural conditions can be taken for granted. However, there remain, often as subordinate or implicit presences in his text, numerous acknowledgements of the continuing significance of natural limits and affordances.

When Smith applies his economic categories to agriculture, fishing and mining, as well as to the purpose of colonial policy, he does engage explicitly and directly with the naturally given conditions and constraints of these practices. Also, and especially in the case of agriculture, he acknowledges cultural and psychological resistances to the new commercial rationality. In this context, my primary focus will be on the conceptual tensions which arise in Smith's consideration of the interface between wealth-creation and its natural conditions. These tensions have a double resonance for us today: first, because Smith's text has itself returned to haunt us; and second, because we too have problems in our relation to nature. Economists, environmental activists, social theorists, policy makers and others are at last addressing the terrifying consequences of an economic 'modernisation' premised upon a wilful 'forgetting' of its dependence upon conditions external to itself. It is possible that Smith, writing *before* the great delusion of progressive emancipation from nature took hold, may have something to offer for us, who attempt to live amongst its consequences.

It would, of course, be quite wrong to begin our investigation of Smith's text as though he were a contemporary of ours and as though the *Wealth of Nations* were just another contribution to the science of economics. Smith wrote in the wake of a thoroughgoing commercialisation of agriculture, and in the context of a striking growth of manufacture and commerce in and between the most economically developed nations. He wrote at the brink of, but still prior to, the great expansionary system of modern industry and the globalisation of trade, and his text is widely regarded as one of the founding moments in the science of economics. The *Wealth of Nations* is obsessively and repetitively concerned with the refutation of 'mercantilism', but it is mercantilism in practice, as a set of disastrous restraints on and distortions of trade, agriculture and industry, rather than as theoretical system, which excites Smith's scorn. Where he does enter into theoretical discourse with his predecessors in economic science, the physiocrats or 'economists', as he calls them, he restricts his discussion, on the grounds that

> That system ... has, so far as I know, never been adopted by any nation, and it at present exists only in the speculations of a few men of great learning and ingenuity in France. It would not, surely, be worth while to examine at great length the errors of a system which never has done, and probably never will do any harm in any part of the world. (IV.ix.2)

Though Smith's full title – *An Inquiry into the Nature and Causes of ...* – clearly situates him as a *philosophe*, as an independent and disinterested seeker after truth in the proper spirit of the Scottish Enlightenment, when he comes to define the discipline of political economy, he does so entirely in terms of its practical purpose:

> Political oeconomy, considered as a branch of the science of a statesman or legislator, proposes two distinct objects; first, to

provide a plentiful revenue or subsistence for the people, or more properly to enable them to provide such a revenue or subsistence for themselves; and secondly, to supply the state or commonwealth with a revenue sufficient for the publick services. (IV.1)

Michel Foucault's much-celebrated pronouncement of the intimacy of knowledge with power is here baldly and frankly affirmed by Smith.

Still, the text is far more heterogeneous and polyvalent than this might suggest. Smith's most commonly adopted voice is that of the wise and prudent adviser to some anonymous legislator or statesman. But the evidence suggests that he was in fact listened to most enthusiastically and immediately by the businessmen of Scotland and the north of England,[1] despite his clear warning that the class of traders and manufacturers 'have generally an interest to deceive and even to oppress the publick, and ... accordingly have, upon many occasions, both deceived and oppressed it' (I.xi.p.10).

So, despite its evident practical interest, Smith's text affects a certain distance from specific social or economic concerns in favour of a dispassionate analysis of the sources of wealth, the causes of economic growth and stagnation, and the mechanisms of distribution of wealth among the various social classes. In places this analysis is presented as formal reasoning from theoretical first principles, but such passages are interspersed with prolonged historical narrative, reports on the economic life of other countries – especially the colonies – and extensive comparative studies with ancient and classical empires. Where Smith does draw practical lessons from his analyses, these are frequently prudential in nature: policies or laws are advocated or opposed in terms of their likely effect in advancing or retarding the production of wealth, which Smith tends to equate with the general interest of society. There are, however, also moments in the text – for example, where he discusses slavery or the treatment of Native Americans – at which Smith takes an explicitly moral stance whose implications may be at variance with purely economic reasoning.

Smith attempts to develop a systematically explanatory economic theory, and, simultaneously, to refine and apply it to a very wide range of descriptive materials and policy issues. In this attempt, he necessarily draws upon (what he supposes to be) the conceptualisations and forms of calculation employed by economic agents themselves. But at the same time, as an intervention in economic policy debates, Smith's text seeks to *transform* those conceptualisations, to consolidate some and to weaken others. My focus here is not so much upon Smith's substantive proposals, but rather on some aspects of his conceptualisation of a range of social practices as the proper domain for economic calculation and for legislative 'deregulation'. In this conceptualisation Smith is engaged on three fronts: first, in advancing a certain view of individual human nature; second, in thinking about the relationships between individual action, group interest and the well-being of society; and third, in defining and extending the *scope* of his framework for analysis. My focus is on the third of these fronts, but it will be necessary to give consideration to the other two if this is to be intelligible.

Human nature, rationality and markets

First, then, the view of individual human nature advanced in Smith's text. In Book I chapter ii, Smith notes 'a certain propensity in human nature ... to truck, barter, and exchange one thing for another' (I.ii.2). This may not be an 'original principle', being probably a consequence of reason and speech: 'Nobody', he says, 'ever saw a dog make a fair and deliberate exchange of one bone for another with another dog.' But elsewhere Smith imagines that, in a 'rude' state of existence, humans met their needs by hunting or collecting, without, presumably, the necessity to 'truck and barter'. When private property in land, a division of labour and the rule of law have been established, our propensity to exchange comes into its own. Under these conditions 'men' deploy their effort, or invest their stock, in various undertakings in which they have an expectation of a gain over and above their expenditure. This is, for Smith, not just one orientation to practical activity among other possibilities. Rather, it is a criterion of rationality, of sanity itself. Given 'tolerable security', he says, a man 'must be perfectly crazy' not to employ his stock in one or other of the profitable ways he has described (II.i.30).

Of course, for this natural propensity of humans to be manifested requires the appropriate institutional setting. Human individuals supply the rationality and the differentiated demands for and supplies of goods, but the institution of the market, with its legal or moral regulation (notice the normative element, 'fairness', in Smith's definition of exchange), is a necessary condition for the cost/gain form of rationality to be expressed in the actual flow of market exchange. Among other things, this is because some quantitative measure of equivalence between products of different kinds is presupposed in the idea of 'fair exchange' itself. This purely quantitative measure, or standard, is the labour-time of others which can be commanded with, or exchanged for, the goods in question. Value, in this sense, what Smith calls 'value in exchange', takes no account of the *kind* of labour involved, or of the substantive properties, or the possible uses of the product in which it inheres. So, the kind of rationality which calculates costs and gains in the market is formal in character, dealing with quantities rather than qualities, seeking to maximise gains and minimise costs.

But Smith continues to think of the whole process of production and distribution of wealth as having a substantive purpose. Indeed, he is inclined to define wealth as 'all the necessaries and conveniencies of life' (I.1), and explicitly excludes from his account of 'the real wealth' of 'all the inhabitants of a great country' that part of their revenue which has to be set aside to replace or maintain their capital stock (II.ii.4–6). Similarly, he recognises that each object of exchange has a value in use, as well as a value in exchange. The specific labours involved in producing these use values may vary in the degree of skill or strength required, their agreeableness or disagreeableness, their honourable or dishonourable character and so on. As a bearer of value in use, a product of human labour (or any other object) satisfies some individual human need or desire.

Though Smith is widely credited with the use/exchange value distinction, in practice his analyses rarely acknowledge it, so that the tensions (for Marx, contradictions) between these two dimensions of capitalist economic activity do not become objects of explicit analysis. Nevertheless, what is striking about Smith's text from the standpoint of the twentieth century is the extent to which what are in fact use-value considerations figure in his analyses. As we shall see, this is a matter of great significance.

One consequence of Smith's evident concern for the purposes of the production of wealth, and for the values in use of products, is his retention of a notion of substantive rationality as applicable even in market economies, alongside the formal rationality associated with cost/gain calculation. This is evident in two interconnected areas: his theory of demand and his account of labour itself. Smith distinguishes what he calls 'effectual' from 'absolute' demand. 'Effectual' demands can be made only by those with *both* requirements *and* the ability to pay for them. Nevertheless, the effectual demand for goods of various kinds is treated by Smith as though it were a direct consequence of people's ordering of their priorities, largely in abstraction from the distribution of revenues between the different classes. This treatment reveals Smith as an adherent of a hierarchical theory of individual human need. He supposes that, as with other animals, it is the means of subsistence which set limits to the expansion of human population. Demand, therefore, is first and foremost demand for food: 'As subsistence is, in the nature of things, prior to conveniency and luxury, so the industry which procures the former, must necessarily be prior to that which ministers to the latter' (III.i.2). Despite Smith's disagreements on other matters with the physiocrats, he shared with them a certain 'agricultural fundamentalism', which, in his case, issues from yet another universal human propensity: 'as to cultivate the ground was the original destination of man, so in every stage of his existence he seems to retain a predilection for this primitive employment' (III.i.3).

After food, says Smith, 'clothing and lodging are the two great wants of mankind'. In the course of an historical transition from the 'rude' or uncultivated to 'advanced' or civilised society there occurs an increase in the productive power of agricultural labour such that a growing proportion of the labour of a society can be devoted to 'satisfying the other wants and fancies of mankind'. Smith includes among these 'wants and fancies' clothing, lodging, household furniture and 'what is called Equipage' (I.xi.c.7). This notion of a hierarchy of needs has important consequences for his economic theory, both determining a 'natural' sequencing of capital accumulation in economic development, and providing him with his distinctive answer to the question of possible limits to the accumulation of wealth: 'The desire of food is limited in every man by the narrow capacity of the human stomach; but the desire of the conveniencies and ornaments of building, dress, equipage, and houshold furniture, seems to have no limit or certain boundary' (I.xi.c.7). So far as Smith takes his argument at this point, it would seem that though demand for some kinds of goods (agricultural products) might be finite, overall demand for the products of labour is potentially limitless. If there are 'limits to growth' they do not, on the face of it, appear to derive from the satiation of human desire.

Turning, now, from the hierarchical view of human need underlying Smith's theory of demand to his account of labour we can find, again, clear indications of substantive rationality, and an associated recognition of the significance of qualitative differentiations. On the surface, his arguments in favour of labour as the 'real measure' of exchange value imply the qualitatative equivalence of different kinds of labour. Labour is, Smith claims, at all times and in all places, of equal value to the labourer: 'In his ordinary state of health, strength and spirits, in the ordinary degree of his skill and dexterity, he must always lay down the same portion of his ease, his liberty, and his happiness' (I.v.7). This suggests that time spent working must always be counted as a cost which is quantitatively measurable and qualitatively unvarying as a sacrifice, for a larger or shorter period, of liberty and happiness.

Yet there are many other passages where Smith acknowledges that some kinds of work are more inherently disagreeable than others. As we have seen, he even thinks of agricultural work as an activity for which we have a natural inclination. Different kinds of work are also held by Smith to be more or less honourable in the view of society. Furthermore, even those variables mentioned in the above quotation – health and strength, skill, dexterity and so on – make for yet other qualitative differences between different kinds of labour. These suggest that, depending on who one is, and what kind of work is being done, one may or may not consider work as a cost at all. Even where work *is* considered as a cost, the commensurability of different *kinds* of experience of work-as-cost is by no means obvious. Leaving aside the problem of circularity this would introduce into the theory, Smith could not easily resolve this problem by simply treating (as he generally does) labour as one marketable commodity among others. Apprenticeships and other 'restrictive practices', the acquisition of the specialised skills required by some jobs and the social honour attaching to them, all militate against any easy flow of labour from one trade to another in response to shifts in demand. Similarly, Smith links population directly with the demand for labour, but given the lack of coincidence in the time-scales of fluctuations in market demand and human maturation, it is hard to see what mechanism would bring this about.

So, Smith's treatment of human need and the category of labour implies that, alongside the formal cost/gain rationality which governs capital accumulation, there must persist areas in which substantive rationality sensitive to qualitative differences continues to operate. The market is an arena in which individuals seek to meet specific and irreducible needs and offer distinctive skills and competences, as well as a means by which wealth is accumulated and circulated. Though Smith is clear about the non-identity of exchange-value and use-value, market exchanges are, for him, still a form of mediation between human needs, purposes and abilities.

As we have seen, there are passages which suggest that the cost/benefit form of rationality, the disposition to treat possessions as stock or capital, to be used as a source of revenue, is an inherent disposition, demarcating the sane and rational from the 'perfectly crazy'. On the other hand, when Smith compares the country gentleman with the former merchant as 'improvers' of the land, he writes of the 'habit' of the latter employing his money in profitable projects, which gives him a 'temper and disposition' in every sort of business. Also, the mercantile habits of 'order, economy and attention' make him more likely to execute any such project successfully, compared with the gentleman whose habit is to use money as an expense, without expecting any return (III.iv.3). Elsewhere, Smith tells us that parsimony increases capital, whilst prodigality and misconduct diminish it, and the growth of capital favours 'industry' as against idleness:

> In mercantile and manufacturing towns, where the inferior ranks of people are chiefly maintained by the employment of capital, they are in general industrious, sober, and thriving ... In those towns which are principally supported by the constant or occasional residence of a court ... they are in general idle, dissolute, and poor. (II.iii.12)

In passages such as these, Smith appears to acknowledge both the dependence of capital accumulation upon individual entrepreneurial virtues and habits, and the effects of capitalist industry on promoting these virtues and habits, especially among the working population. This is consistent with the widely shared Enlightenment view of human educability, of 'environmentalism' in the wider sense, and with the empiricist view of mental operations advocated by Smith's great mentor, the philosopher David Hume. Smith was much more optimistic in his view of the consequences of modern commercial society for individual virtue than some of his associates, most notably Adam Ferguson. Nevertheless, the two were alike in combining (sometimes with dubious consistency) a determinate view of innate human dispositions with sensitivity to the shaping of human personality by habit and experience – what we might now call 'culture'.

The 'innate disposition' view predominates when Smith comes to consider the long-run historical tendency for wealth to accumulate. Smith shared with Ferguson (and Montesquieu who was an important source for both writers in this respect) a concern with the distinctive attributes of modern 'advanced' or 'cultivated' civilisation, by contrast with the savage or barbarous 'rude' states of society largely left behind in western Europe, but still prevailing over much of the known world. A key measure of this transition, for Smith, is the extent to which land has come under cultivation. As soon as agriculture becomes established, human labour can produce from a given area of land more than is necessary for its own maintenance. Population may then grow, labour may be devoted to the meeting of needs and desires beyond mere subsistence, markets are extended and the division of labour in both argiculture and manufacture may be intensified. This view of the 'natural' process of economic development (which, however, as we have seen, may be obstructed or distorted by lack of a legal order, or by restrictive laws and practices, by the accidents of war and so on) relies on Smith's 'innate disposition' view of human nature. There is, so to speak, a constant pressure arising from human nature in favour of progressive cultivation, exchange, division of labour and entrepreneurship:

> the principle, which prompts to expence, is the passion for present enjoyment; which, though sometimes violent and very difficult to be restrained, is in general only momentary and occasional. But the principle which prompts to save, is the desire of bettering our condition, a desire which, though generally calm and dispassionate, comes with us from the womb, and never leaves us till we go into the grave. (II.iii.28)

It is this sober, protestant desire for self-improvement, presented as a natural proclivity of the human species, which enables Smith to treat the progress from 'rude' to 'cultivated', the establishment of private property in land, the growth of exchange, the division of labour and the expansion of social wealth as 'natural' processes, rather than the contingent results of a fortuitous coming together of cultural, legal and material conditions. It is also this view of human nature which provides the implicit rationale for his reconstruction of the histories of ancient and classical empires, as well as medieval Europe, in terms of his own framework of economic categories.

The scope of political economy

We are now in a position to address more directly the question of the scope of these categories. As we have seen, Smith's text is significant both as an event in economic theory and as an influence on economic policy and practice. So the question of 'scope' has two related aspects:

First, how successful is Smith in seeking to extend or consolidate his preferred categories with regard to the material he considers? and

Second, how far might actual social and economic practices be conducted in accordance with these categories, and what might be the consequences and limits of doing so?

In turn, each of these questions might be asked with respect to three dimensions of economic practice:

(1) For each individual human agent, how far, extensively or intensively, can the forms of economic rationality Smith describes and advocates be adopted? In how many aspects of life do individuals deploy these forms of rational calculation? How far might a culture go in constituting individual subjects on this model? Or must we recognise (as I have suggested in some of the earlier reasoning in this chapter) that the formal rationality presupposed in the benevolent functioning of the market itself presupposes a substantive rationality irreducible to the calculation of market advantage? If the latter is the case, then Smith's favoured form of economic life will be sustainable only if it preserves rather than erodes those aspects of individual life which fall outside, but are presupposed by, the economic categories and the practices they represent. These aspects of the self lead a marginal, but still detectable life in Smith's text — the work of the housewife in bearing and bringing up the labourer's children, the normative character of the exchange relation itself ('fairness'), the virtues of the frugal entrepreneur and the industrious worker, the 'ease, liberty and happiness' of the worker, a part only of which is sacrificed to earn the means of subsistence. The list could be multiplied.

(2) With respect to the whole complex of different practices which go to make up the 'physiology' of society, how far might market-induced rationality be extended? Are there, as in individual life, forms of social practice to which the logic of the market is inapplicable, or, more significantly for Smith, practices whose non-market character is a precondition for the market itself? Smith's argument seems to suggest that there are several. The market must exist in a conducive legal or normative context, preserving the 'natural liberty' of property-owners so long as it is consistent with the security of the rest of society, preventing monopoly and granting formal equality to all economic agents. Provision of some public works, such as roads and canals, is essential to the expansion of markets, but may not offer opportunities for profitable investment. Above all, national security, underwritten by the sovereign power, is

not something that Smith imagines can be left to the play of market forces. In fact, he is quite explicit that security takes precedence over opulence, if the two are in conflict. So, Smith not only notes that whole categories of 'unproductive' workers are sustained out of the revenues of the 'productive' classes, but devotes the last book of the *Wealth of Nations* to a justification of general taxation for the maintenance of some of them. However, again unlike Ferguson, Smith seems to take an optimistic view of the relation between the expansion of wealth in commercial society and its moral, legal and political sustaining conditions. He acknowledges, of course, that extravagant government, maladministration and misguided diplomacy (in relation, for example, to the attempt by 'mother' countries to monopolise trade with their colonies) may undermine and obstruct 'improvement' and the accumulation of wealth. But there is no suggestion of any inner, systemic connection, as there was for Ferguson, between the pervasiveness of commercial values and the undermining of public virtue.

(3) Concentrating on the interface between human social practices and 'external' nature, how far may our practice in relation to nature be conducted in accordance with Smith's economic categories? How far may nature itself be commodified? Are there some classes of practice in relation to nature which resist theorisation in terms of Smith's concepts of productive labour, 'stock', commodity, use- and exchange-value? It is here that the problematical relation of the concepts of political economy (and the form of economic life they typify) to their naturally given contexts and conditions comes into view.

As we have seen, Smith invokes a 'natural' process of historical transition from a 'rude', 'unimproved ' to a 'cultivated', 'improved' state of social existence. Given 'tolerable security' and economic liberty, a dynamically self-expanding system of wealth-production, of benefit to the whole of society, can be expected to emerge spontaneously. We saw earlier how the expansion – potentially boundless – of the demand for the products of manufacture also entails an ever-expanding requirement for the materials of manufacture, 'for the fossils and minerals contained in the bowels of the earth'. But Smith is also clear that subsistence takes priority over convenience and ornament in the hierarchy of individual needs, and so in the course of economic development. The basis and the starting point of this dynamic is, therefore, the production of food: agri-culture. So central is this to his thinking that he is inclined to mark human historical progress in terms of the degree of 'inclo-sure', 'improvement' and cultivation of the land.[2]

However, Smith's key objection to the physiocrats concerns their recognition of agriculturalists alone as 'productive'. He extends the accolade of productive labour to include 'artificers, manufacturers and merchants'. Their activity, for Smith, does, unlike the work of menial servants, 'fix and realise itself in some ... vendible commodity', and thereby adds to the revenue of society (IV.ix.31). Much of his argument in the *Wealth of Nations* is devoted to showing the interdependence of agricul-ture, manufacture and trade, and the benefits of the accumula-tion of capital and division of labour in each of these sectors for the growth of wealth in the others. In part, his argument consists in an attempt to show how the heterogeneous practices of mining, fishing, agriculture, manufacture and trade may all be subsumed under the main categories of political economy. This is required if Smith's more general argument about the overall benefits of liberty of economic action is to be sustained. From the standpoint of proprietor or labourer, agriculture and clothing manufacture, for example, have to be seen indiffer-ently as alternative locations for profitable investment of stock, or sources of gainful employment.

The peculiarities of agriculture

Smith's attempt to expand the discourse of political economy takes manufacture and trade as its paradigm, seeking to extend to agriculture the concepts of 'instruments of trade', machinery and fixed and circulating capital. So, for example, shops, ware-houses, workhouses, farmhouses, granaries and stables 'are a sort of instruments of trade, and may be considered in the same light' and the 'improved farm' may also be included in the cate-gory of fixed capital: 'An improved farm may very justly be regarded in the same light as those useful machines which facil-itate and abridge labour, and by means of which, an equal circulating capital can afford a much greater revenue to its employer' (II.i.16). However, elsewhere, Smith recognises sharp disparities between agriculture (and other uses of land) and other types of wealth-producing activity. As we have seen, his version of the hierarchy of human needs, together with his view of population, imply an unceasing demand for agricultural produce. This makes agriculture an exceptionally secure source of revenue. But there are four other sorts of peculiarity which deserve further attention: first, peculiarities having to do with the natural finitude of land; second, the distinctive character of the relationship of agricultural labour to its context and conditions; third, what Smith calls the 'spontaneous production' of nature itself; and fourth, widespread cultural valuations of the land which compete with commercial pressures.

The finitude of the land

Smith treats rent on land as a category of revenue distinct in kind from profits on stock and wages. It is a form of 'monopoly' price (I.xi.a.1), unrelated to any effort or care on the part of the landlord, but deriving from the powers of proprietorship:

> As soon as the land of any country has all become private property, the landlords, like all other men, love to reap where they never sowed, and demand a rent even for its natural produce. The wood of the forest, the grass of the field, and all the natural fruits of the earth, which, when land was in common, cost the labourer only the trouble of gathering them, come, even to him, to have an additional price fixed upon them. He must then pay for the licence to gather them; and must give up to the landlord a portion of what his labour either collects or produces. (I.vi.8)

Clearly, however, landlords are in a position to impose this additional price only if would-be collectors or producers on the land have nowhere else to go. Rent, in other words, is a consequence not just of private property in land, but of private property in *all* of it. Locke's famous provision, that land may justly be appropriated so long as 'there is enough, and as good left in common for others',[3] is plainly not fulfilled. Smith's contrast is with the American colonies, where the rapid expansion of both population and wealth is premised largely on the abundance of land, relative to population, and its consequently low price. So long as the engrossment of land is limited by a requirement upon landowners to improve and cultivate, these are conditions which favour a rapid increase in agricultural production and consequently in other forms of wealth-production. Interestingly, although Smith contrasts the colonists' fittedness to make rapid improvements in a 'waste' and 'thinly inhabited' country with the 'tribes of naked and miserable savages' discovered by Columbus, he does not use Locke's maxim, as had the early colonists themselves, to justify colonial expropriation.[4] He refers, rather, to the 'savage injustice of the Europeans', as 'ruinous and destructive to several of those unfortunate countries' (IV.i.32).

So, under conditions of *relative* abundance of land, finitude is not of economic significance. However, as land is increasingly appropriated and cultivated, proprietors can command a proportion of the value of its produce in the form of rent, a revenue unrelated to any value-adding labour performed by themselves. Since, however, Smith measures the advance of civilisation by the proportion of available land brought under cultivation, and, moreover, attributes to human kind a natural propensity to cultivate, there must be a long-run historical tendency to extend the area of cultivated land and, given the finitude of the land itself, this must be at the expense of wild, 'unimproved' country.

But the latter is a source of objects which meet human needs and demands – such as fruits, wood and game animals. Some of these – wood is the best example – must necessarily become scarcer as the area given over to agriculture increases, so their 'natural' price must rise. 'Useful plants and animals' which 'nature produces in profuse abundance' can have no value in exchange while a country remains uncultivated (I.xi.c.16). However, with the advance of civilisation, demand for them increases, whilst the uncultivated nature which produces them declines in extent. Their price must therefore rise until it becomes profitable to convert land from producing food for human consumption to the provision of animal feed for meat production. In this way, the ratio of arable to cattle farming becomes itself a further mark of the advance of civilisation. It

seems, then, that the finitude of the extent of land in the face
of the extension of agriculture constitutes an absolute limit to
the supply of some goods, whilst other goods may have their
supply artificially increased by improvement and the division
of labour. In either case, though, the checks and balances of
exchange ratios are only mediate effects of extra-social physical limits and natural intransigencies such as climate and the
character of the soil.

The ecology of agricultural work

This takes us on to the second peculiarity of agriculture – the
distinctive relationship of agricultural labour to its context and
conditions. Here, again, we may distinguish several different
respects in which agricultural labour is special: temporal and
spatial inflexibility, non-proportionality and dependency. Each
of these, Smith acknowledges, has economically significant effects.
First, the temporal rhythms of agricultural labour are governed
by the developmental or reproductive rhythms of crop plants and
animals, and by the seasons. This makes specialisation and the
division of labour very difficult to achieve, and explains why
the growth of productivity of agricultural activity falls behind
that attainable in manufacture. Spatially, agriculture is also relatively inflexible, in that 'waste' or 'wild' land has to be cleared,
drained, enclosed and manured, that is 'improved', to make it
suitable for agriculture. Lack of knowledge, technique, capital
or incentive for improvement will necessarily restrict the spatial
extent of agricultural work. But Smith also writes of the climatic
and topographical requirements imposed by some crop plants as
though they constitute an absolute inflexibility. Examples he
gives are specialised wines which are in demand, but also staple
crops such as wheat and rice:

> A good rice field is a bog at all seasons, and at one season bog
> covered with water. It is unfit either for corn, or pasture, or vine-
> yard, or, indeed, for any other vegetable produce that is very
> useful to men: And the lands which are fit for those purposes are
> not fit for rice. (I.xi.b.38)

What we might call 'non-proportionality' is another distinctive feature of agricultural work:

in some employments the same quantity of industry will in different years produce very different quantities of commodities; while
in others it will produce always the same, or very nearly the
same. The same number of labourers in husbandry will, in different years, produce very different quantities of corn, wine, oil,
hops, etc. But the same number of spinners and weavers will
every year produce the same or very nearly the same quantity of
linen and woollen cloth. (I.vii.17)

This is an important disparity, since it constitutes, at least on a
year-by-year basis, a major exception to Smith's central dogma
– that productive activity and investment across the different
sectors of the economy are regulated by 'effectual demand'. In
agriculture, unpredictable vagaries of climate and season intervene between effectual demand and labour so as to obstruct any
tendency on the part of the market to bring them into a regular equilibrium.

Finally, the relationship of agricultural labour to its context
and conditions may be characterised as 'dependent'. In some
ways this feature underlies and explains the other three.
Agriculture, as distinct from manufacturing trades, involves
activities of tending and nurturing organic processes, animal or
plant, which have their own at least *relatively* inflexible spatial,
temporal, topographical and geological conditions. The sorts of
standardisation of physical and chemical processes which are,
and were in Smith's day, characteristic of manufacturing were
not technically feasible in agriculture. With some qualifications,
manufacturing can be carried out more or less anywhere, under
conditions more or less readily controllable. Agriculture cannot,
or in Smith's day, at any rate, *could* not.

Nature as producer

This dependence of agricultural labour on (relatively) non-
manipulable, autonomous organic processes, with their own
conditions and temporalities, is also recognised by Smith in
terms of a positive role of nature itself in agricultural production:

In agriculture too nature labours along with man; and though her
labour costs no expence, its produce has its value, as well as that
of the most expensive workmen. The most important operations

of agriculture seem intended, not so much to increase, though they do that too, as to direct the fertility of nature towards the production of the plants most profitable to man. .... Planting and tillage frequently regulate more than they animate the active fertility of nature; and after all of their labour, a great part of the work always remains to be done by her. (II.v.12)

This acknowledgement of the positive role of nature in agricultural production has two aspects. First, Smith writes of labour as 'directing' as well as increasing the fertility of the soil, and as 'regulating' more than 'animating' the active fertility of nature. This suggests a difference of kind between manufacturing and agricultural labour in the relationship between human intentional action and its conditions, context and outcomes in the two cases (what I have elsewhere referred to as a difference of 'intentional structure'). Though, of course, Smith does not have the benefit of the term 'ecology', his characterisation of their distinctive intentional structures is clearly a recognition of the ecological embedding of agricultural labour processes – an ecological embedding which has definite economic consequences.[5]

Second, Smith describes nature as 'herself' a productive agent. Labour, it now appears, is not a distinctive attribute of human agents (and labouring cattle), but nature, too, is a productive labourer, whose produce has value. This takes us on to the third peculiarity of agriculture – Smith's contention that nature participates in the production of value here in a way it does not in manufacture or other trades.

Smith claims not only that nature is a productive labourer, but also that her contribution can be roughly quantified. Agriculture regularly pays for the maintenance of workers and labouring cattle, together with the profits and replacement of the capital of the farmer, but over and above that, it affords rent for the landlord. So, for Smith, rent is equivalent to 'the work of nature which remains after deducting or compensating every thing which can be regarded as the work of man.' He goes on: 'It is seldom less than a fourth, and frequently more than a third, of the whole produce' (II.v.12). There is clearly a link here with what Smith says elsewhere about the 'spontaneous production of nature' prior to cultivation. When land was in common and uncultivated, the wood, grass and 'natural fruits of the earth' had only to be gathered for need to be satisfied. However, with the coming of private property in land, a price must be paid for 'the licence to gather them', even when no agricultural 'improvement' has been effected (I.vi.8). These spontaneous productions must, it seems, have a value over and above the 'toil and trouble' it takes to gather them, otherwise no one would have the incentive to pay for this licence.

Smith's view of nature as a productive labourer threatens to explode what we might call the underlying metaphysics of his economic theory. This latter, as we have seen, works with an ontology of human individuals, bearers of a hierarchically ordered pattern of needs and desires which they can satisfy only (1) by working to collect or produce useful objects or (2) by exchanging the produce of their work with others, in return for *their* produce. Throughout, Smith thinks of this produce as being made up of products whose raw or 'rude' materials must ultimately be drawn from nature.

Prior to private property and cultivation, labour was primarily devoted to the immediate meeting of need. With an advanced division of labour, private property and the 'improvement' of land, economic action is primarily oriented to production and exchange of commodities, whose key characteristic is their value in exchange. In either state of society, however, labour is a necessary mediator between the needs and desires of human subjects, and external nature. From the standpoint of Smith's economic categories, the latter exists only as a reservoir of means and objects of human labour. In each case, human labouring activity is necessary for both their human use, and, where markets are established, the measure of their value in exchange. 'Nature' does not figure in the categories of Smith's political economy except as object or means of instrumental action – as a source or means of meeting subsistence needs or as a source of revenue. The autonomous existence of nature shows itself in the requirement that 'toil and trouble', as well as skill, dexterity and judgement in the application of labour, are expended in turning it to our purposes. However, nature, beyond its dual role of servicing and resisting human purposes, remains untheorised, in the residual category of 'waste country'. The desirability of 'improving' (Smith's unreflective anthropocentrism

would have made the scare-quotes unthinkable for him) land so
as to render it suitable for 'culture' amounts to a moral requirement on the owners of land. Primogeniture and entails, which
have historically restrained agricultural improvement, are
designated 'absurd' and a 'great evil' (III.ii.6–8).

As we have seen, this instrumental/anthropocentric
perspective sustains Smith's account of the transition from
savagery and barbarism to civilised modernity, his measure of
human historical progress and the defining feature of human
sanity and reason. But our analysis of the special case of agriculture reveals the continued presence of an alternative, contradictory discourse alongside the instrumental/anthropocentric
one. Nature is acknowledged as an active collaborator or partner in a shared project. One striking index of this alternative
discourse is Smith's gendering of nature as it is encountered by
agricultural labour: 'she' labours alongside man, and, after
human labour in planting and tillage is complete, 'a great part
of the labour always remains to be done by her'. In part, no
doubt, Smith's language is governed by the identification of
nature as maternal, as procreative. The associated talk of
'natural fertility' and barrenness goes along with this. But there
may also be an implicit analogy with the domestic division of
labour discussed in this volume by Kathryn Sutherland.
'Nature', says Smith, labours alongside man, 'and though her
labour costs no expense, its produce has its value' (II.v.12).

Specifically agricultural labour, then, presupposes quite a
different ontology to that which predominates in political economy. Nature is not mere 'stuff', to be used in the most efficient
and rational manner obtainable, but rather an active, gendered
subject and partner. Though she may be formally subordinated
through the acquisition of property rights, and, indeed,
'improved', 'regulated' and directed by human rational inge-
nuity, she nevertheless continues to impose her requirements
on 'men': she has her inviolable temporal rhythms and spatial
necessities to which agriculture must adapt.

Of course, for all Smith's much vaunted 'improvement' of
the land, the agriculture he describes is still what we could now
call extensive, organic farming. What he says, for example, about
the ratios of cultivated to uncultivated land, and of arable to

cattle farming, is premised on the assumption that animals are used as a source of power in ploughing, and that their dung is used for manuring. The land which could be ploughed was greater than could be manured by working animals, so that the extent of land which could be cultivated depended on an increase in the price of meat such that it became profitable to keep cattle for meat, and direct fertile land into pasture for them. The agriculture of Smith's day was locked into a relatively tight set of interconnected ecological and financial constraints. The inner tensions and contradictions of the discourse of Smith's political economy are a sensitive indicator of these continuing fetters on the dominant model of economic rationality.

Valuing nature

But there is more, here, than a pragmatic adaptation to certain fairly obvious material realities. The gendering of nature and her role as partner in agricultural labour have definite if inexplicit normative connotations. If nature is a 'she' and a collaborator, then might there not be forms of 'regulation' of 'man's' connections with her that go beyond the merely calculative and prudential? Only rarely does Smith's text betray signs that noninstrumental relations to nature might subsist alongside instrumental ones. In general, as we have seen, progressive improvement and extension of cultivation flows naturally from universal characteristics of human nature where it is not obstructed by inappropriate, absurd or evil laws or customs. However, we have also noticed two passages in which Smith recognises non-economic, or economically irrational, orientations to nature and the land. In one such passage, Smith notes what a 'poor improver' the country gentleman is, in comparison with the merchant-turned-farmer. In part this derives from differences of habit and personality, but also, Smith clearly recognises, it is a difference of cultural orientation. Of the large landed proprietor, Smith says, 'the situation of such a person naturally disposes him to attend rather to ornament, which pleases his fancy, than to profit, for which he has so little occasion' (III.ii.7). The landscaped park, rather than the efficient farm, would, presumably, be the undesirable (to Smith's economical

eye) outcome. But perhaps the most explicit and telling 'erup-
tion' of non-economic values comes in Smith's explanation of the
natural priority of agriculture in historical development. The
'beauty of the country ... the pleasures of a country life, the
tranquillity of mind which it promises' are 'charms' which attract
almost everyone (III.i.3). This seems to be a long way from agriculture as one avenue for profitable investment among others.

But this raises another question: is the full extension of the
categories (and practices) of political economy limited only by
certain late eighteenth-century cultural-normative residues and
temporary ecological peculiarities of agriculture? The rise of
Romantic revaluations of nature as one form of cultural resistance to a purely economic-instrumental treatment of the land,
and the re-emergence of many Romantic themes in our own
'green' and environmentalist movements, suggest that the
answer to the first part of the question may be 'no'. The second
part is, however, much more difficult. Is there something intrinsic to agricultural and related activities which renders them
relatively impervious to the value-maximising abstract instru-
mentalism of capitalist economic calculation? Or have subsequent technical developments in agriculture, such as chemical
fertilisers, mechanisation, the widespread use of pesticides, cold
storage, efficient transportation, genetic manipulation and so
on, rendered Smith's analysis hopelessly outdated? Certainly it
is true that Smith never imagines the technical transformation
which will befall agriculture. However, it remains arguable that
the contradiction within Smith's own discourse, between the
anthropocentric, instrumental rationality of the capitalist
farmer and the concrete, dependent and ecologically embedded
character of the agricultural labour process continues to play
out its practical consequences in the ecological and economic
crises of late twentieth-century agriculture.

The natural conditions of manufacture

Finally, on the *peculiarity* of agriculture, Smith was sharply criticised by J. R. McCulloch, a posthumous editor of his work,
who considered Smith's view that in manufacture 'nature does
nothing - man does all' to be 'manifestly erroneous'. McCulloch

addresses the powers of wind and water, atmospheric pressure and the influence of heat 'in softening and melting metals' as examples of the key role of nature in manufactures. Contrary to Smith's opinion, the 'single advantage of machinery consists, in fact, in its enabling us to press the powers of nature into our service'. McCulloch goes on to expound, in classic form, what would now be called the 'technological optimist' or Promethean view of the power of future invention to expand indefinitely the productive capacity of labour and the social wealth. In this, manufacturing is in sharp *contrast* to agriculture:

> Lands of the first quality are speedily exhausted; and it is in practice found to be impossible, notwithstanding the frequent discoveries and inventions made in the business of agriculture, to go on applying capital indefinitely even to the best lands, without in the end obtaining a diminished return.[6]

McCulloch invokes no less a figure than Ricardo in his argument that what Smith takes to be the great advantage of agriculture over manufacture is, in fact, its great limitation. Ricardo had argued, in effect, that the natural properties of the physical objects and conditions of manufacture (air, water, elasticity of steam and the pressure of the atmosphere) enabled progressive increases in the productive power of labour only in virtue of their abundance, their uniformity of quality and their inappropriability (as private property).

In some ways this criticism is unfair to Smith. As we have seen, a good deal of the *Wealth of Nations* is given over to analysing both intrinsic, ecological and contingent, historical obstacles to capital accumulation in agriculture. However, McCulloch does bring into clear focus the near-complete absence in Smith of any analysis of the naturally given conditions and limits of non-agricultural production. Ricardo, whilst explicitly denying that these do constitute limits, does at least bring them (or some of them) into the discourse of political economy. Both air and water can now, nearing the end of the twentieth century, be readily recognised to be variable in quality, and, in forms appropriate for various social and industrial uses, both of limited abundance *and* privately appropriable.

The materials of capital accumulation

But there is one subset of naturally given conditions which Smith does recognise. These are the primary raw materials and fuels for manufactures of various kinds. We have already seen how, for Smith, boundless desires for manufactured products entail also demand for 'the fossils and minerals contained in the bowels of the earth'. Later, in discussing the relations between fixed and circulating capital, Smith is clear about the incessant demands upon nature which the reproduction and accumulation of capital make. In order to meet consumption needs, and to replace fixed capital, circulating capital must 'in its turn require continual supplies, without which it would soon cease to exist. These supplies are principally drawn from three sources, the produce of land, of mines, and of fisheries' (II.i.27). And Smith does address the conditions which enable the provision of these 'continual supplies'. In connection with his discussion of the sources of rent, he divides the 'rude produce' of land (as distinct from products of 'human industry', such as corn) into three categories: those which 'it is scarce in the power of human industry to multiply at all'; those whose quantity *can* be increased by human industry, in response to demand; and those whose quantity may be increased by human industry only 'uncertainly' and 'within limits' (I.xi.k.1).

Smith's discussion of the economic effects of resource scarcity is, thus, much more complex than is generally recognised.[7] He places 'rare and singular birds and fishes', game, birds of passage and wild fowl in the first category. Demand for these increases with wealth and luxury, whilst supply remains more or less constant, so their price may rise to 'any degree of extravagance'. There is a hint in Smith's text of the status of such goods as what would now be called positional goods, but he does not consider that, for this category of goods, demand might lead to a discontinuation of supply or extinction of the species concerned. The second category of 'rude' produce contains those 'useful plants and animals' which nature produces abundantly, but which can also be cultivated or domesticated when the relative decline in 'wild country' makes it profitable to do so. No special problem of resource scarcity arises here.

The third category of 'rude produce' includes wool, raw hides, fish and precious metals. Fish provide Smith with an example of the *limited* power of human industry to increase their supply: more labour, and machinery, bigger ships and longer distances are required to satisfy an increase in demand for fish. The increase in effort invariably outstrips the increase in fish-supplies. In the case of mining for precious metals, Smith says there are 'no certain limits' to the possible success or failure of attempts to increase supply by 'discovering' more mines. So, the capacity of human industry to expand supply in this type of case is not limited, but rather, uncertain.

In each of these cases, Smith considers only the price implications of relative inflexibility of supply on the market. He leaves unconceptualised the real causes of that inflexibility. Whether or not human activity has the power to increase market supply in response to demand may be a function of : (1) contingent and uneven distribution of the 'good' in question (precious metals); (2) the existence of a fixed and finite stock (precious metals again, land itself); (3) the domesticibility or cultivability (or not) of the 'rude' produce concerned (cattle, vegetable crops); (4) the existence of only-within-limits self-reproducing populations in nature (fish); (5) the extent of 'unimproved' habitat for such self-renewing populations (game, rare birds); and (6) the nature of demand itself, whether it increases with scarcity (positional goods) or decreases with scarcity (e.g. coal, where wood can be used as an alternative). Smith's discussion implicitly or explicitly makes all of these distinctions, but in each case the operative consideration for him is the relation of supply *in the market* to demand, and the implications for prices. Yet it is clear that, depending on the real causes of relative inflexibility of demand, market forces will have profoundly different consequences. Again, although Smith never explicitly addresses questions which would now be considered serious problems in the economics of resource scarcity, his text *is* alive to the problematic interfaces between economic activity and its naturally-given conditions.

Conclusion

Smith's historical disadvantage (that he lived before the massive nineteenth-century expansionary dynamic of industrial technology) may, from the standpoint of ecological economics, have been at the same time a historical advantage: a whole complex of interrelated conditions and constraints affecting mining, agriculture, forestry, transport and so on were a practical challenge which could not easily be ignored in the late eighteenth century. In our own times, the technological optimism which has been all-pervasive since Smith's day is very much on the defensive. Diverse sources of cultural resistance to the logic of ever-advancing commodification and exploitation of nature have gained ground in the wake of the catastrophic ecological consequences of global capital accumulation. Though the interface of economic action with its naturally given conditions is problematic in ways which would have been literally unthinkable in Smith's time, we can still find, in the inner tensions and contradictions of Smith's political economy, much that is of lasting value.

Notes

1 See G. Rudé, *Europe in the Eighteenth Century* (London: Sphere Books, 1974), p. 210.
2 See P. Hulme, 'The Spontaneous Hand of Nature: Savagery, Colonialism and the Enlightenment', in P. Hulme and L. Jordanova, ed., *The Enlightenment and its Shadows* (London: Routledge, 1990), pp. 16–34.
3 J. Locke, 'An Essay Concerning the True Original, Extent and End of Civil Government', in E. Barker, ed., *Social Contract: Essays by Locke, Hume, and Rousseau* (Oxford: Oxford University Press, 1971), p. 18.
4 See Hulme, 'Spontaneous Hand'.
5 See T. Benton, 'Marxism and Natural Limits: An Ecological Critique and Reconstruction', *New Left Review*, 178 (Nov./Dec. 1989), pp. 51–86; and 'Ecology, Socialism and the Mastery of Nature: A Reply to Reiner Grundmann', *New Left Review*, 194 (July/August 1992), pp. 55–74.
6 Adam Smith, *An Inquiry into the Nature and Causes of the Wealth of Nations*, ed. J. R. McCulloch (Edinburgh, 1850), p. 162, note 1.
7 See, for example, E. B. Barbier, *Economics, Natural Resource Scarcity and Development* (London: Earthscan, 1989), ch. 1.

8

The last georgic: *Wealth of Nations* and the scene of writing

KURT HEINZELMAN

Every farmer is more or less of a reader.

William Cobbett[1]

Almost half a century before Adam Smith's *Wealth of Nations* Daniel Defoe conceded the salacious attraction of his own enterprise: 'Writing on Trade was the Whore I really doated upon.'[2] This visceral allure nevertheless helped to keep the subject of economics from becoming, until well into the nineteenth century, wholly the property of professional writers. Even after the Reverend Thomas Malthus became the first economics professor in the English-speaking world (in 1805), economic writing continued to be practised by men (and they were almost exclusively men, then as now) who were not professional economists but rather rhetoricians, like all those other men of letters – preachers, poets, statesmen, singers – whom the *Wealth of Nations* explicitly excludes from the category of economically productive labour (see WN II.iii.2). Writing on trade (and on commerce, exchange, value, rents – the whole discursive formation we now call 'economics') remained the purview of the concerned amateur, the root meaning of which is not an 'expert' but a 'lover', one with singularly possessive desires, if Defoe is to be believed, and one with no economic (i.e., productive) standing, if Smith is to be believed.

The largest subject of this chapter is the topic of writing itself. Specifically, I address how and why the disciplinary

emergence of economics since the late eighteenth century coin-
cides with the reformulation of rhetoric as a discipline-specific
subject, one capable not only of being taught in schools and
universities *by itself alone* (i.e., without literature, particularly
without the classics) but also of being employed thereafter in
the everyday uses of business. At the same time, the *Wealth of
Nations* is one of the last non-literary works in which we can
still see how persuasion, in the absence of statistics, mathemat-
ical models, and even at times sufficient raw data, is partly a
function of that text's literary simulacrum. The simulacrum is,
in the case of the *Wealth*, Virgilian georgic. The literary order
of georgic is complex in terms of its rhetorical and suasive
modes: it is a genre that stands somewhere between belletristic
or 'fine' writing and didactic or informationally motivated writing. As I will show in due course, the georgic also provides the
generic background for much agricultural discourse of the eighteenth century.

Defoe's remark, with which I began, dramatises what literary analysts would call a problem of genre by implicitly raising the question: what kind of writing is economic writing,
particularly in its predisciplinary forms, before economic
discourse as such became institutionalised? As a writer, the
Smithian economist sees himself in a problematic economic role.
He must be, by virtue of Smith's own definition of the nuga-
tory economic value of rhetoric and rhetoricians, an unproductive labourer. This is also a crucial paradox in Virgil's poem and
at the heart of his own cultural dilemma: for Virgil's georgic
poet would want to make the agricultural activities he is
describing (and to some extent prescribing but not participat-
ing in) more central to the culture. But if Smith's own work of
writing, as a labour value, is marginal to the very socio-
economic processes to which the *Wealth* bears witness, he is in
some sense an outsider looking in – a teller of tales and not a
maker of policy, one engaged in the service-oriented practice
of ideological reproduction. (In this regard, the contemporary
American economist Donald McCloskey has challenged all economists to see their writing as more like storytelling than like
constructing quantitative proofs.)[3]

Adam Smith began his own career in 1748 not in the clergy

for which he had been prepared but as an amateur academician
– namely, a lecturer on the subject of writing; and he maintained a lifelong interest in the general question of what writing was for, why clear and concise writing was a culturally
desirable goal, and why English composition ought to be taught
carefully, especially in Scotland. Some twentieth-century scholars have even claimed that Smith played a seminal role in the
modern development of the discipline now called Rhetoric and
Composition. He certainly helped to turn it away from its classical grounding in non-vernacular languages and literature.
According to Wilbur Samuel Howell, Smith altered the emphasis of rhetoric studies from persuasion to communication.[4] As I
have argued elsewhere, Smith was one of a group of post-
Culloden Scots educators who sought to out-English the English
by developing a public awareness of and competence in everyday writing that would make university-trained Scottish young
men increasingly competitive economically and more
cosmopolitan socially.[5] Smith posited rhetoric not as a body of
knowledge containing a pre-existing and prescriptive inven-
tory of formal devices and modes of argumentation to be
mastered but as a praxis, negotiable and utilitarian, with proto-
cols reflective of the enhanced social flexibility and responsive
to the increasingly commercial orientation of universities in
Scotland. 'Prose', Smith told his students, 'is naturally the
Language of Business; as Poetry is of pleasure and amusement.
Prose is the Stile in which all the common affairs of Life all
Business and Agreements are made. No one ever made a Bargain
in verse' (LRBL XXIII.ii.116). That is, Smith's view of the
aesthetic effects of writing was inseparable from his view of the
social ends of writing.

Keith Tribe has astutely observed that the *Wealth of Nations*
as a piece of writing 'only becomes an economic treatise under
certain readings'; it 'does not have a history *qua* economic treatise until some forty years after its first publication'.[6] Tribe thus
usefully introduces, in respect to the *Wealth*, the complex
notion that how one defines the genre and purpose of writing
may be as much an historical as a contemporaneous process.
That is, to identify a kind of writing may entail a retroactive
and belated process rather than an exclusively authorial one,

for genre may not be an entirely originary or intentional determination.

In literary analysis we understand this as the paradox of canonicity. Only after the historicising of gospel discourse, for instance (and in the case of Christian story-telling this takes over a century), can the now canonical gospels be understood as telling *essentially the same* narrative, however radically they differ in both substance and tone. Only then can the ending of Mark's text, which in its earliest form seems 'fragmentary', be 'completed' so as to make Mark's Easter narrative align with the later synoptic gospels, ones which his in some sense has authorised – literally lent his words to.

For us, the *Wealth of Nations* has been historically inscribed within the discourse of economics, and yet, as Tribe further observes, there is a 'humanist conception of the economy' extractable from the *Wealth* that is at odds with its protodisciplinary formulations and that 'did not form a significant element in the constitution of an economic discourse'. Tribe locates this humanist agenda in a tendency to 'convert' (the word is his) Smith's text into a virtual celebration of 'the power of human labour', to 'redefine value as related to men's desires', and then to conceive of 'an economy as an aggregate of [individual] subjects striving to satisfy their wants'.[7] I understand Tribe's use of the term 'humanist', then, to mean two things: it names (1) a way of misreading Smith's argument regarding the accumulation of *national* wealth by reducing it to an agon of needs and desires competing in *individuals*; and (2) a way of clinging to an unwanted, and archaic, belletristic orientation as opposed to a more scientific or at least professional method. Tribe implies that this humanist reading of the *Wealth* is the result of Smithian exegetes rather than a function of Smith's own text. Be that as may be, it is important to see how the humanist perspective attributable to Smith's economic work reproduces Smith's earlier view of the writing process itself, as recorded in his *Lectures on Rhetoric and Belles Lettres* of 1762–63.

Smith's composition model in those lectures was never to be found in belles-lettres alone, although he thought literary texts could have a salutary effect if used to achieve in one's own everyday writing the beneficial effects of imitating others. Smith believed that writing should be productive, and thus his theory of rhetoric circa 1748–65 laid claim to a cultural definition of production directly at odds with his own later view in the *Wealth*. He valued a prose that was simple, natural and possessing a high degree of perspicuity. 'Perspicuity', the first word of Smith's first extant lecture, requires 'a natural order of expression ... what we call easy writing, which makes the sense of the author flow naturally upon our mind without our being obliged to hunt backwards and forwards in order to find it' (LRBL II.i.1, II.i.10). Behind this idea of 'flow', which could be impeded by word-play, equivocation and quibbles, are certain presumptions about how writing can be made 'so plain that one partly asleep may carry the sense along with him' (II.i.10). Smith assumes that writing is a continuous process of clarifying the writer's own thoughts, and he posits the writer–reader relationship as an aggregate of individuals in which reading recapitulates the writer's thought-process, a process that has been managed, apparently invisibly, and transmitted, apparently effortlessly, so as to become the reader's own. This communication model depends upon a concept of reciprocal personal agency in which writing generates information and reading brings about an exchange.

Rhetoric ideally remains value-neutral, therefore, in respect to the writer's subject; it needs to be invisible, to function as a transparency. At the same time, the goal of writing is improvement, to attain by means of writing real effects in the world of business. Smith was able to maintain the value of simplicity and the social virtue of communication because he saw the medium of style as a coefficient of civility. Right rhetoric makes morality accessible to perspicuity. Even if style does not deliver truth, its enabling capabilities make it seem a thing – a commodity – that can be learned from previous communcations, taught and copied, improved upon, lived with. We know from the historical effect of Smith's students (such as Hugh Blair) and of the curricular changes wrought by the students of his students that the new ideology of style equipped one to identify 'errors' in the styles of others and to improve infelicities in one's own. And we know that, in the end, Smithian rhetoric became a pedagogically successful way of normalising the place of language in an acquisitive culture, of confirming perspicuity as a corroborating device of ideology, and of promoting a commonsensical place for literary 'pleasures' in a world of commercial dispensations.

Ironically, Smith's own rhetorical legacy as a teacher of writing depends upon the writing of others. That is, Smith never published his lectures on rhetoric and belles-lettres, and his own manuscripts of these lectures, if they ever existed, have been lost. When we speak of 'Smith's rhetoric' or quote from his lectures, we are actually citing student notes, the most 'complete' version being the set made by one (presumably) student in 1762–63 but not discovered until 1958. In theory, of course, perspicuity, if practised by the lecturer and exercised by the note-taker, should make the extant text as reliable as if the author himself had penned it. Perhaps that is the pedagogical reason why, as John Millar remembered, Smith encouraged his students to take notes (just as James Mill was later to teach his son John Stuart to write clearly by synthesising the notes he took of his father's lectures on economics). And yet other contemporary witnesses recalled that, at least in his later years, Smith 'was in general extremely jealous of the property of his lectures [on rhetoric] and, fearful lest they should be transcribed and published, used often to repeat, when he saw anyone taking notes, that he hated scribblers'.[8] It seems unlikely that Smith's fears were merely aesthetic concerns over the transmission of oral performance into written form or reproductive concerns over the accuracy for posterity of his original 'text'. His fears sound more rawly economic, as if grounded in a wish to possess 'jealously' the mode of production of one's own discourse.

On the one hand, then, humanist faith in the perspicuity of the note-taker; on the other hand, economic anxiety over the motivations of the scribbler: here is the same ambivalence that Tribe has documented in the public reception of the *Wealth of Nations*. Scribbler and note-taker are, in effect, the same person, just as the *Wealth* is simultaneously both a non-disciplinary humanist document and a protodisciplinary economic treatise. The difference is historical context and interpretive perspective. My point is that, in respect to 'the property of his lectures', Smith's own theory of how rhetoric functions cannot account for how the invisible hand of Smithian stylistics is at the mercy of the anonymous hand that uncannily fulfils his fears and expropriates his oral addresses as 'writings'. This entire process may not bespeak, as a humanist faith promises, improvement but rather something very much like commercial exploitation, the dispossession of the property of oneself.

If Defoe thought of economic writing as the whore he both exploited and adored, Smith imagines his writings on economic subjects as part of the whole socio-political infrastructure dedicated to 'improvement' – 'the idol of the age' as William Cowper put it in 1785.[9] Improvement: it is the grammatical subject of the first sentence of the first chapter of the first book of the *Wealth*, and it signals a switch in the ethical orientation of the very act of writing about economics, a switch that underlies, I suggest, the humanist or belletristic aura of Smith's enterprise even as it foreshadows the coming professionalisation of that enterprise. The whole rhetorical burden of the *Wealth* is to remove the personal element in writing about economic subjects, to abstract and codify the idiosyncratic or even perverse desires that may have compelled the individual observer of economic processes to write. A professional cannot call his discourse his whore. What replaces this single (and female) object of desire is the more generalised goal of improvement, an end that may entail personal satisfaction but the pleasure of which is tempered by a larger social utility and straitened with an ethical purpose. Improvement may be an idol but who dares call her a whore?

Textually, the work of improvement – that massive cultural category that so dominated eighteenth-century theory and practice – included the production of didactic genres like sermons (arguably the dominant rhetorical form of the eighteenth century) and travel guides (perhaps the most popular form of secular instruction, at least in the last quarter of the century) as well as, of course, the actual practice of teaching writing, Smith's first academic job. But throughout most of the eighteenth century that infrastructure was tied explicitly to the most popular *poetic* genre of the time, one nominally about improvements in agronomy and one that carried, in fact, the king's own name: the georgic.

The origin of the georgic is the four-book poem by Virgil, written in Latin but with a Greek title, one that specifies only its putative subject: farming.[10] Even for Virgil's contemporaries the *Georgics* was seen as a difficult book concerned with much more than agriculture. By Adam Smith's time the georgic had become a capacious genre that could embrace a host of other stories – from loco-descriptive, seasonal or country-house poems to poetic essays about cider making, sugar production, or London rain-showers, from *sui generis* compositions of intro-spection and meditation like William Cowper's *The Task* to 'realistic' depictions of rural life like George Crabbe's. If works on agricultural methods like Lord Kames's *The Gentleman Farmer* can be called 'a georgic in prose',[11] perhaps the Virgilian georgic with its four-book structure and its emphasis on the progressive movement of history even underlies works like John Millar's anthropological analysis of the four stages of soci-etal development. It has been further postulated that the geor-gic, as much as the romance, is the genre that spawns the modern (i.e., post-eighteenth-century) novel.[12] As this brief catalogue suggests, the georgic, a genre Virgil had thought important enough to spend seven years mastering, was in the eighteenth century on the verge of becoming so diffuse as to be neither identifiable nor critically useful.

By the time Smith wrote the *Wealth of Nations* the georgic had, for a number of reasons, virtually vanished, at least by name, from the repertoire of usable literary genres.[13] As we have already seen, however, genre is not an exclusively authorial determination and may not be readily apparent even to contem-porary readers. In fact, Smith's use of the georgic in the *Wealth* is not merely semantic, a function of thematic content or general metaphorical deployment; he also uses the georgic both allu-sively and as an implicit structural norm. Thus, I am contending that the *Wealth* is belletristic in its very mode of argumentation, its method of making claims, and its procedures for presenting evidence. In this regard I am suggesting that the georgic is an even more determinate influence upon the *Wealth* than on works by the agriculturalists, works in which Virgil's *Georgics* often plays an explicit role.

Often, the agricultural treatise in the first half of the eighteenth century was specifically concerned with saving Virgil for the modern practical farmer. As a kind of writing, these treatises were traditionally filled with gestures of overt erudition and studded with allusions to the classical literature on farming, as indeed Virgil's *Georgics* are. As one Virgilian commentator says, 'This back-to-the-earth poem turns out to be quite bookish',[14] and so is Richard Bradley's encyclopedic effort of 1725, *A Survey of the Ancient Husbandry and Gardening ... the whole rendered familiar to our Climate, with Variety of new Experiments*, which turns out to be more a survey of literary precedent than a variety of experimentation. James Sambrook points out that 'as late as 1733, in his *Practical Husbandman and Planter*, the landscape gardener Stephen Switzer furiously defended the practical usefulness of the *Georgics* against the strictures of Jethro Tull, that pioneer of the Agricultural Revolution'.[15] But even the revolutionary Tull elsewhere confessed himself motivated to publish his views on agriculture by his first having read John Martyn's translation of Virgil's *Georgics*[16] (and it was Martyn's translation of Virgil's poem, one richly various in botanical description, that formed part of *his* 'scientific' credentials for being appointed Professor of Botany at Cambridge University).

The development of the agricultural treatise after mid-century required making a change from what G. E. Fussell calls 'consulting the authority of the ancients' to recognising 'the authority of practice'.[17] Literary historians are familiar with this change, which is starting to occur in British literature at roughly the same time, as not merely a question of how 'authority' is constituted but as a revolution in the meaning of 'originality'. Does originality reside in an apt respect for the ancient and traditional origins of things or in the production of something entirely new, something that is uniquely the manufacture of one's own genius? Indeed, I am arguing that the agricultural treatise, the genre out of which the *Wealth* evolved, dramatically stages this very scene of writing – the friction between authority and originality.[18]

Moreover, it is particularly the case with agricultural writing that this literary problem also becomes a social issue. That generations of agriculturalists should wish to save the ancients for contemporary, practical use may seem inexplicably odd if one is not aware of how writing about agriculture acutely involves two antithetically class-specific activities: day-labour in the fields (i.e., farming) versus the employment of language (i.e., writing and reading). The heavy indebtedness of agricultural writers to literary originals was noted disapprovingly by the Marquis de Mirabeau in 1762, who lamented that the discourse of agriculture should be so entailed to the literary romance of the georgic:

> My zeal for the advancement and perfection of an art [i.e., agriculture] which I have ever acknowledged and boasted the utility of, without pretending to understand the detail and progress of its operations, led me to observe, with vexation, that the new system of husbandry, was no better than a georgical romance, describing the false experiments of a deluded nation.[19]

What is denigrated here as romantic is the singular reliance on textual precedent for experiential claims, but this sort of 'delusion' provided classically trained eighteenth-century agriculturalists with an aesthetic underpinning for their inchoate works of 'scientific' curiosity, one which also bestowed an implicit sense of order. Specifically, these writers were able to postpone the need to ask: (1) whether the farmers for whom their treatises were 'intended' were in fact the ones who would benefit from them; or (2) whether the readers of these agricultural instruction manuals were the ones who would put the instructions into effect. Effaced as literature yet dependent upon a georgic sense of order that was silently grounded in classical (i.e., Virgilian) authority, the agricultural treatise could promote a vision of labour (in the form of husbandry) that was as manageable — and as socially exclusionary — as reading and writing.

Mid-century anxiety that the reading and writing of agriculture were being done incorrectly or by the wrong parties could mitigate concerns like Mirabeau's. The British agriculturalist Walter Harte, for example, claimed in his *Essays on Husbandry* (1764) that agriculture was slipping away from 'the

brightest and most elegant geniuses' and that improvement
would occur only 'if every gentleman were a true rural economist
according to the sense of the antient writers on husbandry'.[20]
The true rural economist in this construction is apparently
someone who can read the 'sense' of, say, Virgil's work on
husbandry and know that his *Georgics* is addressed to no farmer
but to the wealthy and well-connected patron Maecenas and,
through him, to Caesar. Whereas C. Clarke's *The True Theory
and Practice of Husbandry* (1777) specifically addresses gentlemen farmers who wish to regulate their bailiffs more effectively, Lord Kames's *The Gentleman Farmer* (1776) seems to
project an audience among the 'gentlemen of land-estates' who
actually will be themselves the ones farming.[21] According to
Kames's treatise, published in the same year as the *Wealth of
Nations* and explicitly striving for the twin virtues of brevity
and perspicuity that are recommended in Smith's *Rhetoric* (see
p. xiii), farming 'corresponds to that degree of exercise, which
is the best preservative of health'. It 'is equally salutary to the
mind'. Because the farm requires 'constant attention', the
farmer is 'daily gathering knowledge' (p. xv). Of all occupations, agriculture is 'the most consonant to our nature; and the
most productive of contentment, the sweetest sort of happiness'
(p. xvi). Most importantly for this Scotsman, 'no other occupation rivals agriculture, in connecting private interest with that
of the public'. Specifically, it is a form of patriotism: 'In fact, if
there be any remaining patriotism in a nation, it is found among
that class of men [i.e., gentleman-farmers]' (p. xvii). Finally,
says Kames, because farming – unlike, say, hunting – requires
a diligent exercise of rationality, it is also socially progressive
by constituting a form of self-improvement.

Other agricultural writers were more fiscally hard-nosed,
emphasising that agriculture, whatever its Kamesian pay-back
in terms of internal well-being and self-realisation, was first and
foremost a business: 'husbandry, under certain improvements',
said Arthur Young, is 'so much more profitable than most other
businesses'.[22] Young said he was writing not just for 'the whole
tribe of gentleman farmers' but for those 'younger and less able'
men starting out with only a modest initial capital investment.
Agriculture appeals precisely because of the entrepeneurial

promise it extends to even a man of modest means: 'The benefit of being able to employ small sums of money is peculiar to
husbandry.'[23] And the benefit of reading Young's various and
prolific works is that his readers 'may, if they please, gain more
experience in five years, than a common farmer can in twenty'.[24]
Being able to read economises experience and makes it more
productive.

Nathaniel Kent's *Hints to Gentlemen of Landed Property* (2nd
edn, 1776) shares Adam Smith's premise that agriculture is 'the
most useful of all sciences', and he invites 'the intervention and
example of gentlemen of property' in divesting general agricultural practice of what Kent calls 'custom'.[25] In some sense,
though, Kent has a bifurcated audience. While needing the
large, influential gentlemen farmers to spearhead agricultural
reform, Kent's model farm is a small one (pp. 228–9) and his
model farmers are 'such as have been bred up in farm-houses,
or country business from their infancy; whose hands have been
accustomed to labour' (p. 233) and not 'idle fellows, who have
been bred to little trades' (p. 234). Kent imagines, and he is one
of the few agricultural writers before William Cobbett to do so,
that the manager or owner of a given farm (in Smith's terms the
landlord or proprietor) may have different needs, values and
goals from the men and women who work those farms, and that
the former have an obligation to house and provide for the latter.
In a late chapter called 'Reflections on the Great Importance of
Cottages' Kent makes the rudimentary concession that successful farming is a proprietorship earned from the sweat of *other*
men's brows: 'the labourer is one of the most valuable members
of society: without him the richest soil is not worth owning;
his situation then should be considered, and made at least
comfortable, if it were merely out of good policy' (p. 241).
Asserting that cottagers 'are the very nerves and sinews of agriculture', Kent proceeds to offer, like a precursor of Dorothea
Brooke in *Middlemarch*, architectural plans and cost charts for
building adequate quarters to house them. By including the
capital expense of building and maintaining cottages (so that
they will not become what they often are now – 'shattered
hovels' (p. 242)) within his discursive space of agriculture, no
less than by expanding his sense of agricultural subject to

include labourers, yeomen and tenants, Kent's *Hints* makes
class difference part of his rhetorical burden. We might say that
he is combining Clarke's view of farming as the gentlemanly
superintendence of bailiffs with Kames's view of farming as
self-realisation while insisting that the entrepreneurial rewards
of farming as celebrated by Young entail at least a modicum of
social accountability.

Nowhere in the agricultural writings of the period is the
issue of discursive economy – the problem of representing writing itself – as dramatically framed, however, as in the work of
Arthur Young. In the traditional literary order of the georgic,
which I discuss more fully in a moment, writing itself is allied
with labour. Even before Young took up farming for the first
time in 1763, he was a prolific writer, having completed four
novels and several political pamphlets. After only four years of
farming experience he was published for the first time as an
agriculturalist (*The Farmer's Letters* in 1767) and the next year
he produced the first of his many tour books. In 1769, the year
before he published *Rural Oeconomy*, which will be my main
focus here, he published three monographs on subjects ranging
from French nationalism to the management of hogs and the
exportation of corn. In 1770 he published, besides *Rural
Oeconomy*, another four-volume tour book and two *other* treatises on farming (one in two volumes).

Rural Oeconomy begins by offering the sort of modesty
topos which quickly turns into an authorial manifesto. Young
confesses that the demands of agriculture have bereft him of
authority - that is, no previous writers on the subject can help
him: 'So extremely barren do I find my collection of books of
husbandry, on this subject [i.e., the general management of
"practical husbandry"], that upon revision of these papers, I
venture to assure the reader no book ever published has
afforded me a single page' (p. 3). Surely at first we read this
moment as marking Young's break with the georgical romances
of the Virgilian past. And yet, in the absence of Virgilian
authority, Young seeks to bind together the work of farming
and the labour of writing – a thoroughly georgic stratagem: 'It
is the business of the nobility and gentry who practice agriculture, and of authors who practice and write on it, to help

forward the age' (p. 36). As we shall see presently both this
progress myth (of helping to forward the age) and the equation
of farming practice and agricultural writing evidence a Virgilian
cultural faith and are derived from the *Georgics*.

Young underscores the equation when he describes the
writing of agricultural treatises in terms of the same kind of
productive multiplication and improvement that he foresees for
farming:

> The principal part of the last seven years I have lived in such
> retirement, and given so unlimited an attention to matters of
> husbandry, that my constant employment, as well as amusement,
> when out of my fields, has been the registering experiment;
> minuting remarks on most of the branches of agriculture; and
> forming calculations relative to rural oeconomy: – and my papers
> multiplied until they grew into volumes. I have often altered and
> corrected them – and in proportion as I gained experience,
> endeavoured to improve them. (pp. 5–6)

Thus, writing traces the same agenda as farming. Virgil also
worked at *his* georgics for seven years, we may remember.
When at his writing desk (and therefore 'out of my fields'),
Young is inscribing the results of his agricultural experimentation, and these results multiply and grow like the crops in the
fields themselves. The act of editing for improvement tracks
techniques of alteration and correction analogous to those he
has used out of doors. Writing about his experiments without
any written precedent for them, Young refers to his text as 'the
transcript of my experiences' (p. 7) but so pruned and grafted
'that the benefit of reading might be reduced to the labour of
a few months, instead of twice as many years' (pp. 4–5).

To see the reader as one who labours is no idle metaphor
for Young. Underlying his view of 'the benefit of reading' is
the artisanal faith that reading well is a function of improvement. Young rarely identifies his audience by socio-economic
indicator (as in 'gentleman farmer'). Instead, the audience is
made of those who can manage the direct transference of writing to action: the 'practical reader' (p. 5), 'readers of real practice' (p. 1), or, most suggestively, 'the farming reader' (p. 8). In
this insistence that the reader must read in the georgical spirit
of the author, Young becomes a prototype for William Cobbett's

even more ferocious demands on the reader as expressed in his domesticated version of the agricultural treatise, *The English Gardener* (1833):

> As to the manner of studying this book of mine, I would advise the reader to begin by reading it all through, from the beginning to the end; and not to stop here or there, to learn one part of it at a time. If he were to do this three times over, it would only require the time frequently devoted to three or four volumes of a miserable novel.[26]

Cobbett is not jesting entirely. This literal and single-minded, even militaristic, application of oneself to the instructions of the text at hand is what Young asks from his 'farming reader' and is a recurring motif in all agricultural writing.

The principle of 'rural oeconomy' is that readers, like writers, must keep their own books in the form of either descriptive records or account sheets. Implicitly, Young calls for readers to become authors of their own experience, for the authority of experience originates with the self:

> When a man turns over his books, and finds a regular balance of profit and loss on every article, he is enabled to review his business, to consider what have probably been his errors, and wherein he has been most successful. The result of such reflections is true experience, not the random notions that are carried in the memory.[27]

Young envisions an agriculture of accountable productivity that is repeatable and reproducible thanks to these records, these 'books'. Although he began *Rural Oeconomy* by lamenting the absence of textual antecedent, he concludes by imagining a circulatory economy sustained by writing. What Young, the former novelist and narrating farmer, has invented is a new sort of (auto)biographical account that demands the readers' participation in and extension of that narrative into their own fields. This narrative first aestheticises and then universalises labour so that farming, writing/reading and accounting ('keeping books') may become culturally equivalent, albeit economically different, activities.

The *Wealth of Nations* is fundamentally concerned with describing how labours are economically different, how some

are more productive than others, more central to sustaining a
nation's wealth. But the *Wealth* cannot confine itself to addressing labour under market conditions alone, as if 'labour' were
only an economic signifier, any more than it can ignore the idea
of use-value and concentrate entirely on exchange-value. This
is because 'labour' is still for Smith a cultural signifier as well,
with a whole network of significances that govern 'the general
business of society' and not merely with one meaning that
applies to economic business. It is in this sense that we can
speak of 'labour' in the *Wealth* as a device or trope: it is an allegorised term, just as it is in Virgil's *Georgics*. What I have been
trying to show in the agricultural writers is how the concept
of labour becomes acculturated by their more or less overt
appropriation of the term to their own 'work' of writing. The
Wealth does not engage in this sort of acculturation overtly
(though it may reap the benefits of its once having been done).
After all, what has struck virtually every reader of the *Wealth*
since its publication is how it is *unlike* most agricultural writings and how it is free of classical allusion and literary reference, even though Smith, like the agriculturalists and perhaps
like Virgil, holds that 'Agriculture is of all other arts the most
beneficient to society, and whatever tends to retard its improvement is extremely prejudicial to the public interest' (LJ (B) 289).
And of course in the *Wealth* itself Smith develops the specific
ways in which agriculture reflects the public interest: it is the
'great trade of the country' (I.x.c.23); it is the most productive
form of investment (II.v.12); and it produces the most durable
form of wealth (III.iv.24). I am not claiming that the *Wealth*
participates in the literary order of georgic merely because it
bestows a central economic and even cultural value to agricultural production but because of the implicit and continuous
connections the work makes between the concept of labour and
the practice of writing – what might be called its circulatory
system.[28]

     To start with, the georgic, in its Virgilian form, is about
writing. It serves thematically and formally as a bridge between
the singing shepherds of Virgil's early book of pastorals and the
later attempt in his epic to constitute a mythic chronicle or
history. If Virgil's *Eclogues* are spoken or sung by a variety of

personae, then in the *Georgics* the poet is *in propria persona* a character in the poem: ultimately, he identifies himself as Virgil – that is, as someone who is writing and not merely singing or playing the pan-pipes and who has a history. All the characters in the *Georgics* are identified as social agents under the rubric of *labour*, including the poet himself. This is one of the principal characteristics of the georgic: it universalises labour so as to embrace all human effort that strives to order nature. But it also accords a special social function to the writer. He is, in effect, a bridge-builder or networker, not an isolated individual. While writing about agriculture, he is not himself a farmer; he is, rather, a cultural agent whose main task is to connect the cultivation of nature with the policies and aspirations of the ruler – in Virgil's case, Octavian.

As a writer with a specific historical identity, the georgic poet serves to effect the vital social nexus between the pre-political farmer and the statesman (Maecenas) or sovereign (Caesar). Thus, Virgil's poem is finally not about agriculture at all: it is instead the prototype of an open-ended progress narrative in which the writer's critical endeavour is to co-ordinate and reconcile the apparently ceaseless and protean changes promised by Caesar's new imperial *saeculum* with the sense of insurmountable limitation that the farmer knows from his 'hard labour'. Virgil's *Georgics* is the one piece of writing in the classical curriculum of Smith's time that is both millenarian in its plot and fully secular in its apparatus, while according a unique cultural agency to the 'labour' of writing itself.

The *Wealth of Nations* contends that there is something inherently good or beautiful about working the land and implies that the individual farmer is more the custodian of his own work – he possesses the property of his own labour more satisfactorily – than the manufacturing labourer. At the national or socio-political level, agriculture provides, in a uniquely literal way, the ground upon which a culture's greatest and most enduring values are planted:

> The capital of the landlord, ... which is fixed in the improvement of his land, seems to be as well secured as the nature of human affairs can admit of. The beauty of the country besides, the pleasures of a country life, the tranquillity of mind which it promises,

and wherever the injustice of human laws does not disturb it, the independency which it really affords, have charms that more or less attract every body; and as to cultivate the ground was the original destination of man, so in every stage of his existence he seems to retain a predilection for this primitive employment. (III.i.3)

What Smith is developing here is a classical topos which has one point of origin in Virgil's anecdote of 'independency', his tale of the old Corycian gardener in the fourth book of the *Georgics* (IV.125-48), and another point of origin in Virgil's often-quoted odic celebration of the happy husbandman in the second book of the *Georgics* (II.458–74). In the hands of Smith's contemporaries, such as Nathaniel Forster, this sort of passage from the *Wealth* might proceed to a nationalistic allegory like the agriculturally based republic that Forster imagines, based upon 'an hardy, free, and intrepid race of men'.[29] Smith does not go this route, but the recognition that the commercial security one has in land-improvement seems to be derived from the primordial myth of labour that agriculture peculiarly engages is itself a georgic insight, for it is (agricultural) labour, in this expanded and historically 'cultivated' sense, that conquers all, as Virgil's most famous phrase from the *Georgics* puts it (I.145). Smith himself thought that Virgil's poem was meant 'to bring the cultivation of land into fashion' (LJ (B) 297).

Smith does not take the (literary) route of allegorising a mythic love of the land into political terms, but he does practise the Virgilian insistence that labour is an inclusive term, though some forms of labour may be less productive than others and still others (like that of women) may be more or less invisible:

> Farmers and country labourers, indeed, over and above the stock which maintains and employs them, reproduce annually a neat produce, a free rent to the landlord. As a marriage which affords three children is certainly more productive than one which affords only two; so the labour of farmers and country labourers is certainly more productive than that of merchants, artificers and manufacturers. The superior produce of the one class, however, does not render the other barren or unproductive. (WN IV.ix.30)

Here the farming labourers 'reproduce' in the form of a free rent, while the marriage's work of actual reproduction is called productive, without women yet being understood as economic entities. (There is no economic theory before John Stuart Mill's that accounts for productive or economically viable women. See the chapter by Kathryn Sutherland, pp. 97–121 above.) This passage *should* sound odd to us, for its rhetoric is pre-Malthusian but post-Virgilian. Virgil's georgic idea that 'labor omnia vincit' ('labour conquers all') is a direct echo of the earlier assertion in his *Eclogues* that 'amor omnia vincit' ('love conquers all'). In the *Georgics*, 'labor' is constructed entirely on a male model of production and consumption, and its chief antagonist is 'amor' – namely, that desire which depletes both man and beast of the will to battle against immutable fortune. What made the later (i.e. post-Smithian) economics of the Reverend Malthus so notorious was that its attempt to account economically for women forced Malthus to show how 'amor' only leads to reproduction and how reproduction depletes what economic labour, in the form of the work of men's hands, has accumulated. For Malthus, female labour, axiomatically understood as childbearing alone, becomes the activity that undermines by a geometric ratio the economic productivity of male labour.

Smith maintains that the enhanced productivity of one kind of labour does not render another kind 'barren or unproductive.' Take the well-known pin-making illustration. To start with, whatever else it may be, it *is* an illustration, one that derives much of its rhetorical force by means of an allusion, which every educated reader would have understood, to the fourth book of the *Georgics*, Virgil's fable of the bees. Smith explains that in order to see how division of labour works one needs to look at 'a very trifling manufacture' (WN I.i.3) in which all the workers are collected into one location and are 'placed at once under the view of the spectator' (I.i.2). This rhetorical situating of the scene of labour follows Virgil's concession that his analysis of division of labour within the beehive is, for the poet, 'a slight labour' ('in tenui labor' (IV.6), which C. Day Lewis translates 'a featherweight theme') and that his poem is comparing small things to great ('si parva licet componere magnis' (IV.176)). That is to say, Virgil's description of the beehive is also an illustration. My point is that both Virgil and Smith should be seen to illustrate the same thing.

What Smith supposes the division of labour to illustrate is how production can be best improved, but, as Smith is the first to notice, there is a paradox - namely, that labour is more readily divisible in manufacturings than in agriculture, even though it is investment in agricultural production that is primarily responsible for the progress of societal wealth (WN I.i.4). The reason why this paradox does not at once undercut Smith's expostulations is because the paradox is merely rhetorical. That is, Smith is not talking here about improvement as merely an economic (i.e., labour-specific) concept but rather about 'the effects of the division of labour, in the general business of society' (I.i.2). Division of labour in respect to the humble trade of pin-making thus opens out concentrically to embrace all artisanal practices within society: 'It is the great multiplication of the productions of all the different arts, in consequence of the division of labour, which occasions, in a well-governed society, that universal opulence which extends itself to the lowest ranks of the people' (I.i.10). And even as division of labour has this multiplier effect, it also leads Smith inward to the psychological centre of these concentric circles, the innate human 'propensity to truck, barter, and exchange one thing for another' (I.ii.1). Without division of labour this natural inclination would produce 'no such extensive utility' (I.ii.1).

Virgil makes the same point in his equally expansive and comparative description that the bees' social solidarity combats an innate love ('innatus amor') of gain ('habendi') that drives them each to seek its own office ('Cecropias innatus apes amor urget habendi / munere quamque suo' (IV.177–8)). Again, it is love ('amor') that for Virgil libinally drives ('urget') them to pursue their self-interest, and it is the division of labour that calls them back, in spite of their passions, to the communitarian resolve that Virgil's one-line, wholly dactyllic sentence expresses: 'omnibus una quies operum, labor omnibus unus' ('all share their time of labour, their time of rest') (IV.184). Nevertheless, by signing his own poem as a labour, albeit a slight one, Virgil calls attention to the illustrative nature of his anecdote, which is not merely that all labours point to one end, but that all labours are one – that is, they combat the passions, self-interest and 'amor'. Smith does not go so far as Virgil in suggesting that division of labour requires workers to give up their sexuality (IV.198), but he is using labour in the same allegorised sense as Virgil's. Indeed, the point of the whole pin-making scene is allegorical.

What the scene allegorises is Smith's mythic sense of progress, originating as a psychological propensity, combated by a societal reorganisation of innate desires, and directed outward concentrically to all the arts within a culture. In short, not just Book III but the whole of the *Wealth* is dedicated to the idea of progress, the full realisation of which depends upon the Virgilian use of labour as an allegorised term mitigating the effects of 'amor'. Progress in the *Wealth* is grounded neither in agricultural production nor in mercantile commerce, nor in the two together, but in this larger georgic application of labour as a societal bonding agent.

Smith also shares with the Virgilian georgic poet the discharge of the labour that is his own discourse. The *Wealth* itself should be understood as a mediating activity: it is what makes the otherwise somewhat extraneous last books so necessary to Smith's picture of his own service function as a writer. The Smithian economist (if one may call him that) acts as the georgic poet does, to provide a link between productive labourers like farmers and the unproductive but politically central figure of the statesman, 'whose presence is essential to the discourse in providing a unity'.[30] One of the reasons that Smith comes to the conclusion that the expense of supporting the dignity of the sovereign 'should be defrayed by the general contribution of the whole society' (V.i.1) may be that his georgic logic demands it: we all labour to one 'general' good. Indeed, the reverse - that all labour partakes of one societal work - may have been further illustrated to Smith in the final years of the *Wealth*'s composition when the sovereign whose name signified agricultural labour, the farmer-King George III, assumed, with the help of Arthur Young, the management of his own farms at Windsor.

The last mark of the georgic on the *Wealth*'s mode of argument occurs in the turn the dissertation takes in Book V to consider the expense and importance of institutionalised education and particularly the role of writing instruction. Indeed, Mirabeau is quoted earlier by Smith as calling writing one of

the three greatest gifts to mankind (IV.ix.38). It may seem odd
to hear education claimed as a georgic subject, for the *Georgics*
never discuss education specifically, and yet what is the georgic if not a form of writing in which the issue of instruction is
constantly being examined?[31] A georgic is by definition didactic. It lays claim to tutorial value; it seems to impart information. Those who over the centuries have understood the poem
literally, as if Virgil's directions about planting and pruning
and ploughing meant that the poem was transparently 'about'
its overt subjects, illustrate precisely in their single-mindedness
the poem's largest and most ambivalent concern - that we may
be better able to discern the unfailing signs ('Atque haec ut
certis possemus discere signis' (I.351)). For Virgil those 'signs'
are not merely natural and empirical; they are also literary, out
of books. The *Georgics* is one of the most allusive texts we have,
and it requires a thoroughly knowledgeable reader to see that
its instructions are allegorised, like labour itself. To paraphrase
the Cobbett of my epigraph, every farmer must become more,
not less, of a reader.

Which is, I am claiming, the *Wealth*'s challenge also. If the
Wealth of Nations is now seen to have inaugurated the kind of
story-telling that was appropriate to economics, it did so by
drawing upon and modifying the classical Roman story about
farming, which was, as a literary form, slowly being trivialised,
then effaced – in effect, imitated to death. The georgic vanished,
however, only in name, not as a cultural practice. Smith's ways
of telling economic stories presumed a system of public education and quickly required a rhetoric and a style to match, both
of which Smith himself had helped to evolve twenty years
before the *Wealth*'s publication. In this pedagogical revolution
the remnants of the enabling georgic (and the Roman narrative)
tradition would be finally lost more or less for good.[32] And yet,
ironically, in those two decades leading up to 1776 the georgic
concerns of Smith's economic work were already being culturally diffused, not under the old name of 'georgic', still less
under the new name of 'economics', but rather under that of
'rhetoric'. It was through a utilitarian model of communication,
based upon the value of enhanced composition skills not just
in the marketplace of ideas but in the marketplace of exchange-

value itself, that Smith taught his students, who more often now were coming from what Defoe's Robinson Crusoe calls 'the middling classes', a new and precisely *English*-language version of the georgic. He taught them writing, how to effect improvement *through* writing. He taught them that, whatever the cultural worth of reading, to write clear, serviceable prose could bestow and command exchange-value. And Smith instilled this new georgic of literateness even before the compelling, indeed compulsive, importance of economics as a subject had fully created the demand for this differently educated public – that is, for a society which needed to be gainfully articulate as economic agents more than it needed to be erudite assayers of its cultural losses.

Notes

1 William Cobbett, *Journal of a Year's Residence in the United States of America* (Gloucester: Alan Sutton, 1983), p. 195.

2 *A Review of the Affairs of France*, ed. Arthur W. Secord (New York: Facsimile Text Society, 1938), 1 (9), 214a.

3 Donald McCloskey, *If You're So Smart: The Narrative of Economic Expertise* (Chicago: University of Chicago Press, 1990).

4 Wilbur S. Howell, *Eighteenth-Century British Logic and Rhetoric* (Princeton: Princeton University Press, 1991), p. 549.

5 Kurt Heinzelman, 'Rhetoric, Economics, and the Scene of Instruction', in *L'Imaginaire économique*, ed. Philippe Desan, *Stanford French Review*, 15 (1991), pp. 349–71.

6 Keith Tribe, *Land, Labour, and Economic Discourse* (London: Routledge & Kegan Paul, 1978), pp. 113–14.

7 Ibid., p. 112.

8 See Adam Smith, *Lectures on Rhetoric and Belles Lettres*, ed. John M. Lothian (1963: rpt Carbondale: Southern Illinois University Press, 1971), 'Introduction', p. xxii.

9 In Book 3 of *The Task*: see Cowper, *Verse and Letters*, ed. Brian Spiller (London: Rupert Hart-Davis, 1968), p. 462.

10 See Virgil, *Georgics*, ed. Richard F. Thomas (2 vols, Cambridge: Cambridge University Press, 1988). All subsequent references to the poem are cited parenthetically in the text by book and line number.

11 By Richard Feingold in his *Nature and Society: Later Eighteenth-Century Uses of the Pastoral and Georgic* (New Brunswick: Rutgers University Press, 1978), p. 48.

12 By Alan Liu in his *Wordsworth: The Sense of History* (Stanford: Stanford University Press, 1989), p. 20.

13 See my 'Roman Georgic in the Georgian Age: A Theory of Romantic

Genre,' in *Romans and Romantics*, ed. Kurt Heinzelman, *Texas Studies in Language and Literature*, 33 (1991), pp. 182–214.

14 David R. Slavitt, *Virgil* (New Haven: Yale University Press, 1991), p. 46.

15 James Sambrook, *The Eighteenth Century: The Intellectual and Cultural Context of English Literature, 1700–1789* (London: Longman, 1986), p. 173.

16 See G. E. Fussell, *The Classical Tradition in West European Farming* (Newton Abbot: David & Charles, 1972), p. 148.

17 Ibid., p. 148.

18 I am not claiming, of course, that the *Wealth* is an agricultural treatise, though I show at the end of this article how it shares georgic strategies with works from which it is also trying to distance itself. The paradox of being a last or belated georgic is that Smith's book has generic symptoms of the very genre it is trying to divest and discard.

19 Letter from Mirabeau dated 8 November 1762, included as an appendix to Arthur Young's *Rural Oeconomy: or, Essays on the Practical Parts of Husbandry* (London, 1770), p. 488.

20 Quoted in Fussell, *Classical Tradition*, p. 147.

21 Henry Home, Lord Kames, *The Gentleman Farmer* (Edinburgh, 1776), pp. xiii–xiv. Hereafter cited parenthetically in the text by page number.

22 Introduction to *The Farmer's Kalendar* (London: 1771), n.p.

23 Ibid.

24 Young, *Rural Oeconomy*, p. 207. Hereafter cited parenthetically in the text by page number.

25 N. Kent of Fulham, *Hints to Gentlemen of Landed Property* (2nd edn London, 1776), pp. 4, 6. Hereafter cited parenthetically in the text by page number.

26 *The English Gardener* (Oxford: Oxford University Press, 1980), pp. 4–5.

27 Young, *Rural Oeconomy*, p. 205.

28 On this metaphor of circulation as it applies to economics see S. Todd Lowry, 'The Archaeology of the Circulation Concept in Economic Theory,' *Journal of the History of Ideas*, 35 (1974), pp. 429–44; and as it applies to the practice of writing, especially to Arthur Young's, see Jon Klancher, *The Making of English Reading Audiences, 1790–1832* (Madison: University of Wisconsin Press, 1987), pp. 28–37.

29 *Enquiry into the Causes of the Present High Price of Provisions* (London, 1767), p. 115.

30 Tribe, *Land, Labour, and Economic Discourse*, p. 85.

31 William Wordsworth's *The Excursion* (1814), one of his most overtly georgic poems – for which see Annabel Patterson, 'Wordworth's Georgic: Genre and Structure in *The Excursion*', *The Wordsworth Circle*, 9 (1979), pp. 145–54 – devotes its last book to debating ideas of national education.

32. See, for instance, John W. Cairns, 'Rhetoric, Language, and Roman Law: Legal Education and Improvement in Eighteenth-Century Scotland', *Law and History Review*, 9 (1991), pp. 31–58.

Notes on contributors

TED BENTON is Professor of Sociology at the University of Essex. He has published widely in the fields of Marxist theory, and social and environmental philosophy. His most recent book, *Natural Relations* (1993), is an attempt to explore the relationship between ecology, animal welfare and a socialist view of human rights.

STEPHEN COPLEY is Lecturer in English Literature at the University of York. His publications include *Literature and the Social Order in Eighteenth-Century England* (1984), and articles on eighteenth-century polite culture, literature and economics. He is the joint-editor of *Beyond Romanticism: New Approaches to Texts and Contexts 1780-1832* (1992) and *The Politics of the Picturesque* (1994).

KURT HEINZELMAN is Associate Professor of English Literature at the University of Texas, Austin. He is the author of *The Economics of the Imagination*, one of *Choice*'s Outstanding Academic Books of the Year for 1980, and he edited a special issue of *Texas Studies in Literature and Language* entitled *Romans and Romantics* (Summer 1991). He has published widely in the fields of English Romantic literature, British cultural studies and modern poetry.

HEINZ LUBASZ is Lecturer in History at the University of Essex. He has edited *The Development of the Modern State* (1964) and *Revolutions in Modern European History* (1966), and has published articles on Smith and Marx, and on other aspects of the history of social and economic thought.

NOEL PARKER teaches European politics in the Department of Linguistic and International Studies at the University of Surrey. He has previously taught history of ideas, philosophy and political theory at the University of Nice and the Open University. His publications include *Representations of Revolution: Images, Debates and Patterns of Thought on the French Revolution* (1990).

ANDREW SKINNER is Professor of Political Economy at the University of Glasgow. His interests include the development of economic theory in the eighteenth century. He edited Sir James Steuart's *Principles of Political Economy* (1966) and was one of the editors, in the Glasgow Edition of the Works of Adam Smith, of the *Wealth of Nations* and *Essays on Philosophical Subjects*. He recently edited (with P. Jones) a volume of essays entitled *Adam Smith Reviewed* (1992).

KATHRYN SUTHERLAND is Professor of Modern English Literature at the University of Nottingham. Her publications include a selected edition of

Wealth of Nations in the Oxford World's Classics series. She is currently completing a study of women writers and the institutions and narratives of history in the late eighteenth century.

KEITH TRIBE   is Senior Lecturer in Economics at the University of Keele. His publications include *Land, Labour and Economic Discourse* (1978), *Marxism and the Agrarian Question* (1981, with Athar Hussain), *Genealogies of Capitalism* (1981); *Governing Economy* (1988) and *Strategies of Economic Order* (1994). He is currently working on a study of of the development of economic and commercial science in Britain 1870-1960.

Select bibliography

Modern editions of Smith's works

The Glasgow Edition of the Works and Correspondence of Adam Smith (Oxford: Clarendon Press, 1976–83)

I, *The Theory of Moral Sentiments*, ed. A. L. Macfie and D. D. Raphael (1976)

II, *An Inquiry into the Nature and Causes of the Wealth of Nations*, ed. R. H. Campbell, A. S. Skinner and W. B. Todd, 2 vols (1976)

III, *Essays on Philosophical Subjects*, ed. W. P. D. Wightman, J. C. Bryce and I. S. Ross (1980)

IV, *Lectures on Rhetoric and Belles Lettres*, ed. J. C. Bryce (1983)

V, *Lectures on Jurisprudence*, ed. R. L. Meek, D. D. Raphael and P. G. Stein (1978)

VI, *The Correspondence of Adam Smith*, ed. E. C. Mossner and I. S. Ross (1977)

Modern Editions of the *Wealth of Nations*

An Inquiry into the Nature and Causes of the Wealth of Nations, ed. Edwin Cannan, 2 vols (London: Methuen, 1904)

The Wealth of Nations, Books I–III, ed. Andrew Skinner (Harmondsworth: Penguin, 1970; revised 1974)

An Inquiry into the Nature and Causes of the Wealth of Nations, ed. R. H. Campbell, A. S. Skinner and W. B. Todd, 2 vols (Oxford: Clarendon Press, 1976)

The Essential Adam Smith, ed. Robert L. Heilbroner and Laurence J. Malone (Oxford: Oxford University Press, 1986)

The Wealth of Nations, Books I–IV, introd. D. D. Raphael (Everyman's Library, 1910; repr. London: Random Century Group, 1991)

An Inquiry into the Nature and Causes of the Wealth of Nations, A Selected Edition, ed. Kathryn Sutherland (Oxford: Oxford University Press, 1993)

Biographical studies

Campbell, R. H. and A. S. Skinner, *Adam Smith* (London: Croom Helm, 1982)

Rae, John, *Life of Adam Smith* (London, 1895; repr., with additional material by Jacob Viner, New York, 1965)

Ross, Ian, *Life of Adam Smith* (Oxford: Clarendon Press, in preparation)

Stewart, Dugald, 'Account of the Life and Writings of Adam Smith, LL.D.' (1794), in Adam Smith, *Essays on Philosophical Subjects*, ed. W. P. D. Wightman, J. C. Bryce and I. S. Ross (Oxford: Clarendon Press, 1980)

General studies on Smith

Blaug, Mark, *Economic Theory in Retrospect* (4th edn, Cambridge: Cambridge University Press, 1985), Ch. 2

Brown, Maurice, *Adam Smith's Economics: Its Place in the Development of Economic Thought* (London and New York: Croom Helm, 1988)

Bryson, Gladys, *Man in Society: The Scottish Inquiry of the Eighteenth Century* (1945; repr. New York: Augustus M. Kelley, 1986)

Dumont, Louis, *From Mandeville to Marx: The Genesis and Triumph of Economic Ideology* (Chicago: University of Chicago Press, 1977)

Elliott, Nicholas, ed., *Adam Smith's Legacy: His Thought in our Time* (London: ASI (Research) Limited, 1990)

Heinzelman, Kurt *The Economics of the Imagination* (Amherst: University of Massachusetts Press, 1980)

Hirschman, Albert O., *The Passions and the Interests: Political Arguments for Capitalism before its Triumph* (Princeton: Princeton University Press, 1977)

Hollander, Samuel, *The Economics of Adam Smith* (Toronto: University of Toronto Press, 1973)

Hont, Istvan and Michael Ignatieff, ed., *Wealth and Virtue: The Shaping of Political Economy in the Scottish Enlightenment* (Cambridge: Cambridge University Press, 1983)

Hutchison, Terence , *Before Adam Smith: The Emergence of Political Economy 1662–1776* (Oxford: Basil Blackwell, 1988)

McCloskey, Donald N., *The Rhetoric of Economics* (Madison: University of Wisconsin Press, 1985

Macfie, A. L., *The Individual in Society: Papers on Adam Smith*, University of Glasgow Social and Economic Studies, 11 (London: George Allen & Unwin, 1967)

Meek, Ronald L. ed., *Precursors of Adam Smith* (London: Dent, 1973)

Muller, Jerry Z., *Adam Smith in His Time and Ours: Designing the Decent Society* (New York and Oxford: The Free Press, 1993)

Myers, Milton L., *The Soul of Modern Economic Man: Ideas of Self-Interest, Thomas Hobbes to Adam Smith* (Chicago: University of Chicago Press, 1983)

O'Driscoll, Gerald P. Jr, ed., *Adam Smith and Modern Political Economy: Bicentennial Essays on 'The Wealth of Nations'* (Ames, Iowa: Iowa State University Press, 1976)

Raphael, D. D., *Adam Smith* (Past Masters; Oxford: Oxford University Press, 1985)

Reisman, D. A., *Adam Smith's Sociological Economics* (London: Croom Helm, 1976)

Rendall, Jane, *The Origins of the Scottish Enlightenment 1707–76* (London: Macmillan, 1978)

—— 'Virtue and Commerce: Women in the Making of Adam Smith's Political Economy', in *Women in Western Political Philosophy*, ed. Ellen Kennedy and Susan Mendus (Brighton: Harvester Wheatsheaf, 1987), pp. 44–77.

Shell, Marc, *The Economy of Literature* (Baltimore, Md: Johns Hopkins University Press, 1978)

——, *Money, Language, and Thought: Literary and Philosophic Economies from the Medieval to the Modern Era* (Berkeley and Los Angeles: University of Califorenia Press, 1982)

Skinner, Andrew S., *A System of Social Science: Papers relating to Adam Smith* (Oxford: Clarendon Press, 1979)

——, and Thomas Wilson, ed., *The Market and the State: Papers in Honour of Adam Smith* (Oxford: Clarendon Press, 1976)

Tribe, Keith, *Land, Labour, and Economic Discourse* (London: Routledge & Kegan Paul, 1978)

Viner, Jacob, 'Adam Smith and Laissez Faire', *Journal of Political Economy*, 35 (1927), reprinted in *Adam Smith: Critical Assessments*, ed. J. C. Wood (Beckenham: Croom Helm, 1984), vol. 1, pp. 143–67

Werhane, Patricia H., *Adam Smith and his Legacy for Modern Capitalism* (Oxford: Oxford University Press, 1991)

Winch, Donald, *Adam Smith's Politics: An Essay in Historiographic Revision* (Cambridge: Cambridge University Press, 1978)

Wood, C., ed. *Adam Smith: Critical Assessments*, 4 vols (London: Croom Helm, 1984)

Index